SEAMLESS KNIT SWEATERS
in
2 Weeks

SEAMLESS KNIT SWEATERS

in 2 *Weeks*

20 Patterns for Flawless Cardigans, Pullovers, Tees and More

Marie Greene

FOUNDER OF OLIVE KNITS

PAGE STREET
PUBLISHING CO.

PAGE STREET
PUBLISHING CO.

Distributed by Macmillan, sales in Canada by The Canadian Manda Group.

23   22   21   20   19   2   3   4   5

ISBN-13: 978-1-62414-740-1

ISBN-10: 1-62414-740-2

Library of Congress Control Number: 2018960860

Cover and book design by Rosie Stewart for Page Street Publishing Co.

Photography by Belen Mercer

Cover image © Belen Mercer

Printed and bound in the United States

for my grandma,

MARGERY JUNE, WHO TAUGHT ME TO BE A FEARLESS,
RESOURCEFUL KNITTER (AND TO AVOID SEAMS WHENEVER POSSIBLE).

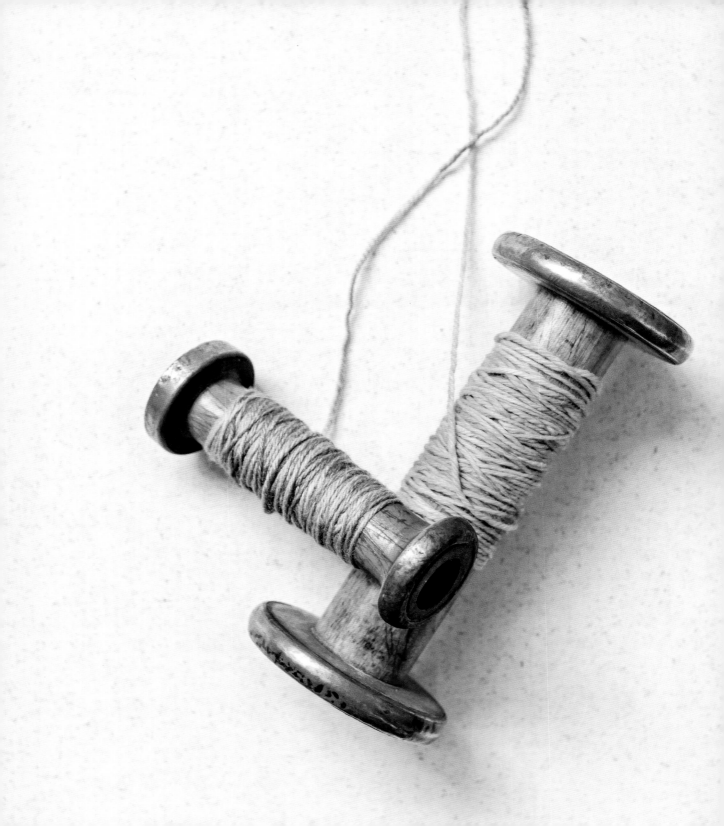

Contents

Introduction

FOUR DAYS AND A FINISHED SWEATER

A few years ago, I challenged myself—a bit unintentionally—to knit an adult-size sweater over the course of a four-day weekend. Deadline knitting is nothing new for me: I love the momentum of a focused project and feel intimately connected when I immerse myself wholeheartedly. But I confess that I'd never attempted such a brief timeline; I wasn't sure if I could do it. It's one thing to knit a bulky sweater in less than a week, but what about a mid-weight sweater with interesting details?

I had a long weekend ahead of me and was motivated by the prospect of finishing the sweater quickly so I could focus on other projects. I shared my plans with my online fiber community to hold myself accountable, and I hit the ground running. I didn't realize it at the time, but the seeds had been planted and a new way of thinking about sweater knitting was taking hold.

I loved the intense familiarity I felt with my four-day sweater as it became part of the flow of each day. I reveled in each milestone—dividing for sleeves, finishing the body, starting the ribbing—and I found myself in a rhythm unlike anything else. Knitting has a natural tempo, to be sure, but this greater level of focus and intention seemed to synchronize my stitches with my heartbeat. And because it was seamless, the pieces grew together stitch by stitch. The project was my constant companion, until—almost overnight—it was finished. Unwoven ends hung like loose spaghetti, but I'd done it; I'd knit a sweater in just over a weekend. What's more, it had been an adventure, not a chore.

Word spread like wildfire in the online community, and it led to a wave of requests for a four-day knitalong. Curiosity had gotten the better of everyone—was I just an incredibly fast knitter, or was this something anyone could achieve? I created an adjustable timeline to account for the range of sizes and we spread the word. Hundreds of knitters signed up for the adventure, knowing that—whether they finished in a few days, or a few weeks—it would likely be the quickest sweater they'd ever make.

The next year, I launched the second official 4 Day Sweater Knitalong with a cardigan called Beekeeper, and this time thousands of knitters from around the world joined in. Year one was impressive, but year two was a revelation. I discovered that I'm not alone in loving the challenge of knitting against the clock. While a four-day timeline isn't a sustainable practice long term, it does illustrate the broader point: knitting a garment can happen more quickly than we might believe.

You can knit an adult sweater in just a few weeks, in any size. If you've ever started a sweater and found it years later in your stash—still missing the sleeves—you may have written off sweater knitting altogether. After all, if a project takes months or years to finish, it can be difficult for most of us to maintain enthusiasm.

But there is another way.

Imagine sweater patterns—for all shapes and sizes—that are designed thoughtfully and efficiently to be achievable in about two weeks. The shaping is strategic, texture is easy to memorize, and the features are striking without being fussy. The best part? They'll fit well and you'll love wearing them.

Wait . . . they'll fit?

There was a time when top-down sweaters had few variations. There were raglans with the impossibly deep arm holes and sharply angled shoulders. And there were the rounded yoke sweaters with very little shaping but lots of versatility for colorwork.

It didn't take me long to recognize the need for seamless sweaters that defied traditional boundaries. Arm holes don't need to be ridiculously deep. Increases don't have to follow the old rules. And seamless sweaters shouldn't fit like a paper sack. Over the years I've developed mock-saddle shoulders and set-in sleeve variations—worked seamlessly, of course—to provide a more interesting canvas for design, while improving the final fit and shaping of my garments. I've incorporated syncopated increases near the sleeve divide to shape the sweaters and streamline fit. Seamless sweaters have more potential than we've given them credit for, and I'm here to save their reputation.

The sweaters on the following pages are streamlined versions of my custom sweater shaping that stay true to the two-week timeline. You'll find pullovers, cardigans, tees and more—each one efficiently designed and easy to wear.

Seamless sweaters knit quickly have changed the way I think about knitting, and it's this energized, immersion experience I hope to bring to you through the sweaters in this book. While four days may not be a reasonable speed for an everyday knit, you'll be surprised what you can happily accomplish in two weeks. You'll find yourself bobbing your head while you knit the granite stitch ridges on the Shoreline Textured Cardigan (page 123), or chatting with friends while zipping along on miles of stockinette on the Meridian Striped Pullover (page 53). You'll find projects that fit the pace of your life, and you'll finish with sweaters you'll love for years to come.

If you're willing to commit, you can knit a sweater in about two weeks and love doing it. Grab your needles, flip through these pages to find your new favorite sweater, and let's get down to business learning how to create a fun, manageable, efficient timeline for your project.

Marie E. Greene

The Strategy of a Seamless Sweater

GAUGE SWATCHING, FINDING YOUR FIT AND DETERMINING YOUR KNITTING SPEED

The sweaters in this book are designed to be knit in a single piece, without seams. Unlike many traditional sweaters which are knit in four parts—with the front, back and two sleeves worked separately and stitched together at the end—all four components of these sweaters are worked together at once. Specific construction details are highlighted at the beginning of each pattern, but the general approach for a seamless sweater, especially one worked top-down, is that the pieces are formed in unison through a series of increases as you work across each right-side row—or every other row, if working the sweater in the round. Markers separate the front, sleeves and back sections, and increases are worked strategically around the markers.

Knitting a seamless sweater accomplishes three things at once: you create the basic fabric, the shape of the fabric and the construction of the final garment. This process naturally cuts out many of the extra steps that can slow down a sweater project. The sweaters in this collection, with the exception of the Archipelago Cocoon Wrap (page 33), begin at the neckline and the body is formed from the neckline down. Read through the pattern before you begin to familiarize yourself with stitch patterns, transitions and shaping that will happen along the way.

I love seamless sweaters something fierce, but they are only as good as the strategies behind their design. Seamless sweaters naturally lack seams which would otherwise provide structure to the garment, and we must employ other techniques to compensate. I do this in the following ways:

- A stable cast-on edge: I use the cable cast-on (page 159) most often because it adds structure to the top edge, which bears much of the weight of the garment.

- Stitch patterns that anchor the yoke: See, for example, the patterning on the Shoreline Textured Cardigan (page 123).

- Clever shaping around the shoulders and neckline: You'll see this used in sweaters throughout the book, such as the Offshore Eyelet Cardigan (page 107), Landmark Cowl-Neck Pullover (page 21) and Sandscape Slipped-Stitch Pullover (page 129), which feature mock-saddle shaping that hugs the shoulders.

- Working the ribbing and trim after the fact, rather than inserting them as you go: This technique provides added stability, as well.

YARN MATTERS

Regardless of construction techniques, a sweater that fits well and stays in place depends on having the right yarn for the job. In seamless sweaters especially, yarn choice is part of the strategy of a good fit. The recommended yarn was chosen for the way it works with the other elements of the design; substitutions may affect the fit, drape, stitch definition and longevity of a design, so it pays to select carefully.

Consider the Fiber Family

If you're unable to use the recommended yarn, it's important to know how to properly consider your alternatives. First, look for yarn in the same general fiber family as what the pattern suggests. If the pattern calls for 100 percent lamb's wool yarn, consider the characteristics of this yarn when choosing an alternative. Lamb's wool, while not soft, will generally hide flaws while showing stitch definition. The fabric will maintain its shape and body, even in stockinette stitch, and won't be prone to excess growth.

Ask yourself:

- Will this yarn have similar drape and sheen?

- Will this yarn enhance or interfere with stitch definition?

- Will this yarn hold up to blocking and gravity for the way this garment is meant to be worn?

Superwash or Not Superwash, That is the Question

Before you substitute a superwash yarn in a design that calls for a non-superwash yarn, or vice versa, consider the design details and what modifications may need to be made to compensate for fiber differences. Substitutions can significantly alter the fit and wearability of your sweater, so it pays to be thoughtful.

Tips to Remember

Superwash yarn will almost always grow several inches, especially in length, beyond non-superwash yarns. You will see this immediately when it comes time to block your sweater. Keep this in mind before modifying your sweater length; it can be a nasty surprise when the sweater grows 4 or 5 inches (10 or 13 cm) unexpectedly. If the pattern was written specifically for a superwash yarn, this growth will already be anticipated in the design. On the other hand, a design that anticipates growth because it's written specifically for a superwash yarn may require you to add length in order to get the same results from a regular, non-superwash wool.

Yarn differences can magnify design details. For example, eyelets or lace patterning naturally lend themselves to growth. If you pair a lace pattern with a superwash yarn, the growth will be enhanced. However, a design with cables and slipped-stitch texture can help the stitches maintain their shape, and may counteract the growth you would normally see in a superwash yarn.

A PROPER GAUGE SWATCH

A gorgeous sweater—that fits—begins with a swatch. This important first step creates a map of the results you can expect from your finished sweater. It provides clues about your tension, yarn behavior, stitch definition and the future fit of your garment. It's the only way to know ahead of time if the yarn and needle combination you've selected will work with your unique knitting style to get the results that the pattern promises. Every knitter is different—even using the

suggested yarn and needle size doesn't mean your results will be exactly the same. Variations in your stitch gauge—even by as little as one or two stitches within your swatch—can affect the final fit.

Gauge information in a pattern generally looks something like this:

20 STITCHES AND 24 ROWS OVER 4" (10 CM)

This example gives us both stitch gauge and row gauge. Both are important to the final fit.

Stitch Gauge

Per our example, if you have 20 whole stitches in a 4" (10 cm) blocked swatch, your finished sweater should match the measurements provided in the pattern schematic. For example, if the total number of stitches at the bust is 200, then at a gauge of 20 stitches in 4" (10 cm)—or 5 st per 1" (2.5 cm)—the resulting bust measurement would be 40" (100 cm). The number of stitches at the bust (200) divided by the stitches per inch (2.5 cm) (5) = final bust measurement of 40" (100 cm).

"Close" Isn't Really Close

I can't tell you how often I've heard a knitter say that the gauge was "close," only to express frustration that the finished sweater doesn't fit. The slight difference of a stitch or two in the gauge swatch seems irrelevant, but when magnified across the full body of your sweater, it can make a big difference. Let's talk about how close "close" really isn't.

Using the previous example of 20 stitches in 4" (10 cm) as our baseline, if you have 22 stitches instead, your resulting fit (for 200 stitches at the bust) would be 36" (91 cm) vs. the expected 40" (100 cm). It's a noticeable difference caused by just two extra stitches in a 4" (10 cm) space.

On the other hand, if you have two fewer stitches over 4" (10 cm), your results will vary in the opposite direction. For example, using this same baseline, if you have 18 stitches over 4" (10 cm) instead of 20 stitches, the resulting measurement would be approximately 44" (111 cm). When you're expecting a sweater with a fit of 40" (100 cm), being "off" by just two stitches in either direction can mean a sweater that fits two sizes smaller or larger than you anticipated. If you want the right results, it's important to make every effort to ensure that your gauge is accurate.

Measure the Interior—Not the Edges—of Your Swatch

Speaking of accuracy, to ensure that you are able to measure full, complete stitches for your swatch, it is important to knit your swatch piece slightly wider and longer than the area you will be measuring for gauge. For example, if the recommended gauge should be 20 stitches and 24 rows, cast on 24–26 stitches and knit closer to 30 rows before binding off. This ensures that you will be able to measure a full 4" (10 cm) over the interior of the swatch—away from the edges. Since the edge stitches are not full, complete stitches (or rows), they should not be included in your measurement.

Don't Forget Row Gauge

I used to be a "knit first, ask questions later" kind of knitter. Maybe you can relate? Not only was I haphazard (at best) about stitch gauge, but row gauge never crossed my radar. I had no idea it was important, and it was only once I began to design sweaters that it occurred to me just how important row gauge really was—especially when you're knitting a garment top-down.

Two Reasons to Check Your Row Gauge

First, unlike pieced sweaters, which are generally knit to a specified measurement, the upper body of a top-down, seamless sweater is knit to a specified number of rows. Because of this, if you have too many or too few rows in your gauge, then the measurement from the top of your shoulder to the underarm will vary from what the pattern indicates. This measurement is the one that's most affected by a row gauge issue, and it can make for a less comfortable fit.

Second, row gauge affects yarn consumption. If you find that you often run short on yarn, consider your row gauge as a possible culprit. Having more rows in your 4" (10 cm) swatch means significantly more rows in the sweater overall. While most patterns—mine included—estimate yardage a little higher to account for slight variations, you may still run into trouble if your row gauge is not accurate.

Measuring stitch gauge.

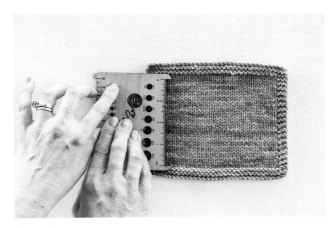

Measuring row gauge.

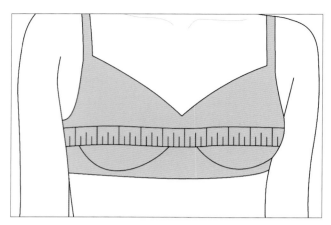

Full bust measurement.

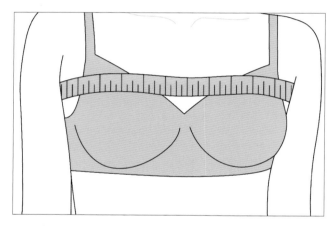

Upper bust measurement.

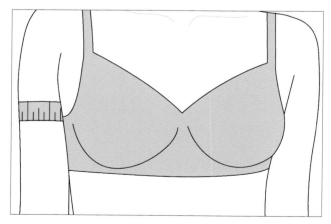

Arm circumference measurement.

SIZE & FIT

If there was one standard size that worked for everyone, making our own garments would be boring. Half the fun of creating a sweater for yourself is being able to decide how you want it to fit. But in order to get the results you expect, it's important to know about sizing and ease, and how to apply your own measurements to get the fit you want. There's nothing more frustrating than to pour your knitting hopes and dreams into a sweater, only to be left with a garment that doesn't fit. I want you to love your sweater.

Know Your Measurements

Before selecting a sweater size, start by figuring out what size YOU are. You'll need three primary measurements right away:

- Your full bust measurement

- Your upper bust measurement

- Your arm circumference at the widest point

Let's Get Your Measurements!

- Wearing a bra and a t-shirt or tank top, take a measuring tape and wrap it around your back, bringing it to the front so that it meets right at the midpoint of your bust. Make sure the measuring tape is horizontally even all the way around and doesn't sag down in the back as you measure—and don't pull too tight. This is your full bust measurement.

- For your upper bust measurement, take the measuring tape and wrap it around your back and over the upper part of your bust. This may be several inches above the midpoint of your bust and should rest comfortably atop. This measurement will usually be smaller than your full bust measurement.

- Next, wrap the measuring tape around your bicep and check your arm circumference. You want the measurement of the widest part of your arm so you can compare it to the widest part of the sleeve.

WHAT SIZE SHOULD I MAKE?

There is a difference between the "size" and the "finished measurements" of a pattern, and this difference will provide insight into the way the garment should fit. When you select a sweater off the rack at your favorite department store, you will likely have a selection in a range of sizes XS through XXL or beyond. If you were to choose two different sweaters, both size L, you would likely notice differences in the measurements from one to the other. Just because it is the same "size" doesn't mean the measurements will be exactly the same. Some sweaters are meant to fit loosely, some are meant to hug the body and others fall somewhere in between. In one brand we can wear a medium (M), but in another brand we might be a large (L). Sizing differences vary from pattern to pattern, designer to designer and decade to decade based on fashion trends.

Size

The size, as listed on a sweater label (or in our case, the pattern description) is meant to convey which bust sizes the sweater is intended to fit. Within this book, you'll see these sizes referred to in ranges that look like this: 30/32" (34/36, 38/40, 42/44, 46/48, 50/52) (76/81 cm [86/91, 97/102, 107/112, 117/122, 127/132]). When you read the word "size" within the pattern or anywhere within this book, this is the set of numbers being referred to. The first step in choosing your size is to determine where your actual bust measurement falls within the size ranges offered. For example, if your full bust measurement (at the widest point) is 31" (78.7 cm), begin by taking a closer look at the finished measurements for size 30/32 and go from there.

Finished Measurements

A sweater is meant to have a specific fit based on the designer's vision. While the size tells you which bust measurements the sweater is designed to fit, the finished measurements are the actual results you will get when the sweater is complete. The difference between these two sets of numbers equals how much ease the sweater will have when you are finished.

Ease

Ease is the word used to describe the fit of a garment in relation to your body. It indicates whether a garment will be baggy, tight or somewhere in between. The sweaters in this book are written to fit with positive ease. But since our bodies rarely fit into a cookie-cutter mold, and personal tastes vary, you can adjust your fit by selecting a different size for a fit with more or less ease. The finished measurements and the ease associated with them are contingent on getting the correct gauge as stated in the pattern. It's worth noting that ease is also contingent on choosing the correct size in the first place. The type of ease and how much of it is included can be a tricky business, because it varies from pattern to pattern; knitting the same size from one design to the next doesn't necessarily mean the fit will be the same.

Positive ease is the average default for most sweater patterns. It means knitting a garment with finished measurements that are larger than the measurements of your body, usually by several inches. For example, if you have a 32" (81 cm) bust and you knit a sweater with 3" (7.6 cm) positive ease, the resulting piece will measure 35" (89 cm) at the bust. Positive ease is the comfort zone for many knitters, and it's how most sweaters are designed. Approximately 2–3" (5–7.6 cm) of positive ease is a good baseline, and it gives most of us the wiggle room we need to feel comfortable in our clothes and have freedom of movement. Positive ease allows for a little fluctuation in our size, too, which never hurts. Please note: There is such a thing as too much positive ease, so remember that less is sometimes more. Too much extra ease becomes oversized and sloppy. If this isn't the look you're going for, be careful about how much extra ease you allow.

Because positive ease is already included in the designs throughout this book, it is not necessary to go up to a larger size. If you're at the lower end of the size range, you may prefer a size smaller.

Negative ease means you'll have a finished sweater that measures smaller than the measurements of your body—usually in the bust, with the corresponding fit in the arms being proportional. If you'd like to accentuate small shoulders/waist and a curvy bust, negative ease might give you the results you want, but it's less common and not for everyone.

Zero ease means that the bust of your garment is equal to the measurements of your body. Zero ease works well when a close fit is desired—but not as snug as negative ease. It is especially nice for lightweight cardigans that are meant to be worn over a sundress or sleeveless shirt. For those with curvy figures and small waists, zero ease (or even negative ease) can be a flattering style.

Different Ease = Different Style

Some designs are meant to be worn loose, some are meant to be fitted; styles vary, and so do personal preferences. The benefit of knitting your own sweaters is that you get to decide the fit you want. The intended ease helps to standardize a pattern so that it will have enough room to fit comfortably for most knitters, but it's your job to choose the size that works best for the fit you like.

Pick a Size, Any Size

When you have determined your bust measurement and arm circumference, verify that your gauge is accurate. It can't be said enough: gauge is crucial. Now, it's time to pick a size. If you're in between sizes or at the lower end of the stated size range, the positive ease will often allow you to knit the smaller size. If you have narrow shoulders and smaller arms but a large bust, consider choosing a size midway between your upper bust measurement and your full bust measurement. For example, my full bust measures 38 inches [97 cm] and my upper bust measures 34 inches [86 cm], so I can often get away with knitting a size 36. It depends on whether I want a more tailored fit or a roomy fit. Always compare your body measurements with the finished measurements of the sweater—both the bust and arm—to verify that this is the right option for you. Rarely will you need to knit a larger sweater than the recommended size, unless you need to accommodate a larger arm circumference.

Sizing Tip

The reality of fit is this: what fits your bust might not fit your arms and vice versa. If your arms measure two, three or even four sizes larger than the size you'd normally make for your bust, you can go up to the size that will fit your arms best which means the rest of the sweater will be larger, as well. Or you can perform a little math wizardry by playing with the number of increases in order to adjust your fit. Unless pattern modification is already your specialty, I recommend waiting until you are very comfortable with it—maybe knit it once to get a feel for it—before you attempt a complicated modification.

For the adventurous knitter: My quick advice for arm modifications includes mixing and matching the sleeve instructions to include the cast-on number for the size you need for your arms with the body/bust instructions, and the cast-on number for the size you need for your bust. This adjustment can help you customize your fit in either direction, but it can get a bit tricky and you'll need to create your own road map to help you navigate the adjustments along the way.

GOAL KNITTING

Have you ever looked at a project and wondered how long it would take to knit?

Me, too.

The answer depends on the project, but if you're serious about knitting efficiently and/or you're on a deadline, the seamless sweater is the way to go. Let's talk about what makes a seamless sweater tick, and how to set goals for a successful and timely knit.

If you've been knitting any length of time, you probably already have an idea of how long it takes you to complete an ordinary knitting project, give or take. For me, a fingering weight sweater in my size (36/38) usually takes about two weeks, barring unexpected events; a worsted weight sweater takes me about a week at a normal pace. I knit several hours each day; three to four hours is my ideal. I can achieve that with an hour of knitting before work, knitting a bit in the afternoon and knitting at night before bed. Granted, the timing depends on how many projects I'm working on, how motivated I am and how much wine/coffee I've had. Results vary in both directions.

Determining your general knitting speed can help you break your sweater project into manageable goals. This can help you decide how many hours you'll want to knit each day, and how many days a week to work on your project. Knitting a sweater in two weeks isn't an unrealistic goal, but it does require some commitment to the result. Giving yourself a timeline with milestones along the way will help guarantee your success. As you'll see on the following pages, even just one to two hours of focused knitting a day can help you knit a sweater in a few weeks.

But before we get ahead of ourselves, let me say this: challenging yourself to knit quickly is just a fun way to test your knitting chops; it's not meant to be stressful. Sometimes when we hurry, we put unnecessary stress on ourselves and the project we're working on. That can ruin the fun of the experience. Knitting under a short deadline also requires us to let go of certain nit-pickiness that might otherwise slow us down. Don't let yourself get too focused on perceived imperfections—often they'll be cured with blocking. Most of all, remember that a handknit garment isn't meant to look factory-made, so give yourself permission to be a maker, and put your stamp of individuality into the garment you create.

Let's get started.

I'm sure you've heard the rumor that the humble gauge swatch is the backbone of a successful sweater (see page 12 for everything you need to know about swatching for sweaters). But there's more to swatching than just checking for size and fabric. You can also knit a "time-gauge" swatch for your project to get an estimate of how long it will take you—in actual knitting time—to complete. If you're on a deadline, or just plain curious, this extra step can help you make heads or tails of the amount of time you'll actually spend knitting on any particular project. Keep in mind it's just an estimate, and if seeing the hard numbers takes the fun out of it, skip this process altogether.

HOW TO ESTIMATE YOUR KNITTING SPEED WITH A TIME-GAUGE SWATCH

- Cast on roughly 100 stitches using the yarn and needles you plan to use for your sweater and work two rows flat in stockinette stitch. If you are swatching for a project in the round, join your stitches in the round and work in stockinette stitch from there.

- Measure the next 5 yards (4.5 m) of your working yarn and tie a slip knot at the 5-yard (4.5-m) mark.

- Grab a stopwatch and get comfortable.

- Start the timer and knit at a comfortable pace until you reach the 5-yard (4.5-m) mark, then stop the timer. Note: If the majority of the sweater you're testing for is worked in a specific texture stitch, work your swatch in texture. Otherwise, test your time using stockinette stitch.

> **TIP:** Remember to breathe and work at a steady, reasonable pace. The goal isn't to see how fast you can possibly knit, but rather to gauge your normal knitting speed.

- Make note of the yardage listed for the sweater and size you plan to make. Compare it to the results of your time-gauge swatch.

Compare your results using the following example:

My chosen sweater, Shelter Cove (page 38) calls for 938 yards (858 m) for size 38/40.

Minutes to knit 5 yards (4.5 m) based on my time-gauge swatch: 5.65 (divide this number by 5 to get the yard-per-minute number = 1.13 yards (1 m) per minute, or YPM)

938 yards (858 m) multiplied by 1.13 yards (1 m) per minute = 1060 minutes

Divide the minutes into hours: 1060 divided by 60 = 17.6 hours

If I wanted to knit this sweater in 4 days, I would take 17.6 hours divided by 4 days = 4.4 hours of focused knitting per day. If my goal was to knit the sweater in 2 weeks, I'd take 17.6 hours divided by 14 days = 1.3 hours of focused knitting per day. Not bad, right?

Remember: Every time you check your phone, take a potty break or make another pot of coffee, your knitting pace slows. The idea is to take a look at the estimate and be able to say: Wow. If I only need 1.3 hours of focused knitting, then if I give myself 2 hours a day to work on this, I can easily stay on track without feeling rushed.

Things to Keep in Mind

Once you have your ideal time established, round up by 2 to 3 hours to account for the variables that slow things down—a dropped stitch, a knot in the yarn, a cable snafu. Give yourself wiggle room.

Knowing the numbers can help you decide how to approach your goal in terms of setting aside the appropriate amount of time for your sweater, how many hours per day you'll want to knit, etc. That said, it's still an estimate. You might get into a groove and knit faster than usual or have more interruptions than you anticipate. In the end, the numbers are just there to give you something to aim for. They're not set in stone.

Above all else, you're the boss of your knitting. If you want to take your time or race to the finish, either way it's up to you.

Always put your health first. If long stretches of knitting bother your hands, arms or other parts of your body, take a break. Pacing yourself and doing what's best for you is more important than how quickly you finish.

Long-Weekend Knits

RELAXING REPETITION & BREEZY DETAILS

When a long weekend arrives, I'm immediately inspired to cast on a new project. Okay, let's be honest, I'm also inspired on a Tuesday for no reason at all, but I think we can agree that there's something motivating about an extra day or two on the weekend.

The sweaters on the following pages are designed to keep your interest with only sporadic periods of focus required so you can knit for long stretches, but easily put down your project and pick it up again without losing your spot. You'll find these projects perfect for knitting in your favorite comfy chair with access to a few basic tools—get your cable needles ready! The relatively simple textures are easy to memorize and result in sweaters that look significantly more dynamic than your average "quick knit." If you have time for occasional attention to a chart or don't mind a slightly less portable project, like Archipelago (page 33), these sweaters will keep you engaged without sacrificing efficiency.

The breezy details and relaxing repetition of the sweaters in this section are perfect for a cozy weekend at home—you'll be knitting and wearing these long-weekend knits in no time.

Landmark Cowl-Neck Pullover

Playing favorites with sweaters is no easy task, but I admit I have a soft spot for this one. Maybe it's the unusual details, or maybe I'm just a sucker for a honey-colored sweater, but I find myself reaching for Landmark every time I head toward the coast, which is always a bit cooler than it is inland. In fact, it was one of only two sweaters I took with me on a recent cross-country trip where I knew I'd be spending time in variable coastal weather. Featuring a wide cable with horizontal "landmarks" of texture along the way, this cowl-neck pullover is an elegant classic with modern details and a comfortable fit.

TIMELINE

Long sleeves and a cowl-neck—plus cables!—work up more quickly than you might expect thanks to bulky weight yarn. Most sizes will find it easy to complete in 7 to 10 days of attentive knitting.

MATERIALS

Yarn	• Bulky | Woolfolk Luft | 55% ultimate Merino wool, 45% organic Pima cotton | 109 yards (100 m) in 50 g | 732 yards (814, 904, 993, 1123, 1257) (669 m [744, 827, 908, 1027, 1149])
Yarn Notes	• Luft is a light-as-a-feather chained Merino with a halo of color that creates a soft, airy fabric with surprising stitch definition for its style.
Needles	• U.S. size 9/5.5 mm (24–32" [60–80 cm]) circular needle (body) • U.S. size 9/5.5 mm (12" [30 cm]) circular needle or DPN (sleeves) • U.S. size 8/5 mm (24–32" [60–80 cm]) circular needle (lower body ribbing) • U.S. size 8/5 mm (16" [40 cm]) circular needle (neckline) • Note: Use needle size necessary to obtain gauge.
Gauge	• 16 st and 20 rows with larger needle over 4" (10 cm) in stockinette stitch
Notions	• Yarn needle • Stitch markers • Cable needle

STITCH GLOSSARY

bet	between
BOR	beginning of round/row
CO	cast on
dec	decrease
DPN	double point needle/s
ea	each
inc	increase
k	knit
k2tog	knit 2 st at once (dec 1)
kfb	knit into front and back of same st (inc 1)
m	marker/markers
M1u	make one under by knitting under the bar before the next st—similar to a M1L or M1R, but don't twist the stitch; it should leave a small hole (inc 1)
mX	marker "X" indicates which marker (i.e, mA, mB, mC, etc.)
M1L	make one st that leans left (inc 1)
M1R	make one st that leans right (inc 1)
p	purl
pmX	place marker, "X" indicates which marker (i.e, pmA, pmB, pmC, etc.)
rem m	remove marker

(continued)

STITCH GLOSSARY

rep	repeat
rs	right side
sm	slip marker/markers
smX	slip marker, "X" indicates which marker (i.e, smA, smB, smC, etc.)
ssk	slip, slip, knit together (dec 1)
st	stitch/stitches
ws	wrong side
[ ]	brackets always indicate a repeat

SIZES

Bust sizes 30/32" (34/36, 38/40, 42/44, 46/48, 50/52) (76/81 cm [86/91, 97/102, 107/112, 117/122, 127/132])

RECOMMENDED EASE

Positive ease is included for a comfortable fit. See finished measurements for final ease as compared to your actual bust measurement. If you are between sizes, refer to the final measurements to determine which size to choose. In many cases you'll find that the smaller of the two sizes will be best.

CONSTRUCTION

Landmark features unique shaping that hints at a set-in sleeve. Worked top-down, the initial neckline is established by working back and forth (flat) until you join to work in the round. The cowlneck is worked afterward, and it can be worked inside-out if you prefer to knit instead of purl.

NOTE: Rows and rounds apply to all sizes unless otherwise indicated. Be sure to read ahead and mark sections that are specific to your size before you begin. Also note the irregular pace of increases: pay close attention as they shift.

QUICK TIP: Pay special attention to the nontraditional pace of increases. The first few rows feature increases on the front/back sections, but not the sleeves, to create the shoulder saddle. The increases then transition away from the front and back, and are worked only on the sleeves until shaping near the sleeve divide begins. It's an interesting construction—not at all difficult—but be sure to read the row instructions carefully as it's easy to miss the change in increases if you're in the groove and forget to look. Stitch Count Check-In points are provided to keep you on track.

LANDMARK PATTERN

With U.S. size 9/5.5 mm (24-32" [60-80 cm]) circular needle, cast on 44 (52, 52, 66, 74, 84) st using cable cast-on method. Do not join.

ROW 1 – SET UP (RS): Kfb, pmA, k8 (10, 10, 14, 16, 18), pmB, kfb, k24 (28, 28, 34, 38, 44), kfb, pmC, k8 (10, 10, 14, 16, 18), pmD, kfb (4 st inc).

ROW 2 (WS): P across, slipping m as you go.

ROW 3 (RS): K2, smA, k to mB (no inc), smB, k1, M1L, k to 1 st before mC, M1R, k1, smC, k to mD (no inc), smD, k2 (2 st inc).

ROW 4 (WS): As row 2.

ROW 5 (RS): As row 3 (2 st inc).

ROW 6 (WS): As row 2.

STITCH COUNT CHECK-IN

FRONTS (EA): 2
SLEEVES (EA): 8 (10, 10, 14, 16, 18)
BACK: 32 (36, 36, 42, 46, 52)

SIZES 30/32, 34/36, 38/40 ROW 7 (RS): Co 1 st using knitted cast-on worked tightly*, then k to 1 st before mA, M1R, k1, smA, k1 (2, 2, -, -, -), M1u, [k2, M1u] rep bet brackets three times total, k1 (2, 2, -, -, -), smB, k1, M1L, k to 1 st before mC, M1R, k1, smC, k1 (2, 2, -, -, -), M1u, [k2, M1u] rep bet brackets three times total, k1 (2, 2, -, -, -), smD, k1, M1L, k to end (12 st inc + CO).

SIZES 42/44, 46/48, 50/52 ROW 7 (RS): Co 1 st using knitted cast-on worked tightly*, then k to 1 st before mA, M1R, k1, smA, k - (-, -, 2, 3, 4), M1u, [k2, M1u] rep bet brackets five times total, k - (-, -, 2, 3, 4), smB, k1, M1L, k to 1 st before mC, M1R, k1, smC, k - (-, -, 2, 3, 4), M1u, [k2, M1u] rep bet brackets five times total, k - (-, -, 2, 3, 4), smD, k1, M1L, k to end (16 st inc + CO).

ROW 8 (WS): Co 1 st using knitted cast-on worked purlwise*, then p across row, slipping m as you go.

*GOING FORWARD, all stitches cast-on on the right side will be worked using the knitted cast-on method (page 159), and all stitches cast-on on the wrong side will be worked using the knitted cast-on method worked purlwise (page 160). Always knit the new stitch/es on the right side and purl the new stitch/es on the wrong side as you work through the rows.

ALL sizes continue.

ROW 9 (RS): Co 1 st, then k to 1 st before mA, M1R, k1, smA, k1, M1L, k to 1 st before mB, M1R, k1, smB, k1, M1L, k to 1 st before mC, M1R, k1, smC, k1, M1L, k to 1 st before mD, M1R, k1, smD, k1, M1L, k to end (8 st inc + CO).

ROW 10 (WS): As row 8.

ROW 11 (RS): Co 1 (1, 1, 2, 2, 2) st, then k to 1 st before mA, M1R, k1, smA, k1, M1L, k to 1 st before mB, M1R, k1, smB, k1, M1L, k to 1 st before mC, M1R, k1, smC, k1, M1L, k to 1 st before mD, M1R, k1, smD, k1, M1L, k to end (8 st inc + CO).

ROW 12 (WS): Co 1 (1, 1, 2, 2, 2) st, then p across row, slipping m as you go.

STITCH COUNT CHECK-IN

FRONTS (EA): 8 (8, 8, 9, 9, 9)
SLEEVES (EA): 16 (18, 18, 24, 26, 28)
BACK: 38 (42, 42, 48, 52, 58)

ROW 13 (RS): Co 1 (2, 2, 2, 4, 4) st, then k to 1 st before mA, M1R, k1, smA, k1, M1L, k to 1 st before mB, M1R, k1, smB, k1, M1L, k to 1 st before mC, M1R, k1, smC, k1, M1L, k to 1 st before mD, M1R, k1, smD, k1, M1L, k to end (8 st inc + CO).

ROW 14 (WS): Co 1 (2, 2, 2, 4, 4) st, then p across row, slipping m as you go.

ROW 15 (RS): Co 2 (2, 2, 4, 4, 4) st, then k to 1 st before mA, M1R, k1, smA, k1, M1L, k to 1 st before mB, M1R, k1, smB, k1, M1L, k to 1 st before mC, M1R, k1, smC, k1, M1L, k to 1 st before mD, M1R, k1, smD, k1, M1L, k to end (8 st inc + CO).

ROW 16 (WS): Co 2 (2, 2, 4, 4, 4) st, then p across row, slipping m as you go.

Landmark shoulder and back detail.

ROW 17 (RS): Co 4 st, then k to 1 st before mA, M1R, k1, smA, k1, M1L, k to 1 st before mB, M1R, k1, smB, k1, M1L, k to 1 st before mC, M1R, k1, smC, k1, M1L, k to 1 st before mD, M1R, k1, smD, k1, M1L, k to end (8 st inc + CO).

ROW 18 (WS): Co 4 st, then p across row, slipping m as you go.

ROW 19 (RS): Co 8 (10, 10, 10, 10, 16) st, then k to 1 st before mA, M1R, k1, smA, k1, M1L, k to 1 st before mB, M1R, k1, smB, k to mC (no inc), smC, k1, M1L, k to 1 st before mD, M1R, k1, smD, k1, M1L, k to end (6 st inc + CO) Cut yarn, leaving a tail.

NECKLINE JOIN: Rejoin the yarn just after mD, leaving a tail to weave in later. This marks the new BOR. Slide the stitches after mD to the left needle so they "meet" with the other stitches on the front section (all stitches between mD and mA are now the "front"). K across, joining the front stitches as you reach the gap (be careful not to twist stitches) and knit to end of round (no inc).

Landmark sleeve detail.

STITCH COUNT CHECK-IN

FRONT: 46 (50, 50, 56, 60, 66)
SLEEVES (EA): 24 (26, 26, 32, 34, 36)
BACK: 44 (48, 48, 54, 58, 64)

NEXT ROUND (INC): At BOR, k19 (21, 21, 24, 26, 29), pmE, k12, pmF, k19 (21, 21, 24, 26, 29), smA, k1, M1L, k to 1 st before mB, M1R, k1, smB, k to mC, smC, k1, M1L, k to 1 st before mD, M1R, k1 (4 st inc + CO).

NEXT ROUND (NO INC): K across, slipping m as you go.

NEXT ROUND (INC): At BOR, k to mE, smE, begin Center Cable over 12 st starting with round 1*, smF, k19 (21, 21, 24, 26, 29), smA, k1, M1L, k to 1 st before mB, M1R, k1, smB, k to mC, smC, k1, M1L, k to 1 st before mD, M1R, k1 (4 st inc).

*****PLEASE** read through the Center Cable Directions (page 25) and make note of the variation on the second repeat to extend the Granite Stitch past the borders of the Center Cable.

NEXT ROUND (NO INC): K across, slipping m as you go and maintaining Center Cable next round between mE and mF on the front.

REP THE ABOVE TWO ROUNDS, working Center Cable rounds in order and rep until you reach the following:

STITCH COUNT CHECK-IN

FRONT: 46 (50, 50, 56, 60, 66)
SLEEVES (EA): 36 (38, 40, 46, 48, 50)
BACK: 44 (48, 48, 54, 58, 64)

NEXT ROUND (FRONT/BACK INC BEGIN AGAIN): At BOR, k1, M1L, k2, M1L, k to mE, smE, work Center Cable next round, smF, k to 3 st before mA, M1R, k2, M1R, k1, smA, k1, M1L, k to 1 st before mB, M1R, k1, smB, k1, M1L, k2, M1L, k to 3 st before mC, M1R, k2, M1R, k1, smC, k1, M1L, k to 1 st befores mD, M1R, k1 (12 st inc).

NEXT ROUND (NO INC): K across, slipping m as you go and maintaining Center Cable next round between mE and mF on front.

REP these two rounds 4 (5, 3, 4, 5, 5) times more.

STITCH COUNT CHECK-IN

FRONT: 66 (74, 66, 76, 84, 90)
SLEEVES (EA): 46 (50, 48, 56, 60, 62)
BACK: 64 (72, 64, 74, 82, 88)

NEXT ROUND (EXTRA INC): At BOR, k1, M1L, k2, M1L, k2, M1L, k to mE, smE, work Center Cable next round, smF, k to 5 st before mA, M1R, k2, M1R, k2, M1R, k1, smA, k1, M1L, k to 1 st before mB, M1R, k1, smB, k1, M1L, k2, M1L, k2, M1L, k to 5 st before mC, M1R, k2, M1R, k2, M1R, k1, smC, k1, M1L, k to 1 st before mD, M1R, k1 (16 st inc).

NEXT ROUND (NO INC): K across, slipping m as you go and maintaining Center Cable Chart (page 26) next round between mE and mF on front.

REP these two rounds 0 (0, 2, 2, 2, 2) times more.

STITCH COUNT CHECK-IN

FRONT: 72 (80, 84, 94, 102, 108)
SLEEVES (EA): 48 (52, 54, 62, 66, 68)
BACK: 70 (78, 82, 92, 100, 106)

DIVIDE FOR SLEEVES: NEXT ROUND (NO INC): K across front in pattern (maintaining Center Cable Chart, keeping mE and mF in place) to mA, rem mA and place sleeve stitches onto waste yarn (loosely, so you can try it on later), then CO 0 (0, 2, 2, 2, 4) st underarm and join to back section, removing mB in the process, k to mC and rem mC, place sleeve stitches onto waste yarn (loosely, so you can try it on later), then CO 0 (0, 2, 2, 2, 4) st underarm and join to front, removing mD in the process and replacing it at the center of the underarm (in the center of the newly cast-on st)—mD now denotes BOR.

STITCH COUNT CHECK-IN

142 (158, 170, 190, 206, 222) st in lower body

CONTINUE lower body in the round, maintaining Center Cable Chart panel until body measures 12" (30 cm) from underarm (at sleeve divide).

NEXT ROUND, transition to U.S. size 8/4.5 mm (24-32" [60-80 cm]) circular needle (or one size smaller than needle used for body) and k one round—at the same time dec 1 (2, 2, 1, 2, 0) st somewhat evenly using k2tog. You should end with a multiple of 3. On the next round transition to ribbing as follows: [k2, p1] rep bet brackets to end of round. Continue in ribbing as established until lower rib measures 2.5" (6.25 cm). Bind off in pattern with medium tension. Lower edge should not be restrictive. If it is, bind off a bit more loosely.

SLEEVES: With U.S. size 9/5.5 mm (12" [30 cm]) circular needle (or same size needle used for body), pick up sleeve st from waste yarn—including st cast-on under the arm - 48 (52, 56, 64, 68, 72) st. Pm at center of underarm to mark BOR. Knit sleeve in the round in stockinette st for 2" (5 cm).

NEXT ROUND: K2, k2tog, k to 4 st before m, ssk, k2 (2 st dec).

CONTINUE working sleeve in the round in stockinette stitch, working a dec round as established approximately every 2.5" (2.5, 2.5, 2, 2, 1.5) (6.25 cm [6.25, 6.25, 5, 5, 3.8]), until sleeve measures 19" (48.25 cm) and you have 32 (36, 40, 46, 48, 50) st. Begin the two-round granite stitch series as follows: [p2tog] rep bet brackets to end of round. Next round: [kfb] rep bet brackets to end of round. Work three more rounds in stockinette stitch. Rep the two-round granite stitch series once more. Work two rounds in stockinette stitch, then bind off in pattern with medium tension.

NECKLINE: With U.S. size 8/5 mm (16" [40 cm]) circular needle (or one size smaller than that used for body), pick up nearly every available stitch around neckline and join to work in the round. Work in reverse stockinette (purl every row on the rs) until cowl-neck measures 7" (17.75 cm). Bind off loosely in pattern (you may use a stretchy bind-off if needed).

BLOCKING: Wet block flat, drawing neckline straight up and pinning flat until dry. Turn as necessary for even drying.

CENTER CABLE DIRECTIONS

NOTE: The blackened squares on the chart mean "no stitch"—meaning the stitch that had been in that space is no longer there. These non-stitches are not represented in the written directions below.

ROUND 1: P1, c10f, p1.
ROUNDS 2-8: P1, k10, p1.
ROUND 9: P1, c10f, p1.
ROUNDS 10-16: P1, k10, p1.
ROUND 17 (GRANITE STITCH ROUND 1): P1, [p2tog] rep bet brackets five times total, p1.
ROUND 18 (GRANITE STITCH ROUND 2): P1, [kfb] rep bet brackets five times total, p1.
ROUNDS 19-25: P1, k10, p1.

REGARDLESS OF WHETHER YOU USE THE CHART OR WRITTEN DIRECTIONS, PLEASE READ BEFORE YOU BEGIN.

The Center Cable Chart is repeated down the front of the body with a slight variation ONLY on the second repeat. Work rounds 1–25 of the Cable Chart once. On the second repeat, when you reach round 17, extend the Granite Stitch by working in pattern to 6 st before mE, [p2tog] three times, smE, work round 17 of the Cable Chart to mF, smF, [p2tog] three times, then work to end of round in pattern. On the next round (Center Cable Chart round 18 and Granite Stitch round 2), work in pattern to 6 st before mE, [kfb] three times, smE, work round 18 of the Center Cable Chart to mF, smF, [kfb] three times, then work to end of round in pattern.

Work all other repeats per the written directions or chart.

CENTER CABLE CHART

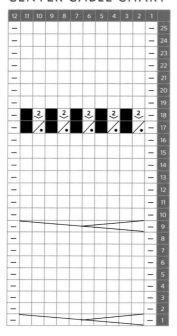

	c10f	Cable 10 forward. (rs) Place 5 st on cn, hold to front, k5 then k5 from cn
☐	k	(rs) Knit
☑2	kfb	Knit Front Back. (rs) Knit into front and back of same st (inc 1)
☐	p	(rs) Purl
☑	p2tog	Purl 2 Together. (rs) Purl 2 st togehter at once (dec 1)
■	x	No stitch. (rs) Represents a st that is no longer there due to dec

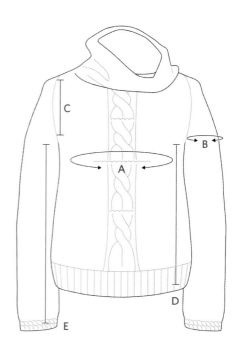

FINISHED MEASUREMENTS

A) BUST:
34.5" (38.5, 42, 46.5, 50.5, 54.5) (86.3 cm [96.3, 105, 116.3, 126.3, 136.3])

B) SLEEVE AT WIDEST POINT:
12" (13, 14, 16, 17, 18) (30 cm [32.5, 35, 40, 42.5, 45])

C) TOP OF SHOULDER TO UNDERARM:
9.4" (10, 10.4, 11.2, 11.8, 12) (23.9 cm [25.4, 26.4, 28.4, 30, 30.5])

D) LENGTH OF BODY FROM UNDERARM:
14.5" (36.8 cm) prior to blocking

E) LENGTH OF SLEEVE FROM UNDERARM:
20.5" (52.1 cm) prior to blocking

Cobble Beach Dotted Tee

Every capsule wardrobe needs a tee, don't you think? There's nothing I love more than a v-neck tee, in particular. The angled neckline is flattering for almost any figure and having a little extra neck/upper chest exposed allows for more breathability, especially if you tend to get a bit warm in sweaters or live in a hot climate. This understated and versatile design features delicate details that catch the sunlight, especially in fair to medium colorways. Darker yarns may disguise the bobbles entirely. You might layer Cobble Beach over a tank top or sundress, or wear it under a jacket in cooler weather for a different look.

TIMELINE

This lightweight tee features time-saving short sleeves and a cropped length. Most knitters will find this an approachable project to knit in about 5 to 7 days.

MATERIALS

Yarn	• Sport | HiKoo Rylie | 50% baby alpaca, 25% mulberry silk, 25% linen | 274 yards (251 m) per 100 g | 684 yards (760, 836, 920, 1012, 1115) (625 m [695, 764, 841, 925, 1020])
Yarn Notes	• Worked in a blend of baby alpaca, mulberry silk and linen, Cobble Beach should be lightweight with medium drape and sheen. The fiber content encourages slight growth with blocking, and the silk accentuates the subtle bobble detail along the bottom. Substitutions may create different results.
Needles	• U.S. size 4/3.5 mm (24-32" [60-80 cm]) circular needle (body) • U.S. size 4/3.5 mm (12" [30 cm]) circular needle or DPN (sleeves) • U.S. size 2/3 mm (12" [30 cm]) circular needle or DPN (sleeve cuff) • U.S. size 3/3.25 mm (24-32" [60-80 cm]) circular needle (lower body ribbing and neckline) • Note: Use needle size necessary to obtain gauge.
Gauge	• 22 st and 30 rows with largest needle over 4" (10 cm) in stockinette stitch
Notions	• Yarn needle • Stitch markers • Waste yarn

STITCH GLOSSARY

bet	between
BOR	beginning of round/row
CO	cast on
dec	decrease
ea	each
inc	increase
k	knit
k2tog	knit 2 st at once (dec 1)
kfb	knit into front and back of same st (inc 1)
m	marker/markers
mX	marker "X" indicates which marker (i.e, mA, mB, mC, etc.)
M1L	make one st that leans left (inc 1)
M1R	make one st that leans right (inc 1)
p	purl
pmX	place marker, "X" indicates which marker (i.e, pmA, pmB, pmC, etc.)
rem m	remove marker
rep	repeat
rs	right side
sl	slip

(continued)

STITCH GLOSSARY

sm	slip marker/markers
smX	slip marker, "X" indicates which marker (i.e, smA, smB, smC, etc.)
ssk	slip, slip, knit together (dec 1)
st	stitch/stitches
ws	wrong side
[ ]	brackets always indicate a repeat

SIZES

Bust sizes 30/32" (34/36, 38/40, 42/44, 46/48, 50/52) (76/81 cm [86/91, 97/102, 107/112, 117/122, 127/132])

RECOMMENDED EASE

Positive ease is included for a comfortable fit. See finished measurements for final ease as compared to your actual bust measurement. If you are between sizes, refer to the final measurements to determine which size to choose. In many cases you'll find that the smaller of the two sizes will be best.

CONSTRUCTION

Cobble Beach is cast-on and worked flat until the v-neck shaping is complete. The sweater is then joined to work in the round from there. The body is primarily stockinette stitch with subtle dotted texture along the bottom. The neckline and short sleeves are finished last— though you can do them sooner, if you prefer.

NOTE: Rows and rounds apply to all sizes unless otherwise indicated. Be sure to read ahead and mark sections that are specific to your size before you begin.

LENGTH TIP: Changing the style of your sweater is sometimes as easy as adding—or subtracting—from the length. Keep in mind that the garment will grow with blocking if you're using the recommended fiber blend, so it's best to stop 2-3 inches (5-7.6 cm) before your ideal length.

COBBLE BEACH PATTERN

With U.S. size 4/3.5 mm (24-32" [60-80 cm]) circular needle (or size to obtain gauge), cast on 34 (50, 74, 82, 92, 102) st using cable cast-on method. Do not join.

ROW 1 - SET UP (RS): K2, pmA, kfb, k0 (4, 12, 14, 18, 22), kfb, pmB, kfb, k24 (32, 40, 44, 46, 48), kfb, pmC, kfb, k0 (4, 12, 14, 18, 22), kfb, pmD, k2 (6 st inc).

ROW 2 (WS): P across, slipping m as you go.

ROW 3 (RS): K1, kfb, smA, k1, M1L, k to 1 st before mB, M1R, k1, smB, k1, M1L, k to 1 st before mC, M1R, k1, smC, k1, M1L, k to 1 st before mD, M1R, k1, smD, kfb, k1 (8 st inc).

ROW 4 (WS): As row 2.

ROW 5 (RS): K to 1 st before mA, M1R, k1, smA, k1, M1L, k to 1 st before mB, M1R, k1, smB, k1, M1L, k to 1 st before mC, M1R, k1, smC, k1, M1L, k to 1 st before mD, M1R, k1, smD, k1, M1L, k to end (8 st inc).

ROW 6 (WS): As row 2.

REP rows 5 and 6 until you have the following:

STITCH COUNT CHECK-IN

FRONTS (EA): 8
SLEEVES (EA): 16 (20, 28, 30, 34, 38)
BACK: 40 (48, 56, 60, 62, 64)

NEXT ROW (RS): K to 3 st before mA, M1R, k2, M1R, k1, smA, k1, M1L, k to 1 st before mB, M1R, k1, smB, k1, M1L, k to 1 st before mC, M1R, k1, smC, k1, M1L, k to 1 st before mD, M1R, k1, smD, k1, M1L, k2, M1L, k to end (10 st inc).

NEXT ROW (WS) and all ws rows unless otherwise indicated: P across, slipping m as you go.

SIZES 30/32, 34/36, 38/40, 42/44, 46/48 NEXT ROW (RS): K to 1 st before mA, M1R, k1, smA, k1, M1L, k to 1 st before mB, M1R, k1, smB, k1, M1L, k to 1 st before mC, M1R, k1, smC, k1, M1L, k to 1 st before mD, M1R, k1, smD, k1, M1L, k to end (8 st inc).

SIZE 50/52 NEXT ROW (RS): K to 3 st before mA, M1R, k2, M1R, k1, smA, k1, M1L, k to 1 st before mB, M1R, k1, smB, k1, M1L, k to 1 st before mC, M1R, k1, smC, k1, M1L, k to 1 st before mD, M1R, k1, smD, k1, M1L, k2, M1L, k to end (10 st inc).

ALL SIZES NEXT ROW (RS): K to 3 st before mA, M1R, k2, M1R, k1, smA, k1, M1L, k to 1 st before mB, M1R, k1, smB, k1, M1L, k to 1 st before mC, M1R, k1, smC, k1, M1L, k to 1 st before mD, M1R, k1, smD, k1, M1L, k2, M1L, k to end (10 st inc).

SIZES 30/32, 34/36, 38/40 NEXT ROW (RS): K to 1 st before mA, M1R, k1, smA, k1, M1L, k to 1 st before mB, M1R, k1, smB, k1, M1L, k to 1 st before mC, M1R, k1, smC, k1, M1L, k to 1 st before mD, M1R, k1, smD, k1, M1L, k to end (8 st inc).

SIZES 42/44, 46/48, 50/52 NEXT ROW (RS): K to 3 st before mA, M1R, k2, M1R, k1, smA, k1, M1L, k to 1 st before mB, M1R, k1, smB, k1, M1L, k to 1 st before mC, M1R, k1, smC, k1, M1L, k to 1 st before mD, M1R, k1, smD, k1, M1L, k2, M1L, k to end (10 st inc).

STITCH COUNT CHECK-IN

FRONTS (EA): 14 (14, 14, 15, 15, 16)
SLEEVES (EA): 24 (28, 36, 38, 42, 46)
BACK: 48 (56, 64, 68, 70, 72)

> **SIZES 30/32, 34/36 NEXT ROW (RS):** K to 3 st before mA, M1R, k2, M1R, k1, smA, k1, M1L, k to 1 st before mB, M1R, k1, smB, k1, M1L, k to 1 st before mC, M1R, k1, smC, k1, M1L, k to 1 st before mD, M1R, k1, smD, k1, M1L, k2, M1L, k to end (10 st inc).
>
> **NEXT ROW (WS):** P across, slipping m as you go.
>
> **NEXT ROW (RS):** K to 1 st before mA, M1R, k1, smA, k1, M1L, k to 1 st before mB, M1R, k1, smB, k1, M1L, k to 1 st before mC, M1R, k1, smC, k1, M1L, k to 1 st before mD, M1R, k1, smD, k1, M1L, k to end (8 st inc).
>
> **NEXT ROW (WS):** P across, slipping m as you go.

> **SIZES 38/40, 42/44, 46/48, 50/52 NEXT ROW (RS):** K to 3 st before mA, M1R, k2, M1R, k1, smA, k1, M1L, k to 1 st before mB, M1R, k1, smB, k1, M1L, k to 1 st before mC, M1R, k1, smC, k1, M1L, k to 1 st before mD, M1R, k1, smD, k1, M1L, k2, M1L, k to end (10 st inc).
>
> **NEXT ROW (WS):** P across, slipping m as you go.

REP the rows within the box for your size until you reach the following:

STITCH COUNT CHECK-IN

FRONTS (EA): 29 (29, 34, 35, 35, 36)
SLEEVES (EA): 44 (48, 56, 58, 62, 66)
BACK: 68 (76, 84, 88, 90, 92)

> **SIZE 30/32 NEXT ROW (RS):** K to 3 st before mA, M1R, k2, M1R, k1, smA, k1, M1L, k to 1 st before mB, M1R, k1, smB, k1, M1L, k to 1 st before mC, M1R, k1, smC, k1, M1L, k to 1 st before mD, M1R, k1, smD, k1, M1L, k2, M1L, k to end (10 st inc).
>
> **NEXT ROW (WS):** P across, slipping m as you go.
>
> **NEXT ROW (RS):** K to 1 st before mA, M1R, k1, smA, k1, M1L, k to 1 st before mB, M1R, k1, smB, k1, M1L, k to 1 st before mC, M1R, k1, smC, k1, M1L, k to 1 st before mD, M1R, k1, smD, k1, M1L, k to end (8 st inc).
>
> **NEXT ROW (WS):** P across, slipping m as you go.

> **SIZES 34/36, 38/40, 42/44, 46/48, 50/52 NEXT ROW (RS):** K to 3 st before mA, M1R, k2, M1R, k1, smA, k1, M1L, k to 1 st before mB, M1R, k1, smB, k1, M1L, k to 1 st before mC, M1R, k1, smC, k1, M1L, k to 1 st before mD, M1R, k1, smD, k1, M1L, k2, M1L, k to end (10 st inc).
>
> **NEXT ROW (WS):** P across, slipping m as you go.

REP the rows within the box for your size until you reach the following:

STITCH COUNT CHECK-IN

FRONTS (EA): 41 (45, 50, 51, 51, 52)
SLEEVES (EA): 60 (64, 72, 74, 78, 82)
BACK: 84 (92, 100, 104, 106, 108)

SIZES 30/32, 34/36, 38/40, 42/44, 46/48 NEXT ROW (RS): K to 3 st before mA, M1R, k2, M1R, k1, smA, k1, M1L, k to 1 st before mB, M1R, k1, smB, k1, M1L, k to 1 st before mC, M1R, k1, smC, k1, M1L, k to 1 st before mD, M1R, k1, smD, k1, M1L, k2, M1L, k to end (10 st inc).

SIZE 50/52 NEXT ROW (RS): K to 5 st before mA, M1R, k2, M1R, k2, M1R, k1, smA, k1, M1L, k to 1 st before mB, M1R, k1, smB, k1, M1L, k2, M1L, k to 3 st before mC, M1R, k2, M1R, k1, smC, k1, M1L, k to 1 st before mD, M1R, k1, smD, k1, M1L, k2, M1L, K2, M1L, k to end (14 st inc).

NEXT ROW (WS): P across, slipping m as you go.

SIZES 30/32, 34/36 NEXT ROW (RS): K to 3 st before mA, M1R, k2, M1R, k1, smA, k1, M1L, k to 1 st before mB, M1R, k1, smB, k1, M1L, k to 1 st before mC, M1R, k1, smC, k1, M1L, k to 1 st before mD, M1R, k1, smD, k1, M1L, k2, M1L, k to end (10 st inc).

SIZES 38/40, 42/44, 46/48 NEXT ROW (RS): K to 3 st before mA, M1R, k2, M1R, k1, smA, k1, M1L, k to 1 st before mB, M1R, k1, smB, k1, M1L, k2, M1L, k to 3 st before mC, M1R, k2, M1R, k1, smC, k1, M1L, k to 1 st before mD, M1R, k1, smD, k1, M1L, k2, M1L, k to end (12 st inc).

SIZE 50/52 NEXT ROW (RS): K to 5 st before mA, M1R, k2, M1R, k2, M1R, k1, smA, k1, M1L, k to 1 st before mB, M1R, k1, smB, k1, M1L, k2, M1L, k to 3 st before mC, M1R, k2, M1R, k1, smC, k1, M1L, k to 1 st before mD, M1R, k1, smD, k1, M1L, k2, M1L, K2, M1L, k to end (14 st inc).

NEXT ROW (WS): P across, slipping m as you go.

SIZE 30/32 Move ahead to Divide for Sleeves.

SIZES 34/36, 38/40, 42/44, 46/48 NEXT ROW (RS): K to 3 st before mA, M1R, k2, M1R, k1, smA, k1, M1L, k to 1 st before mB, M1R, k1, smB, k1, M1L, k2, M1L, k to 3 st before mC, M1R, k2, M1R, k1, smC, k1, M1L, k to 1 st before mD, M1R, k1, smD, k1, M1L, k2, M1L, k to end (12 st inc).

SIZE 50/52 NEXT ROW (RS): K to 5 st before mA, M1R, k2, M1R, k1, smA, k1, M1L, k to 1 st before mB, M1R, k1, smB, k1, M1L, k2, M1L k to 5 st before mC, M1R, k2, M1R, k2, M1R, k1, smC, k1, M1L, k to 1 st before mD, M1R, k1, smD, k1, M1L, k2, M1L, k2, M1L, k to end (16 st inc).

NEXT ROW (WS): P across, slipping m as you go.

SIZES 34/36, 38/40 Move ahead to Divide for Sleeves.

SIZES 42/44, 46/48, 50/52 NEXT ROW (RS): K to 5 st before mA, M1R, k2, M1R, k2, M1R, k1, smA, k1, M1L, k to 1 st before mB, M1R, k1, smB, k1, M1L, k2, M1L, k2, M1L k to 5 st before mC, M1R, k2, M1R, k2, M1R, k1, smC, k1, M1L, k to 1 st before mD, M1R, k1, smD, k1, M1L, k2, M1L, k2, M1L, k to end (16 st inc).

NEXT ROW (WS): P across, slipping m as you go.

SIZE 42/44: Move ahead to Divide for Sleeves.

SIZES 46/48, 50/52 NEXT ROW (RS): K to 5 st before mA, M1R, k2, M1R, k1, smA, k1, M1L, k to 1 st before mB, M1R, k1, smB, k1, M1L, k2, M1L, k2, M1L k to 5 st before mC, M1R, k2, M1R, k2, M1R, k1, smC, k1, M1L, k to 1 st before mD, M1R, k1, smD, k1, M1L, k2, M1L, k2, M1L, k to end (16 st inc).

NEXT ROW (WS): P across, slipping m as you go.

SIZES 46/48, 50/52 Rep these two rows once more, then move ahead to Divide for Sleeves.

STITCH COUNT CHECK-IN

FRONTS (EA): 45 (51, 56, 60, 66, 70)
SLEEVES (EA): 64 (70, 78, 82, 90, 94)
BACK: 88 (100, 110, 120, 134, 140)

DIVIDE FOR SLEEVES: K across front to mA, rem mA and place sleeve st onto waste yarn (loosely, so you can try it on later). CO 2 (3, 3, 4, 4, 6) st underarm and join to back section, replacing mA in the center of the st cast-on under the arm, rem mB as you reach it. K to mC, rem mC, and place sleeve st onto waste yarn (loosely, so you can try it on later). CO 2 (3, 3, 4, 4, 6) st underarm, replacing mD in the center of of the underarm st, and k to end. Cut working yarn, leaving a tail.

JOIN IN THE ROUND: Rejoin yarn just after mD, leaving a tail to weave in later. This marks the new BOR. Slide the st after mD to the left needle so they "meet" with st on the other front section (all st between mD and mA are now the "front"). K across front, joining the two sections as you reach the gap (be careful not to twist st), and k to end of round (including new st cast-on under the arm).

STITCH COUNT CHECK-IN

182 (208, 228, 248, 274, 292) st in lower body

Work lower body in stockinette st in the round until body measures 8" (20 cm). Work one last round in stockinette st, and at the same time inc 4 (2, 0, 4, 2, 2) st somewhat evenly spaced using M1R and M1L - 186 (210, 228, 252, 276, 294) st (or a multiple of 6).

LOWER BODY DETAIL ROUND 1: [K5, k1-p1-k1-p1 into next st] rep bet brackets to end of round.

ROUND 2: [K5, sl3, p1, pass 3 slipped st one at a time over purled st] rep bet brackets to end of round.

ROUNDS 3–6: Knit.

ROUND 7: K2, [k1-p1-k1-p1 into next st, k5] rep bet brackets to end of round, ending k3.

ROUND 8: K2, [sl3, p1, pass 3 slipped st one at a time over purled st, k5] rep bet brackets to end of round, ending k3.

ROUNDS 9–12: Knit.

REP rounds 1–12 until lower body measures 12–14" (30.5–35.5 cm) from underarm, ending on a knit round. Transition to U.S. size 3/3.25 mm (24–32" [60–80 cm]) circular needle (or one size smaller than that used for the body) and k one round. At the same time dec 2 (2, 0, 0, 0, 2) st evenly using k2tog to end with a multiple of 4. On the next round begin lower ribbing as follows: [k2, p2] rep bet brackets to end of round. Rep ribbing round until lower ribbing measures 2" (5 cm).

SLEEVES: With U.S. size 4/3.5 mm (12" [30 cm]) circular needle (or the same size as used for the body), pick up sleeve st from waste yarn (including st cast-on under the arm where applicable) 66 (73, 81, 86, 94, 102) st. Pm at center of underarm to mark BOR. Knit sleeve in the round in stockinette st for 1.5" (3.8 cm).

DEC ROUND: K2, k2tog, k to 4 st before m, ssk, k2 (2 st dec).

KNIT in the round for 1.5" (3.8 cm), then work one more dec round as established (2 st dec). Knit in the round for an additional 1.5" (3.8 cm) more and on the last round, dec 2 (1, 1, 2, 2, 2) st in the same manner as before—60 (68, 76, 80, 88, 96) st.

TRANSITION to U.S. size 2/3 mm (12" [30 cm]) circular needle or DPN and k one round, then begin ribbing: [k2, p2] rep bet brackets to end of round. Work ribbing as established until sleeve cuff measures 1.5" (3.8 cm). Bind off in pattern with medium/loose tension. Cuff should not feel restrictive; if it does, bind off more loosely.

NECKLINE: With U.S. size 3/3.25 mm (24–32" [60–80 cm]) circular needle, pick up st around the neckline (approximately 7 of every 8 st) starting at the center front on the rs, and working around the neckline to the other side. Turn and work back and forth in stockinette st for 4 rows, ending ready to work a rs row. Bind off on the rs with medium tension. Fold the corner of the front right trim corner over the left trim corner (stated sides are as if you were wearing it) and tack this down at the center with a darning needle and additional yarn. When blocking, place pins along the neckline to ensure it dries evenly and smooth.

WET block flat, turning as needed for even drying.

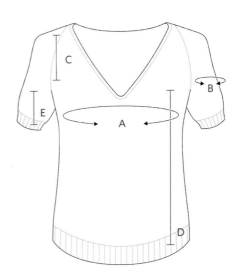

FINISHED MEASUREMENTS

A) BUST: 33.1" (37.8, 41.5, 45.1, 49.8, 53.1) (82.7 cm [94.5, 103.6, 112.7, 124.5, 132.7])

B) SLEEVE AT WIDEST POINT: 12" (13.1, 14.5, 15.6, 17.1, 18.5) (30 cm [32.7, 36.4, 39.1, 42.7, 46.4])

C) DROP FROM TOP OF SHOULDER TO UNDERARM: 8.5" (9.1, 9.6, 10, 10.8, 11.1) (21.7 cm [23, 24.4, 25.4, 27.4, 28.1])

D) LENGTH OF BODY FROM UNDERARM: 14–16" (35.6–40.6 cm)

E) LENGTH OF SLEEVE FROM UNDERARM: 5.5" (13.97 cm)

Archipelago Cocoon Wrap

Archipelago is a modern wrap that fits somewhere between a shrug and a cocoon. It's loose-fitting with generous, flexible ease and can be slipped over just about anything for a show-stopping final layer. To be honest, its origin was a bit of a surprise; a miscalculation led to a different width/length ratio than I first anticipated. It was a happy accident, though, as the result is one of my most beloved pieces in this collection.

TIMELINE

With very little focus required, Archipelago's only limitation is its size—and therefore portability—as it begins to grow. Knit in an aran weight yarn with long stretches of stockinette, this simple wrap sweater can be easily knit in 7 to 10 days.

MATERIALS

Yarn	• Aran | The Fibre Co. Arranmore | 80% Merino wool, 10% cashmere, 10% silk | 175 yards (160 m) per 100 g | 1000 yards (1050, 1100) (914 m [960, 1006])
Yarn Notes	• The recommended yarn is an elegant wool tweed with just a touch of cashmere and silk. This soft, slubby fiber will have heavy drape that maintains its shape with wear, and is surprisingly light considering it's a heavier weight fiber.
Needles	• U.S. size 9/5.5 mm (24-32" [60-80 cm]) circular needle (body) • U.S. size 7/4.5 mm (40-60" [100-150 cm]) circular needle (ribbing) • Note: Use needle size necessary to obtain gauge.
Gauge	• 18 st and 20 rows with larger needle over 4" (10 cm) in stockinette stitch
Notions	• Yarn needle • Cable needle • Stitch markers (including locking stitch markers) • Waste yarn

STITCH GLOSSARY

bet	between
BOR	beginning of round/row
c12f	cable 12 front (slip 6 st to cable needle, hold to front, k6, then k6 from cable needle)
CO	cast on
ea	each
k	knit
m	marker/markers
mX	marker "X" indicates which marker (i.e, mA, mB, mC, etc.)
p	purl
pm	place marker
pmX	place marker, "X" indicates which marker (i.e, pmA, pmB, pmC, etc.)
psso	pass slipped stitch over
rep	repeat
rs	right side
sl	slip
sm	slip marker/markers
smX	slip marker, "X" indicates which marker (i.e, smA, smB, smC, etc.)
slwyib	slip one stitch (without working it) holding yarn in back
slwyif	slip one stitch (without working it) holding yarn in front
ws	wrong side
[ ]	brackets always indicate a repeat

SIZES

Small, Medium, Large

RECOMMENDED EASE

Positive, flexible ease for all sizes

CONSTRUCTION

Archipelago is knit in one piece from side to side, with a chunky cable along the top edge (to provide support across the shoulders). The simple i-cord edges are worked as you go, and the body is joined by adding ribbing around the sleeves.

SHAPING TIP: The cocoon shape is unusual. It's taller than it is wide (the cable ridge is the "top"). It is only when you join the corners to work the ribbing for the sleeves that the final shape begins to make sense. Resist the urge to add width or length, as you'll be surprised at how much room you'll have when the construction is complete.

ARCHIPELAGO PATTERN

With U.S. size 9/5.5 mm (24–32" [60–80 cm]) circular needle (or size to obtain gauge), cast on 190 st using cable cast-on method.

ROW 1 (RS): K1, slwyif, k1, pmA, k163, pmB, p1, k12, p1 (this will be the shoulder cable section), pmC, k7, pmD, k1, slwyif, k1.

ROW 2 (WS): Slwyif, k1, slwyif, smD, p7, smC, k1, k12, k1, smB, p to mA, smA, swyif, k1, swyif.

ROW 3 (RS): K1, slwyif, k1, smA, k to mB, smB, work Cable Chart row 1 (chart [page 37] or written directions), smC, k7, smD, K1, slwyif, k1.

ROW 4 (WS): Slwyif, k1, slwyif, smD, p7, smC, work Cable Chart next row, smB, p to mA, smA, swyif, k1, swyif.

ROW 5 (RS): K1, slwyif, k1, smA, k to mB, smB, work Cable Chart next row, smC, k7, smD, K1, slwyif, k1.

ROW 6 (WS): Slwyif, k1, slwyif, smD, p7, smC, work Cable Chart next row, smB, p to mA, smA, swyif, k1, swyif.

REP rows 5 and 6, working Cable Chart rows 1–30 in order as you proceed, until body measures approximately 28" (32, 36) (70 cm [80, 90]), binding off on a Cable Chart row 11 in pattern with medium tension.

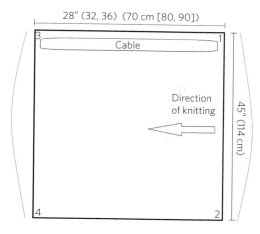

RIBBING & CLOSURE: Using the diagram as a reference, bring point 1 to point 2 and pin with a locking marker. Then bring point 3 to point 4 and pin. The space created when joining point 1 to point 2 will become the left sleeve (if you were wearing it). The space created when joining point 3 to point 4 will become the right sleeve. If you look at the garment laid flat, the cable row should be horizontal along the top edge (this will be over your shoulders). The points you've closed with locking markers should mark the sleeves on either side. Pick up and knit 176 stitches around the first arm hole/sleeve, pm to denote BOR and work in [k4, p4] ribbing in the round (on the rs) for 6 rounds.

NEXT ROUND (DEC): [k4, p1, p2tog, p1] rep bet brackets to end of round.

NEXT ROUND: [K4, p3] rep bet brackets to end of round.

REP the above round four more times (for a total of five).

NEXT ROUND (DEC): [K4, p1, p2tog] rep bet brackets to end of round.

NEXT ROUND: [K4, p2] rep bet brackets to end of round.

REP the above round two more times (for a total of three).

NEXT ROUND (DEC): [K4, p2tog] rep bet brackets to end of round.

NEXT ROUND: [K4, p1] rep bet brackets to end of round.

REP this round two more times (for a total of three).

Archipelago side view.

Archipelago cable detail.

NEXT ROUND: [K2, sl1, k2tog, psso] rep bet brackets to end of round.

BIND OFF in knit with medium tension.

NOTE: If you would like your sleeve opening wider, you can skip the final set of decreases and continue in the [k4, p1] rib for an additional row before binding off.

TO WEAR: The cable portion should lay horizontally across your shoulders.

CABLE DIRECTIONS

ROW 1: P1, k12, p1.
ROW 2: K1, p12, k1.
ROW 3: P1, k12, p1.
ROW 4: K1, p12, k1.
ROW 5: P1, c12f, p1.
ROW 6: K1, p12, k1.
ROW 7: P1, k12, p1.
ROW 8: K1, p12, k1.
ROW 9: P1, k12, p1.
ROW 10: K1, p12, k1.
ROW 11: P1, k12, p1.
ROW 12: K1, p12, k1.
ROW 13: P1, k12, p1.
ROW 14: K1, p12, k1.
ROW 15: P1, k12, p1.
ROW 16: K1, p12, k1.
ROW 17: P1, c12f, p1.
ROW 18: K1, p12, k1.
ROW 19: P1, k12, p1.
ROW 20: K1, p12, k1.
ROW 21: P1, k12, p1.
ROW 22: K1, p12, k1.
ROW 23: P1, c12f, p1.
ROW 24: K1, p12, k1.
ROW 25: P1, k12, p1.
ROW 26: K1, p12, k1.
ROW 27: P1, k12, p1.
ROW 28: K1, p12, k1.
ROW 29: P1, k12, p1.
ROW 30: K1, p12, k1.
REP rows 1–30 to establish cable across the body of the garment.

CABLE CHART

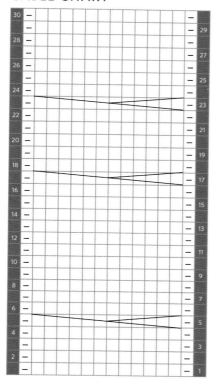

KEY

☐	k	(rs) Knit. (ws) Purl.
☐	p	(rs) Purl. (ws) Knit.
⟋⟍	c12f	Cable 12 front. (rs) Slip 6 st to cable needle, hold to front, k6, then k6 from cable needle.

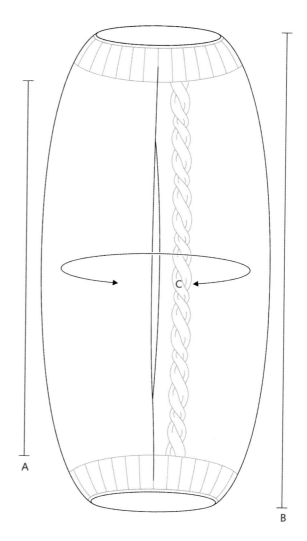

FINISHED MEASUREMENTS

A) WIDTH BEFORE RIBBING:
28" (32, 36) (70 cm [80, 90]) across back from edge to edge (before sleeve ribbing)

B) WIDTH WITH RIBBING:
35" (39, 45) (71.1 cm [99.1, 114.3]) across from sleeve edge to sleeve edge (including ribbing)

C) LENGTH:
45" (114 cm) from top to bottom (the "top" being the cable edge)

Shelter Cove V-Neck Pullover

I live in the Pacific Northwest where a good wool sweater can be worn in place of a jacket most of the year, and I can't help but reach for this one when the temperature drops. There's something special about a sweater on a blustery day! Shelter Cove is easy to slip on and go and seems to work with just about everything in my closet. With a flattering v-neck (not too deep) and strategic shaping around the arms to enhance fit, it's a quick-knit sweater that I think you'll love.

TIMELINE

Knit in an aran weight wool with an easily-memorized cable pattern, this sweater can realistically be finished in 7 to 10 days by motivated knitters.

Gauge	• 18 st and 20 rows with larger needle over 4" (10 cm) in stockinette stitch
Notions	• Yarn needle • Stitch markers • Waste yarn

MATERIALS

Yarn	• Heavy worsted | Sherwood Yarn BFL Brown Masham | 75% BFL, 25% brown Masham | 175 yards (160 m) per 100 g | 760 yards (844, 938, 1032, 1156, 1295) (695 m [772, 858, 944, 1057, 1184])
Yarn notes	• The recommended yarn is relatively dense with rich undertones from the addition of brown Masham wool. It shows texture well and looks just as beautiful in the stockinette stitch sections of the sweater as it does on the cables. The desired fabric should have medium density—not too stiff, with slight drape after blocking. Using a non-superwash wool will ensure that the sweater will not grow significantly with blocking; keep this in mind if you do want to add length. Non-superwash wool also will maintain its density and warmth with wear.
Needles	• U.S. size 8/5 mm (24-32" [60-80 cm]) circular needle (body) • U.S. size 8/5 mm (12" [30 cm]) circular needle or DPN (sleeves) • U.S. size 7/4.5 mm (24-32" [60-80 cm]) circular needle (lower body ribbing) • U.S. size 6/4 mm (12" [30 cm]) circular needle (sleeve cuff) • U.S. size 6/4 mm (24" [60 cm]) circular needle (neckline) • Note: Use needle size necessary to obtain gauge.

STITCH GLOSSARY

bet	between
BOR	beginning of round/row
CO	cast on
dec	decrease
DPN	double point needle/s
ea	each
inc	increase
k	knit
k2tog	knit 2 st at once (dec 1)
m	marker/markers
mX	marker "X" indicates which marker (i.e, mA, mB, mC, etc.)
M1L	make one st that leans left (inc 1)
M1R	make one st that leans right (inc 1)
p	purl
pmX	place marker, "X" indicates which marker (i.e, mA, mB, mC, etc.)
rem m	remove marker

(continued)

STITCH GLOSSARY

rep	repeat
rs	right side
sm	slip marker/markers
smX	slip marker, "X" indicates which marker (i.e, smA, smB, smC, etc.)
ssk	slip, slip, knit together (dec 1)
st	stitch/stitches
ws	wrong side
[ ]	brackets always indicate a repeat

SIZES

Bust sizes 30/32" (34/36, 38/40, 42/44, 46/48, 50/52) (76/81 cm [86/91, 97/102, 107/112, 117/122, 127/132])

RECOMMENDED EASE

Positive ease is included for a comfortable fit. See finished measurements for final ease as compared to your actual bust measurement. If you are between sizes, refer to the final measurements to determine which size to choose. In many cases you'll find that the smaller of the two sizes will be best.

CONSTRUCTION

Shelter Cove is worked back and forth from the beginning until the neck shaping is established. The two sides of the front are worked separately until joined at the center of the v-neck. The sweater is joined in the round at the completion of the neck shaping. The working yarn is rejoined at the side to establish the new starting point, and it's worked in the round from there.

NOTE: Rows and rounds apply to all sizes unless otherwise indicated. Be sure to read ahead and mark sections that are specific to your size before you begin.

QUICK TIP: Keep your edge stitches along the v-neck tidy by pulling the first stitch tight as you begin each new row. This makes the stitches easier to pick up later, and creates a cleaner neckline edge.

SHELTER COVE PATTERN

With U.S. size 8/5 mm (24–32" [60–80 cm]) circular needle, cast on 54 (64, 74, 76, 100, 108) st using cable cast-on method. Do not join.

ROW 1 – SET UP (RS): K1 (1, 2, 2, 3, 3), M1R, k1, pmA, k1, M1L, k8 (12, 14, 14, 22, 26), M1R, k1, pmB, k1, M1L, k28 (30, 34, 36, 42, 42), M1R, k1, pmC, k1, M1L, k8 (12, 14, 14, 22, 26), M1R, k1, pmD, k1, M1L, K1 (1, 2, 2, 3, 3) (8 st inc).

ROW 2 (WS): P across, slipping m as you go.

ROW 3 (RS): K1, M1R, k to 1 st before mA, M1R, k1, smA, k1, M1L, k to 1 st before mB, M1R, k1, smB, k1, M1L, k to 1 st before mC, M1R, k1, smC, k1, M1L, k to 1 st before mD, M1R, k1, smD, k1, M1L, k to 1 st before end, M1L, k1 (10 st inc).

ROW 4 (WS): As row 2.

REP rows 3 and 4 until you reach the following:

STITCH COUNT CHECK-IN
FRONTS (EA): 29 (31, 34, 32, 29, 29)
SLEEVES (EA): 38 (44, 48, 46, 50, 54)
BACK: 58 (62, 68, 68, 70, 70)

SIZES 30/32, 34/36, 38/40 Move ahead to Neckline Join.

SIZES 42/44, 46/48, 50/52 NEXT ROW (RS): K1, M1R, k to 3 st before mA, M1R, k2, M1R, k1, smA, k1, M1L, k to 1 st before mB, M1R, k1, smB, k1, M1L, k to 1 st before mC, M1R, k1, smC, k1, M1L, k to 1 st before mD, M1R, k1, smD, k1, M1L, k2, M1L, k to 1 st before end, M1L, k1 (12 st inc).

SIZES 42/44, 46/48, 50/52 NEXT ROW (WS): As row 2.

SIZE 42/44 Move ahead to Neckline Join.

SIZES 46/48, 50/52 NEXT ROW (RS): K1, M1R, k to 3 st before mA, M1R, k2, M1R, k1, smA, k1, M1L, k to 1 st before mB, M1R, k1, smB, k1, M1L, k to 1 st before mC, M1R, k1, smC, k1, M1L, k to 1 st before mD, M1R, k1, smD, k1, M1L, k2, M1L, k to 1 st before end, M1L, k1 (12 st inc).

SIZES 46/48, 50/52 NEXT ROW (WS): As row 2.

SIZES 46/48, 50/52 NEXT ROW (RS): K1, M1R, k to 3 st before mA, M1R, k2, M1R, k1, smA, k1, M1L, k to 1 st before mB, M1R, k1, smB, k1, M1L, k to 1 st before mC, M1R, k1, smC, k1, M1L, k to 1 st before mD, M1R, k1, smD, k1, M1L, k2, M1L, k to 1 st before end, M1L, k1 (12 st inc).

SIZES 46/48, 50/52 NEXT ROW (WS): As row 2.

STITCH COUNT CHECK-IN

FRONTS (EA): 29 (31, 34, 35, 38, 38)
SLEEVES (EA): 38 (44, 48, 48, 56, 60)
BACK: 58 (62, 68, 70, 76, 76)

NECKLINE JOIN: Cut working yarn, leaving a tail long enough to weave-in later. Slide all stitches after mD (this is the right front section if you were wearing the sweater) to the left needle to "meet" with the other half of the front stitches. Rejoin working yarn at mD to denote new beginning of round (BOR).

NEXT ROUND (INC): Starting at mD and with new working yarn, k1, M1L, k across front (joining the right to left front as you reach it, taking care not to twist the st) to 1 st before mA, M1R, k1, smA, k1, M1L, k to 1 st before mB, M1R, k1, smB, k1, M1L, k to 1 st before mC, M1R, k1, smC, k1, M1L, k to 1 st before mD, M1R, k1 (8 st inc).

Your garment is now joined in the round and will continue in the round from this point forward.

NEXT ROUND (NO INC): K, slipping m as you go.

NEXT ROUND (INC): K1, M1L, k22 (24, 27, 28, 31, 31), pm1, work Center Panel starting with round 1 over 16 st, pm2, k to 1 st before mA, M1R, k1, smA, k1, M1L, k to 1 st before mB, M1R, k1, smB, k1, M1L, k to 1 st before mC, M1R, k1, smC, k1, M1L, k to 1 st before mD, M1R, k1 (8 st inc).

NOTE: Center Panel will be worked between m1 and m2 from this point forward.

NEXT ROUND (NO INC): K, slipping m as you go.

REP the above two rounds 4 (1, 0, 0, 0, 0) time/s more, slipping the m as you reach them. (If no rep for your size, move to the next line of instruction.)

NEXT ROUND (EXTRA INC ROUND): K1, M1L, k2, M1L, k to m1, sm1, work Center Panel next row, sm2, k to 3 st before mA, M1R, k2, M1R, k1, smA, k1, M1L, k to 1 st before mB, M1R, k1, smB, k1, M1L, k2, M1L, k to 3 st before mC, M1R, k2, M1R, k1, smC, k1, M1L, k to 1 st before mD, M1R, k1 (12 st inc).

NEXT ROUND (NO INC): K, slipping m as you go.

REP the above two rounds 0 (1, 1, 2, 3, 2) time/s more. (If no rep for your size, move to the next line of instruction.)

STITCH COUNT CHECK-IN

FRONT: 74 (76, 80, 86, 96, 92)
SLEEVES (EA): 52 (54, 56, 58, 68, 70)
BACK: 74 (76, 80, 86, 96, 92)

SIZE 30/32 Move ahead to Divide for Sleeves.

SIZES 34/36, 38/40, 42/44, 46/48, 50/52 NEXT ROUND (DOUBLE EXTRA INC ROUND): K1, M1L, k2, M1L, k2, M1L, k to m1, sm1, work Center Panel next row, sm2, k to 5 st before mA, M1R, k2, M1R, k2, M1R, k1, smA, k1, M1L, k to 1 st before mB, M1R, k1, smB, k1, M1L, k2, M1L, k2, M1L, k to 5 st before mC, M1R, k2, M1R, k2, M1R, k1, smC, k1, M1L, k to 1 st before mD, M1R, k1 (16 st inc).

SIZES 34/36, 38/40, 42/44, 46/48, 50/52 NEXT ROUND (NO INC): K, slipping m as you go.

SIZES 34/36, 38/40, 42/44, 46/48, 50/52 Rep the above two rounds - (0, 1, 1, 1, 3) times more, then move ahead to Divide for Sleeves.

STITCH COUNT CHECK-IN

FRONT: 74 (82, 92, 98, 108, 116)
SLEEVES (EA): 52 (56, 60, 62, 72, 78)
BACK: 74 (82, 92, 98, 108, 116)

DIVIDE FOR SLEEVES: K to m1, sm1, work Center Panel next row, sm2, k to mA, rem mA and place sleeve st on waste yarn (loosely, so you can try it on later). CO 2 (2, 2, 4, 4, 4) st at the underarm, removing mB in the process and replacing it at the center of the underarm (in the center of the newly cast-on st). K to mC and rem mC, place sleeve st on waste yarn (loosely). CO 2 (2, 2, 4, 4, 4) st at the underarm, removing mD in the process and replacing it at the center of the underarm (in the center of the newly cast-on st)—mD now denotes BOR. You will have two markers (BOR/mD and mB) at the center of each underarm and two markers (m1 and m2) to denote Center Panel.

STITCH COUNT CHECK-IN

152 (168, 188, 204, 224, 240) st in lower body

MAIN BODY NEXT ROUND: K to m1, sm1, work Center Panel next round over 16 st, sm2, k to end of round, slipping mB when you pass it.

REP this round, working Center Panel Chart rounds 1–16 in order and rep down the center of the front of the body until lower body measures approximately 13–14" (33–35.5 cm) from underarm and you have completed round 16 of the Center Panel. On the next round, transition to U.S size 7/4.5 mm (24–32" [60–80 cm]) circular needle (or one size smaller than that used for the body), and knit one round. On the next round begin lower ribbing as follows: [k2, p2] repeat between brackets to end of round. Repeat the ribbing round until lower ribbing measures 2" (5 cm). Bind off in pattern with medium tension.

SLEEVES: With U.S. size 8/5 mm (12" [30 cm]) circular needle or DPN (or the same size as used for the body) pick up sleeve stitches from waste yarn (including st cast-on under the arm where applicable)—54 (58, 62, 66, 76, 82) st. Pm at center of underarm to mark BOR. Knit sleeve in the round in stockinette st for 1" (2.5 cm).

NEXT ROUND: K2, k2tog, k to 4 st before m, ssk, k2 (2 st dec).

CONTINUE sleeve in stockinette stitch in the round, working a decrease row as established approximately every 2" (2.5, 2, 2, 1.5, 1.5) (5 cm [6.4, 5, 5, 3.8, 3.8]) until you have 40 (44, 44, 48, 52, 60) stitches and sleeve measures approximately 18–19" (46–48 cm) from the underarm. On the next round, transition to U.S. size 6/4 mm (12" [30 cm]) and work one more round in stockinette. Begin cuff ribbing on the next round: [k2, p2] repeating between brackets to end of round. Continue in established ribbing until cuff measures 2" (5 cm). Bind off in pattern with medium tension.

REP for second sleeve.

NECKLINE: Starting at front center of the neckline, and using U.S. size 6/4 mm (24" [60 cm]) circular needle, pick up st along neckline edge all the way around, picking up a multiple of 4 + 2 for ribbing (see page 161) (picking up nearly every stitch). Work neckline in [k2, p2] ribbing (rep bet brackets) to end of row, ending k2. Work flat (back and forth) as established until ribbing measures 1.25" (3.2 cm). Bind off in pattern with medium tension. Note: If the edge feels restrictive, you've bound-off too tightly. If the edge appears to be wavy or loose, you've bound-off too loosely.

Shelter Cove front view.

BIND-OFF TIP: You can adjust your tension by relaxing or tensing your hands as you work the bind-off row, and providing a little more or a little less space between stitches, as needed for the results you want. I recommend re-working the bind-off row if the first attempt doesn't provide the results you want.

WEAVE-IN ends and wet block, pinning flat, especially along the sides of the Center Panel. Let dry, turning as needed.

CENTER PANEL DIRECTIONS

ROUND 1: K3, k2tog, p1, k1, m1R, p2, m1L, k1, p1, ssk, k3.
ROUND 2: K4, p1, k1, p4, k1, p1, ktbl, k3.
ROUND 3: K2, k2tog, p1, k1, m1R, p4, m1L, k1, p1, ssk, k2.
ROUND 4: K3, p1, k1, p6, k1, p1, ktbl, k2.
ROUND 5: K1, k2tog, p1, k1, m1R, p6, m1L, k1, p1, ssk, k1.
ROUND 6: K2, p1, k1, p8, k1, p1, ktbl, k1.
ROUND 7: K2tog, p1, k1, m1R, p8, m1L, k1, p1, ssk.
ROUND 8: K1, p1, k1, p10, k1, p1, ktbl.
ROUND 9: M1L, k1, p1, ssk, p8, k2tog, p1, k1, m1R.

ROUND 10: K3, ktbl, p8, k4.
ROUND 11: K1, m1L, k1, p1, ssk, p6, k2tog, p1, k1, m1R, k1.
ROUND 12: K4, ktbl, p6, k5.
ROUND 13: K2, m1L, k1, p1, ssk, p4, k2tog, p1, k1, m1R, k2.
ROUND 14: K5, ktbl, p4, k6.
ROUND 15: K3, m1L, k1, p1, ssk, p2, k2tog, p1, k1, m1R, k3.
ROUND 16: K5, p1, ktbl, p2, k1, p1, k5.

CENTER PANEL CHART

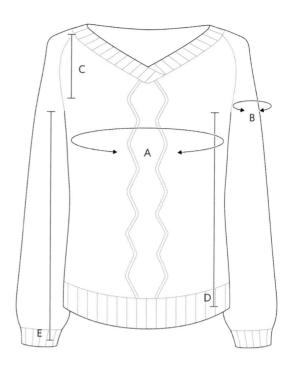

KEY			
□	k	(rs) Knit	
⧄	k2tog	Knit two together at once (dec 1)	
⅄	M1L	Make one left. Insert tip of right needle into bar bet st from the back (purlwise), slip this st onto left needle and knit through the back loop (left angled increase). See Chapter 7 (page 159).	
─	p	(rs) Purl	
⅄	M1R	Make one right. Insert tip of right needle into bar bet st from the front (knitwise), slip this st onto left needle and knit through the front (right angled increase). See Chapter 7 (page 159).	
⧅	ssk	Slip, slip, knit. [Slip st as if to knit] twice, then place both st back on left needle and knit together through back (dec 1).	

FINISHED MEASUREMENTS

A) BUST:
33.8" (37.3, 41.8, 45.3, 49.8, 53.3)/ 84.4 cm (93.3, 104.4, 113.3, 124.4, 133.3)

B) SLEEVE AT WIDEST POINT:
12" (12.9, 13.8, 14.7, 16.9, 18.2) / 30 cm (32.2, 34.4, 36.7, 42.2, 45.6)

C) DROP FROM TOP OF SHOULDER TO UNDERARM:
9.6" (10, 10.6, 11, 12.2, 13)/ 24 cm (25, 26.5, 27.5, 30.5, 32.5)

D) LENGTH OF BODY FROM UNDERARM:
15–17" (37.5–42.5 cm)

E) LENGTH OF SLEEVE FROM UNDERARM:
20–21" (50–52.5 cm)

High Tide Cable Tee

Early knitting lessons with my grandmother came complete with boxes of vintage knitting magazines. Maybe I swooned over one too many leaflets from the 1960s, but I credit them with my soft spot for mock turtlenecks. Significantly modernized, High Tide features some of what I loved about those vintage styles—the neckline, wide cable and half-sleeves—but with a roomier fit for those who prefer a less form-fitting style. Perfect for getting started over a long weekend at home, the front cable is a breeze to track once you've gotten it established. You'll find yourself free of the pattern once you pass the sleeve divide and can zip through the body in no time.

TIMELINE

Like most sweaters in this chapter, High Tide balances details strategically for a quick finish. Those with time to knit can finish this sweater in about a week, but even a slower paced knitter can reach the finish line in about 10 days.

MATERIALS

Yarn	• Worsted weight | Shibui Knits Drift | 85% extra fine Merino, 15% cashmere | 110 yards (101 m) per 50 g | 850 yards (930,1000,1080,1176,1270) (777 m [850, 914, 988, 1075, 1161])
Yarn Notes	• The recommended yarn results in an elegant style with medium body, slight drape and a hint of sheen. However, this flexible style could be knit in a range of yarns with equally successful results.
Needles	• U.S. size 7/4.5 mm (24-32" [60-80 cm]) circular needle (body) • U.S. size 7/4.5 mm (12" [30 cm]) circular needle or DPN (sleeves) • U.S. size 6/4 mm (24-32" [60-80 cm]) circular needle (lower ribbing) • U.S. size 5/3.75 mm (12" [30 cm]) circular needle or DPN (sleeve cuff) • U.S. size 5/3.75 mm (16" [40 cm]) circular needle (neckline)
Gauge	• 20 st and 25 rows with larger needle over 4" (10 cm) in stockinette stitch
Notions	• Yarn needle • Stitch markers • Cable needle

STITCH GLOSSARY

bet	between
BOR	beginning of round/row
CO	cast on
dec	decrease
DPN	double point needle/s
ea	each
inc	increase
k	knit
k2tog	knit 2 st at once (dec 1)
kfb	knit into front and back of st (inc 1)
m	marker
mX	marker "X" indicates which marker (i.e, mA, mB, mC, etc.)
M1L	make one st that leans left (inc 1)
M1R	make one st that leans right (inc 1)
p	purl
pmX	place marker "X" indicates which marker (i.e, pmA, pmB, pmC, etc.)
rem m	remove marker
rep	repeat
rs	right side
sm	slip marker

(continued)

STITCH GLOSSARY

smX	slip marker, "X" indicates which marker (i.e, smA, smB, smC, etc.)
ssk	slip, slip, knit together (dec 1)
st	stitch/stitches
ws	wrong side
[ ]	brackets always indicate a repeat

SIZES

Bust sizes 30/32" (34/36, 38/40, 42/44, 46/48, 50/52) (76/81 cm [86/91, 97/102, 107/112, 117/122, 127/132])

RECOMMENDED EASE

Positive ease is included for a comfortable fit. See finished measurements for final ease as compared to your actual bust measurement. If you are between sizes, refer to the final measurements to determine which size to choose. In many cases you'll find that the smaller of the two sizes will be best.

CONSTRUCTION

High Tide is knit seamlessly from top to bottom with positive ease. It's a relatively mindless project with just enough visual interest to keep the process entertaining, without being fussy. The pattern is easy to memorize and—with the added benefit of half-sleeves—you'll be finished in no time.

NOTE: Rows and rounds apply to all sizes unless otherwise indicated. Be sure to read ahead and mark sections that are specific to your size before you begin.

TIDY NECKLINE TIP: Positive ease gives this design a relaxed, loose fit. If you prefer less wiggle room in your sweater, consider going down a size. Use the finished measurements for both the bust and arm to verify that the smaller size will work for you before you proceed.

HIGH TIDE PATTERN

With U.S. size 7/4.5 mm (24–32" [60–80 cm]) circular needle, cast on 42 (44, 48, 56, 70, 80) st using cable cast-on method.

ROW 1 (RS): K1, pmA, k1, M1L, k4 (4, 4, 8, 12, 14), M1R, k1, pmB, k1, M1L, k26 (28, 32, 32, 38, 44), M1R, k1, pmC, k1, M1L, k4 (4, 4, 8, 12, 14), M1R, k1, pmD, k1 (6 st inc).

ROW 2 (WS): P across, slipping m as you go.

ROW 3 (RS): As row 1.

ROW 4 (WS): As row 2.

ROW 5 (RS): Kfb, smA, k1, M1L, k to 1 st before mB, M1R, k1, smB, k1, M1L, k to 1 st before mC, M1R, k1, smC, k1, M1L, k to 1 st before mD, M1R, k1, smD, kfb (8 st inc).

ROW 6 (WS): As row 2.

ROW 7 (RS): K1, M1R, k1, smA, k1, M1L, k to 1 st before mB, M1R, k1, smB, k1, M1L, k to 1 st before mC, M1R, k1, smC, k1, M1L, k to 1 st before mD, M1R, k1, smD, k1, M1L, k1 (8 st inc + CO).

ROW 8 (WS): As row 2.

STITCH COUNT CHECK-IN

FRONTS (EA): 3
SLEEVES (EA): 14 (14, 14, 18, 22, 24)
BACK: 36 (38, 42, 42, 48, 54)

ROW 9 (RS): CO 1 st using knitted cast-on worked knitwise*, k to 1 st before mA, M1R, k1, smA, k1, M1L, k to 1 st before mB, M1R, k1, smB, k1, M1L, k to 1 st before mC, M1R, k1, smC, k1, M1L, k to 1 st before mD, M1R, k1, smD, k1, M1L, k to end (8 st inc + CO).

ROW 10 (WS): CO 1 st using knitted cast-on worked purlwise*, then p across, slipping m as you go.

*GOING FORWARD, all stitches cast-on on the right side will be worked using the knitted cast-on method, and all stitches cast-on on the wrong side will be worked using the knitted cast-on method worked purlwise. Always knit the new stitch/es on the right side and purl the new stitch/es on the wrong side as you work through the rows.

ROW 11 (RS): Rep row 9.

ROW 12 (WS): Rep row 10.

ROW 13 (RS): CO 2 st, k to 1 st before mA, M1R, k1, smA, k1, M1L, k to 1 st before mB, M1R, k1, smB, k1, M1L, k to 1 st before mC, M1R, k1, smC, k1, M1L, k to 1 st before mD, M1R, k1, smD, k1, M1L, k to end (8 st inc + CO).

ROW 14 (WS): CO 2 st, then p across, slipping m as you go.

ROW 15 (RS): CO 4 (4, 4, 4, 4, 6) st, k to 1 st before mA, M1R, k1, smA, k1, M1L, k to 1 st before mB, M1R, k1, smB, k1, M1L, k to 1 st before mC, M1R, k1, smC, k1, M1L, k to 1 st before mD, M1R, k1, smD, k1, M1L, k to end (8 st inc + CO).

ROW 16 (WS): CO 4 (4, 4, 4, 4, 6) st, then p across, slipping m as you go.

ROW 17 (RS): CO 4 (4, 4, 4, 6, 6) st, k to 1 st before mA, M1R, k1, smA, k1, M1L, k to 1 st before mB, M1R, k1, smB, k1, M1L, k to 1 st before mC, M1R, k1, smC, k1, M1L, k to 1 st before mD, M1R, k1, smD, k1, M1L, k to end (8 st inc + CO).

ROW 18 (WS): CO 4 (4, 4, 4, 6, 6) st, then p across, slipping m as you go.

ROW 19 (RS): CO 16 (18, 22, 22, 24, 26), k to 1 st before mA, M1R, k1, smA, k1, M1L, k to 1 st before mB, M1R, k1, smB, k1, M1L, k to 1 st before mC, M1R, k1, smC, k1, M1L, k to 1 st before mD, M1R, k1, smD, k1, M1L, k to end (8 st inc + CO).

CUT yarn, leaving a tail.

STITCH COUNT CHECK-IN
FRONTS (EA): 58 (60, 64, 64, 70, 76)
SLEEVES (EA): 26 (26, 26, 30, 34, 36)
BACK: 48 (50, 54, 54, 60, 66)

NECKLINE JOIN: Rejoin yarn just after mD, leaving a tail to weave in later. This marks the new BOR. Slide the stitches after mD to the left needle so they "meet" with the other stitches on the front section (all stitches between mD and mA are now the "front")— 58 (60, 64, 64, 70, 76) st between mD and mA. K this round, joining at the front stitches when you reach the gap (be careful not to twist stitches) and knit to end of round (no inc).

High Tide shoulder and back view.

NEXT ROUND (NO INC): At new BOR (mD) K17 (18, 20, 20, 23, 26), pm1, p2, k20, p2, pm2, k17 (18, 20, 20, 23, 26), sm, k to end of round, slipping m as you go.

*m1 and m2 denote Center Cable Chart

NEXT ROUND (INC): K1, M1L, k to m1, sm1, work Center Cable Chart first round (then subsequent rounds in order when you rep this row), sm2, k to 1 st before mA, M1R, k1, smA, k1, M1L, k to 1 st before mB, M1R, k1, smB, k1, M1L, k to 1 st before mC, M1R, k1, smC, k1, M1L, k to 1 st before mD, M1R, k1 (8 st inc).

NEXT ROUND: K the round, slipping m as you go and maintaining Center Cable next row as established.

REP these two rounds until you have the following:

STITCH COUNT CHECK-IN
FRONT: 94 (96, 100, 100, 106, 112)
SLEEVES (EA): 62 (62, 62, 66, 70, 72)
BACK: 84 (86, 90, 90, 96, 102)

SIZE 30/32 Move ahead to Divide for Sleeves.

SIZES 34/36, 38/40, 42/44, 46/48, 50/52 NEXT ROUND (EXTRA INC): K1, M1L, k2, M1L, k to m1, work Center Cable Chart next round, sm2, k to 3 st before mA, M1R, K2, M1R, k1, smA, k1, M1L, k to 1 st before mB, M1R, k1, smB, k1, M1L, k2, M1L, k to 3 st before mC, M1R, k2, M1R, k1, smC, k1, M1L, k to 1 st before mD, M1R, k1 (12 st inc).

SIZES 34/36, 38/40, 42/44, 46/48, 50/52: K the round, working Center Cable Chart next row and slipping m as you go.

REP the above two rounds – (1, 1, 0, 1, 2) times more.

STITCH COUNT CHECK-IN

FRONT: - (104, 108, 104, 114, 124)
SLEEVES (EA): - (66, 66, 68, 74, 78)
BACK: - (94, 98, 94, 104, 114)

SIZE 34/36 Move ahead to Divide for Sleeves.

SIZES 38/40, 42/44, 46/48, 50/52 NEXT ROUND (DOUBLE EXTRA INC): K1, M1L, k2, M1L, k2, M1L, k to m1, sm1, work Center Cable Chart next round, sm2, k to 5 st before mA, M1R, k2, M1R, K2, M1R, k1, smA, k1, M1L, k to 1 st before mB, M1R, k1, smB, k1, M1L, k2, M1L, k2, M1L, k to 5 st before mC, M1R, k2, M1R, k2, M1R, k1, smC, k1, M1L, k to 1 st before mD, M1R, k1 (16 st inc).

SIZES 38/40, 42/44, 46/48, 50/52 K the round, working Center Cable Chart next row, slipping m as you go.

REP these two rounds until you have the following:

STITCH COUNT CHECK-IN

FRONT: - (-, 114, 122, 132, 142)
SLEEVES (EA): - (-, 68, 74, 80, 84)
BACK: - (-, 104 112, 122, 132)

DIVIDE FOR SLEEVES: K to m1, sm1, work Center Cable Chart next round, sm2, k to mA, and place sleeve st on waste yarn (loosely, so you can try it on later). CO 0 (0, 2, 4, 4, 4) st using knitted cast-on method (see Chapter 7 [page 159])—keep mA and replace it at the center of the st under the arm. Rem mB and join to back, k to mC. Place sleeve st on waste yarn (loosely, so you can try it on later), removing mC in the process. CO 0 (0, 2, 4, 4, 4) st, under the arm and keep mD (replacing at at the center of the underarm stitches) to denote BOR.

STITCH COUNT CHECK-IN

178 (198, 222, 242, 262, 282) st in lower body

High Tide front view detail.

LOWER BODY: K to m1, sm1, work Center Cable Chart next round, sm2, k to end, slipping remaining m as you go.

WORK Lower Body Round for 1" (2.5 cm), then begin optional bust darts as follows: At BOR, k10, pm3, ssk, work in established pattern to 12 st before mA, k2tog, pm4, k10, smA, k to end of round.

NEXT ROUND: K (maintaining Center Cable Chart as established).

REP these two rounds two times more (for a total of 6 st dec on the front).

From this point forward, work the Lower Body Round (no additional dec) until body measures approximately 12" (30 cm) from underarm and you have completed a round 10 of the Center Cable Panel. With U.S. size 6/4 mm (24–32" [60–80 cm]) circular needle (or one size smaller than that used for the body), work one round more in pattern.

LOWER RIBBING: With the new smaller needle, work in [k1, p1] ribbing, rep bet brackets to end of round. Rep ribbing every round until lower rib measures 2" (5 cm). Bind off in pattern with medium tension. Lower edge should not feel restrictive. If it does, bind off more loosely.

SLEEVES: With U.S. size 7/4.5 mm (12" [30 cm]) circular needle or DPN, place sleeve st from waste yarn onto needle and pick up st cast-on under the arm 62 (66, 70, 78, 84, 88) st. Pm at center of underarm to denote BOR.

[Work in the round in stockinette st for 1.5" (3.8 cm). Dec round: K2, k2tog, k to 4 st before m, ssk, k2, sm.]

REP bet [ ] twice more. Transition to U.S. size 5/3.75 mm (12" [30 cm]) circular needle or DPN and dec 0 (0, 0, 0, 0, 1) additional st on the final round work in [k1, p1] ribbing for 1.5" (3.8 cm). Bind off in pattern with medium tension.

REP for second sleeve.

NECKLINE: With U.S. size 5/3.75 mm (16" [40 cm]) circular needle, pick up every st around the neckline, ending with a multiple of 2, join to work in the round and work in [k1, p1] ribbing until neckline measures 2.5" (6.25 cm). Bind off in pattern with medium/loose tension. Note: In order to ensure a comfortable fit over the head and neck, pick up no fewer than 100 st for the neckline. This is only a concern for smaller sizes who will need to remember to pick up every available stitch; larger sizes will easily be picking up more than 100.

WET block flat, pinning the cable neatly and turning as needed until dry.

CENTER CABLE DIRECTIONS
ROUNDS 1–5: P2, k20, p2.
ROUND 6: P2, C10b, C10f, p2.
ROUNDS 7–10: P2, k20, p2.
REP rounds 1–10 to establish pattern.

CENTER CABLE CHART

24	23	22	21	20	19	18	17	16	15	14	13	12	11	10	9	8	7	6	5	4	3	2	1	
−	−																					−	−	10
−	−																					−	−	9
−	−																					−	−	8
−	−																					−	−	7
−	−																					−	−	6
−	−																					−	−	5
−	−																					−	−	4
−	−																					−	−	3
−	−																					−	−	2
−	−																					−	−	1

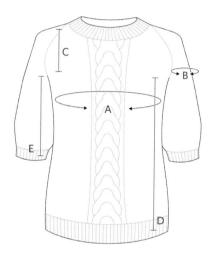

FINISHED MEASUREMENTS

A) BUST:
33.6" (37.6, 42.4, 46.4, 50.4, 54.4) (84 cm [94, 106, 116, 126, 136])*

B) SLEEVE AT WIDEST POINT:
12.4" (13.2, 14, 15.6, 16.8, 17.6) (31 cm [33, 35, 39, 42, 44])

C) TOP OF SHOULDER TO UNDERARM:
9.6" (10.24, 10.56, 11.2, 11.84, 12.32) (24.38 cm [26.01, 26.82, 28.45, 30.07, 31.29])

D) LENGTH OF BODY FROM UNDERARM:
14" (35.5 cm) prior to blocking

E) SLEEVE LENGTH FROM UNDERARM:
6" (15.24 cm) prior to blocking

*Measurements take into account 2" [5 cm] loss of ease due to front cable.

Staycation Knits

HINTS OF TEXTURE & GRAPHIC FEATURES

The staycation concept must have come from a knitter. I have no proof of its origin but there's nothing lovelier than uninterrupted knitting time in my favorite spot on my own deck. Getting away from it all from the comfort of home is the ideal prescription for the sweaters in this chapter. Unlike Long-Weekend Knits, which require a little added focus from the outset, these Staycation Knits invite you to dive-in now and focus later for a truly relaxing knit. Hints of texture and graphic features in the lower body of these designs, like the chevrons down the sides of Stowaway (page 72) or the slipped-stitch patterning and pleat on Seaside (page 58), give you something to look forward to along the way, but most don't begin until after the initial shaping is complete. Any extra focus you might need is no problem, because you're home and your knitting tools are right at hand.

Meridian Striped Pullover

Your favorite, much-loved sweatshirt has a new rival: Meridian. This casual, sporty pullover features a relaxed fit in the body, wide stripes on the sleeves and twisted stitch ribbing for visual interest. It's a relatively mindless project, thanks to its endless stockinette stitch worked in the round, that results in a comfortable, wearable sweater for casual days. Confession: I've been known to pair this sweater with yoga pants and call it good; it's *that* cozy.

TIMELINE

With little to no technical components to navigate and only a couple of quick color changes, Meridian's primary time consumption comes from sheer volume of stitches in the long body and sleeves, making it more approachable for long stretches of knitting at home. If you can get into a groove with few interruptions, you'll find this an achievable knit in 10 to 12 days. Stockinette stitch worked in the round tends to be the quickest and most efficient stitch for most knitters, which lends itself to a quicker project overall.

MATERIALS

Yarn	• DK | Knitted Wit Polwarth Shimmer DK | 85% Polwarth wool, 15% silk | 330 yards (302 m) per 115 g | MC: 845 yards (939, 1141, 1255, 1405, 1573) (773 m [859, 1043, 1148, 1285, 1438]) | CC: 50-65 yards (45-59 m)
Yarn Notes	• Worked in hand-dyed, non-superwash Polwarth silk, your sweater should have light drape, medium sheen and a relaxed fit. Take care to work your swatch with both colors, and wet block to check color-fastness before you begin.
Needles	• U.S. size 7/4.5 mm (24-32" [60-80 cm]) circular needle (body) • U.S. size 7/4.5 mm (12" [30 cm]) circular needle (sleeves) • U.S. size 6/4 mm (24-32" [60-80 cm]) circular needle (lower body ribbing) • U.S. size 5/3.75 mm (12" [30 cm]) circular needle (sleeve cuff) • U.S. size 5/3.75 mm (16-24" [40-60 cm]) circular needle (neckline) • Note: Use needle size necessary to obtain gauge.

Gauge	• 18 st and 25 rows with larger needle over 4" (10 cm) in stockinette stitch
Notions	• Yarn needle • Stitch markers • Waste yarn

STITCH GLOSSARY

bet	between
BOR	beginning of round/row
CC	contrast color
CO	cast on
dec	decrease
ea	each
inc	increase
k	knit
ktbl	knit st through back loop
k2tog	knit 2 st at once (dec 1)
m	marker/markers
MC	main color
mX	marker "X" indicates which marker (i.e, mA, mB, mC, etc.)
M1L	make one st that leans left (inc 1)
M1R	make one st that leans right (inc 1)
p	purl

(continued)

STITCH GLOSSARY

pmX	place marker, "X" indicates which marker (i.e, pmA, pmB, pmC, etc.)
rem m	remove marker
rep	repeat
rs	right side
sm	slip marker/markers
smX	slip marker, "X" indicates which marker (i.e, smA, smB, smC, etc.)
ssk	slip, slip, knit together (dec 1)
st	stitch/stitches
ws	wrong side
[ ]	brackets always indicate a repeat

SIZES

Bust sizes 30/32" (34/36, 38/40, 42/44, 46/48, 50/52) (76/81 cm [86/91, 97/102, 107/112, 117/122, 127/132])

RECOMMENDED EASE

Positive ease is included for a comfortable fit. See finished measurements for final ease as compared to your actual bust measurement. If you are between sizes, refer to the final measurements to determine which size to choose. In many cases you'll find that the smaller of the two sizes will be the best choice.

CONSTRUCTION

Meridian is worked back and forth at the beginning until the neck shaping is established. The sweater is joined in the round at the completion of the neck shaping and worked top-down to the hem. The sleeves and neckline ribbing are worked last.

NOTE: Rows and rounds apply to all sizes unless otherwise indicated. Be sure to read ahead and mark sections that are specific to your size before you begin.

TIP FOR WORKING WITH TWO COLORS: Working with more than one color can have unpredictable results, depending on the yarn and colorway. Take care to work your swatch with both colors, and wet block the swatch to check for color-fastness before you begin.

MERIDIAN PATTERN

With U.S. size 7/4.5 mm (24-32" [60-80 cm]) circular needle and MC, cast on 35 (45, 67, 71, 75, 85) st using cable cast-on method. Do not join.

ROW 1 - SET UP (RS): K2, pmA, kfb, k0 (2, 8, 8, 10, 12), kfb, pmB, kfb, k25 (31, 41, 45, 45, 51), kfb, pmC, kfb, k0 (2, 8, 8, 10, 12), kfb, pmD, k2 (6 st inc).

ROW 2 (WS): P across, slipping m as you go.

SIZE 30/32 ONLY ROW 3 (RS): K2, smA, K1, M1L, k2, M1R, k1, smB, k2, M1L, k to 2 st before mC, M1R, k2, smC, k1, M1L, k 2, M1R, k1, smD, k2 (6 st inc).

SIZES 34/36, 38/40, 42/44, 46/48, 50/52 ROW 3 (RS): K2, smA, k2, M1L, k to 2 st before mB, M1R, k2, smB, k2, M1L, k to 2 st before mC, M1R, k2, smC, k2, M1L, k to 2 st before mD, M1R, k2, smD, k2 (6 st inc).

All sizes continue.

ROW 4 (WS): P across, slipping m as you go.

ROW 5 (RS): K1, M1R, k1, smA, k2, M1L, k to 2 st before mB, M1R, k2, smB, k2, M1L, k to 2 st before mC, M1R, k2, smC, k2, M1L, k to 2 st before mD, M1R, k2, smD, k1, M1L, k to end (8 st inc).

ROW 6 (WS): P across, slipping m as you go.

ROW 7 (RS): CO 0 (0, 0, 0, 0, 1) st using knitted cast-on worked tightly*, k to 2 st before mA, M1R, k2, smA, k2, M1L, k to 2 st before mB, M1R, k2, smB, k2, M1L, k to 2 st before mC, M1R, k2, smC, k2, M1L, k to 2 st before mD, M1R, k2, smD, k2, M1L, k to end (8 st inc + CO).

ROW 8 (WS): CO 0 (0, 0, 0, 0, 1) st using knitted cast-on worked purlwise*, p across row (including newly cast-on st), slipping m as you go.

*GOING FORWARD, all stitches cast-on on the right side will be worked using the knitted cast-on method, and all stitches cast-on on the wrong side will be worked using the knitted cast-on worked purlwise. Always knit the new stitch/es on the right side and purl the new stitch/es on the wrong side as you work through the row.

ROW 9 (RS): CO 0 (1, 1, 1, 1, 1) st, k to 2 st before mA, M1R, k2, smA, k2, M1L, k to 2 st before mB, M1R, k2, smB, k2, M1L, k to 2 st before mC, M1R, k2, smC, k2, M1L, k to 2 st before mD, M1R, k2, M1L, k to end (8 st inc + CO).

ROW 10 (WS): CO 0 (1, 1, 1, 1, 1) st, p across row, slipping m as you go.

STITCH COUNT CHECK-IN
FRONTS (EA): 5 (6, 6, 6, 6, 7)
SLEEVES (EA): 12 (14, 20, 20, 22, 24)
BACK: 37 (43, 53, 57, 57, 63)

ROW 11 (RS): CO 0 (1, 2, 2, 2, 2) st, k to 2 st before mA, M1R, k2, smA, k2, M1L, k to 2 st before mB, M1R, k2, smB, k2, M1L, k to 2 st before mC, M1R, k2, smC, k2, M1L, k to 2 st before mD, M1R, k2, smD, k2, M1L, k to end (8 st inc + CO).

ROW 12 (WS): CO 0 (1, 2, 2, 2, 2) st and p across row, slipping m as you go.

ROW 13 (RS): CO 1 (1, 2, 2, 2, 4) st, k to 2 st before mA, M1R, k2, smA, k2, M1L, k to 2 st before mB, M1R, k2, smB, k2, M1L, k to 2 st before mC, M1R, k2, smC, k2, M1L, k to 2 st before mD, M1R, k2, smD, k2, M1L, k to end (8 st inc + CO).

ROW 14 (WS): CO 1 (1, 2, 2, 2, 4) st and p across row, slipping m as you go.

ROW 15 (RS): CO 1 (2, 4, 4, 4, 4) st, k to 2 st before mA, M1R, k2, smA, k2, M1L, k to 2 st before mB, M1R, k2, smB, k2, M1L, k to 2 st before mC, M1R, k2, smC, k2, M1L, k to 2 st before mD, M1R, k2, smD, k2, M1L, k to end (8 st inc + CO).

ROW 16 (WS): CO 1 (2, 4, 4, 4, 4) st and p across row, slipping m as you go.

Meridian back view.

ROW 17 (RS): CO 4 (4, 4, 6, 6, 6) st, k to 2 st before mA, M1R, k2, smA, k2, M1L, k to 2 st before mB, M1R, k2, smB, k2, M1L, k to 2 st before mC, M1R, k2, smC, k2, M1L, k to 2 st before mD, M1R, k2, smD, k2, M1L, k to end (8 st inc + CO).

ROW 18 (WS): CO 4 (4, 4, 6, 6, 6) st and p across row, slipping m as you go.

ROW 19 (RS): CO 15 (15, 17, 17, 17, 17) st, k to 2 st before mA, M1R, k2, smA, k2, M1L, k to 2 st before mB, M1R, k2, smB, k2, M1L, k to 2 st before mC, M1R, k2, smC, k2, M1L, k to 2 st before mD, M1R, k2, smD, k2, M1L, k to end (8 st inc + CO). Cut yarn, leaving a tail.

STITCH COUNT CHECK-IN
FRONT: 47 (53, 63, 67, 67, 73)
SLEEVES (EA): 22 (24, 30, 30, 32, 34)
BACK: 47 (53, 63, 67, 67, 73)

Meridian shoulder and rib detail.

NECKLINE JOIN: Rejoin yarn just after mD, leaving a tail to weave in later. This marks the new BOR. Slide the stitches after mD to the left needle so they "meet" with the other stitches on the front section (all stitches between mD and mA are now the "front"). Knit across, joining the front stitches as you reach the gap (be careful not to twist stitches) and knit to end of round.

NEXT ROUND (INC): At BOR, k2, M1L, k to 2 st before mA, M1R, k2, smA, k2, M1L, k to 2 st before mB, M1R, k2, smB, k2, M1L, k to 2 st before mC, M1R, k2, smC, k2, M1L, k to 2 st before mD, M1R, k2 (8 st inc).

NEXT ROUND (NO INC): K the round, slipping m as you go.

REP these two rounds until you have the following number of stitches:

STITCH COUNT CHECK-IN
FRONT: 79 (87, 97, 101, 99, 105)
SLEEVES (EA): 54 (58, 64, 64, 64, 66)
BACK: 79 (87, 97, 101, 99, 105)

NEXT ROUND (EXTRA INC): K2, M1L, k2, M1L, k to 4 st before mA, M1R, k2, M1R, k2, smA, k2, M1L, k to 2 st before mB, M1R, k2, smB, k2, M1L, k2, M1L, k to 4 st before mC, M1R, k2, M1R, k2, smC, k2, M1L, k to 2 st before mD, M1R, k2 (12 st inc).

NEXT ROUND (NO INC): K the round, slipping m as you go.

REP these two rounds 0 (0, 0, 0, 1, 1) more times. You should have the following number of stitches:

STITCH COUNT CHECK-IN
FRONT: 83 (91, 101, 105, 107, 113)
SLEEVES (EA): 56 (60, 66, 66, 68, 70)
BACK: 83 (91, 101, 105, 107, 113)

SIZES 30/32, 34/36, 38/40 Move ahead to Divide for Sleeves.

SIZES 42/44, 46/48, 50/52 NEXT ROUND (DOUBLE EXTRA INC): K2, M1L, k2, M1L, k2, M1L, k to 6 st before mA, M1R, k2, M1R, k2, M1R, k2, smA, k2, M1L, k to 2 st before mB, M1R, k2, smB, k2, M1L, k2, M1L, k2, M1L, k to 6 st before mC, M1R, k2, M1R, k2, M1R, k2, smC, k2, M1L, k to 2 st before mD, M1R, k2 (16 st inc).

NEXT ROUND (NO INC): K the round, slipping m as you go.

SIZES 42/44, 46/48, 50/52 Rep the above two rounds 0 (1, 1) times. Then move ahead to Divide for Sleeves.

STITCH COUNT CHECK-IN
FRONT: 83 (91, 101, 111, 119, 125)
SLEEVES (EA): 56 (60, 66, 68, 72, 74)
BACK: 83 (91, 101, 111, 119, 125)

DIVIDE FOR SLEEVES: K across front to mA, rem mA and place sleeve stitches onto waste yarn (loosely, so you can try it on later). CO 2 (2, 2, 2, 4, 6) st underarm and join to back section, removing mB in the process. K to mC and rem mC, then place sleeve stitches onto waste yarn (loosely, so you can try it on later). CO 2 (2, 2, 2, 4, 6) st underarm and join to front, removing mD in the process and replacing it at the center of the underarm; mD now denotes BOR.

STITCH COUNT CHECK-IN
170 (186, 206, 226, 246, 262) st in lower body

LOWER BODY: Knit the lower body in stockinette stitch in the round until body measures 14.5" (36.8 cm) from underarm. Transition to U.S. size 6/4 mm (24-32" [60-80 cm]) circular needle—or one size smaller than that used for the body—on next round and knit one round on the smaller needle. AT THE SAME TIME, decrease 2 (3, 2, 1, 0, 4) st somewhat evenly using k2tog to end with a multiple of 3. Begin lower ribbing as follows: [p2, ktbl] repeat between brackets to end of round. Repeat this round until ribbing measures 2.5" (6.4 cm). Bind off with medium tension in pattern. Note: Bottom edge should not feel tight or restrictive. If it does, bind off more loosely.

SLEEVES: With U.S. size 7/4.5 mm (12" [30 cm]) circular needle or DPN (or the same size as used for the body) and MC, pick up sleeve stitches from waste yarn (including st cast-on under the arm where applicable) 58 (62, 68, 70, 76, 80) st. Pm at center of underarm to mark BOR. Knit in the round in stockinette st for 2" (5 cm).

NEXT ROUND: K2, k2tog, k to 4 st before m, ssk, k2 (2 st dec).

TRANSITION to CC at the start of the next round. Work 14 rounds in CC, then 5 rounds in MC, then another 14 rounds in CC. At the same time, work a decrease round as indicated approximately every 1.5" (3.8 cm) until sleeve measures approximately 17" (43 cm) from underarm, and you have the following number of stitches: 39 (42, 48, 48, 57, 60). Note: You may need to work one more or one less dec to reach these counts to end with a multiple of 3. On the last row, transition to U.S. size 5/3.75 mm (12" [30 cm]) circular needle or DPN (or two sizes smaller than used for sleeve) for cuff and begin ribbing as follows: [p2, ktbl] rep between brackets to end of round. Continue in established ribbing (repeating [p2, ktbl] on every round) until cuff measures 3" (7.6 cm). Bind off in pattern with medium tension.

REP for second sleeve.

NECKLINE: With U.S. size 5/3.75 mm (16-24" [40-60 cm]) circular needle (or needle two sizes smaller than that used for the body), pick up stitches around the neckline in the following manner: Pick up every available stitch along the shoulders and back, and approximately 6 of every 7 st along the front, ending with a multiple of 3. Work neckline in [p2, ktbl] ribbing in the round until neck ribbing measures 1.5" (3.8 cm). Bind off in pattern with medium tension.

WEAVE-IN ends and wet block, soaking thoroughly, then rinse well. Pin flat and allow to dry completely, turning as needed for even drying.

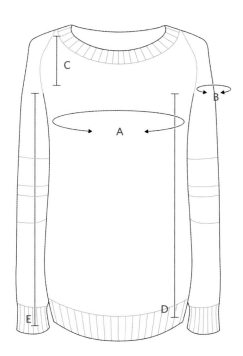

FINISHED MEASUREMENTS

A) BUST:
37.8" (41.3, 45.8, 80.2, 54.7, 58.2) (94.4 cm [103.3, 114.4, 125.6, 136.7, 145.6])

B) SLEEVE AT WIDEST POINT:
12.9" (13.8, 15.1, 15.6, 16.9, 17.8) (32.2 cm [34.4, 37.8, 38.9, 42.2, 44.4])

C) TOP OF SHOULDER TO UNDERARM:
9" (9.4, 9.9, 10.2, 10.7, 10.9) (22.76 cm [23.98, 25.2, 26.01, 27.23, 27.64])

D) LENGTH OF BODY FROM UNDERARM:
17" (43.18 cm) prior to blocking

E) LENGTH OF SLEEVE FROM UNDERARM:
20" (50.8 cm) prior to blocking

Seaside Pleated Cardigan

I love the versatility of three-quarter sleeves for year-round wear. Seaside starts off simply, easing you into texture features that are rhythmic and intuitive, giving you something to look forward to throughout the process. Slipped stitches and a charming back pleat create a cardigan you'll find yourself reaching for again and again. The short length is flattering on any figure, especially when worn over a longer top or dress.

TIMELINE

The open-front, shortened sleeves and minimalist details support a reasonable 7- to 10-day timeline for average knitters with motivation to finish quickly.

MATERIALS

Yarn	• Worsted | The Fibre Co. Cumbria | 60% Merino wool, 30% Masham wool and 10% mohair | 238 yards (218 m) per 100 g | 715 yards (792, 879, 968, 1084, 1214) (654 m [724, 804, 885, 991, 1110])
Yarn Notes	• Worked in natural wool, Seaside will not grow significantly with blocking and should have reasonable, softened stitch definition.
Needles	• U.S. size 7/4.5 mm (32" [80 cm]) circular needle (body) • U.S. size 6/4 mm (32" [80 cm]) circular needle (lower body ribbing) • U.S. size 7/4.5 mm (12" [30 cm]) circular needle or DPN (sleeve) • U.S. size 5/3.75 mm (12" [30 cm]) circular needle or DPN (sleeve cuff) • U.S. size 5/3.75 mm (32-40" [80-100 cm]) circular needle (neckline/front band) • Note: Use needle size necessary to obtain gauge.
Gauge	• 20 st and 26 rows with largest needle over 4" (10 cm) in stockinette stitch
Notions	• Yarn needle • Stitch markers, including a locking marker • Waste yarn

STITCH GLOSSARY

bet	between
BOR	beginning of round/row
CO	cast on
dec	decrease
ea	each
inc	increase
k	knit
k2tog	knit 2 st at once (dec 1)
kfb	knit into the front and back of the same stitch (inc 1)
m	marker/markers
mX	marker "X" indicates which marker (i.e, mA, mB, mC, etc.)
M1L	make one st that leans left (inc 1)
M1R	make one st that leans right (inc 1)
p	purl
pmX	place marker, "X" indicates which marker (i.e, pmA, pmB, pmC, etc.)
rem m	remove marker
rep	repeat
rs	right side
sl2wyif	slip 2 st (without working them) holding the yarn in front
sm	slip marker/markers

(continued)

STITCH GLOSSARY

smX	slip marker, "X" indicates which marker (i.e, smA, smB, smC, etc.)
ssk	slip, slip, knit together (dec 1)
st	stitch/stitches
ws	wrong side
[ ]	brackets always indicate a repeat

SIZES

Bust sizes 30/32" (34/36, 38/40, 42/44, 46/48, 50/52) (76/81 cm [86/91, 97/102, 107/112, 117/122, 127/132])

RECOMMENDED EASE

Positive ease is included for a comfortable fit. See finished measurements for final ease as compared to your actual bust measurement. If you are between sizes, refer to the final measurements to determine which size to choose. In many cases you'll find that the smaller of the two sizes will be the best choice.

CONSTRUCTION

Seaside is worked top-down and knit flat, with enough coverage in front that you could close it with a shawl pin if you wanted to. The subtle back pleat gives the sweater about 2" (5 cm) of extra room in the back, which adds to the casual swing of the finished piece.

NOTE: Rows and rounds apply to all sizes unless otherwise indicated. Be sure to read ahead and mark sections that are specific to your size before you begin.

COLOR TIP: While a solid or tonal colorway makes for a classic look, this cardigan could be just as interesting in a variegated yarn, or with contrast color for the ribbing and trim.

SEASIDE PATTERN

With U.S. size 7/4.5 mm (32" [80 cm]) circular needle, cast on 38 (48, 58, 80, 90, 104) st using cable cast-on method. Do not join.

ROW 1 – SET UP ROW (RS): Kfb, pmA, kfb, k2 (4, 6, 14, 18, 22), kfb, pmB, kfb, k26 (32, 38, 44, 46, 52), kfb, pmC, kfb, k2 (4, 6, 14, 18, 22), kfb, pmD, kfb (8 st inc).

ROW 2 AND ALL WS ROWS UNTIL OTHERWISE INDICATED (WS): P across, slipping m as you go.

ROW 3 (RS): K1, M1R, k1, smA, k1, M1L, k to 1 st before mB, M1R, k1, smB, k1, M1L, k to 1 st before mC, M1R, k1, smC, k1, M1L, k to 1 st before mD, M1R, k1, smD, k1, M1L, k to end (8 st inc).

ROWS 5, 7, 9, 11, 13 (RS): K to 1 st before mA, M1R, k1, smA, k1, M1L, k to 1 st before mB, M1R, k1, smB, k1, M1L, k to 1 st before mC, M1R, k1, smC, k1, M1L, k to 1 st before mD, M1R, k1, smD, k1, M1L, k to end (8 st inc).

STITCH COUNT CHECK-IN

FRONTS (EA): 8
SLEEVES (EA): 18 (20, 22, 30, 34, 38)
BACK: 42 (48, 54, 60, 62, 68)

ROW 15 (RS): K1, M1R, k to 1 st before mA, M1R, k1, smA, k1, M1L, k to 1 st before mB, M1R, k1, smB, k1, M1L, k to 1 st before mC, M1R, k1, smC, k1, M1L, k to 1 st before mD, M1R, k1, smD, k1, M1L, k to 1 st before end, M1L, k1 (10 st inc).

ROWS 17, 19 (RS): K to 1 st before mA, M1R, k1, smA, k1, M1L, k to 1 st before mB, M1R, k1, smB, k1, M1L, k to 1 st before mC, M1R, k1, smC, k1, M1L, k to 1 st before mD, M1R, k1, smD, k1, M1L, k to end (8 st inc).

STITCH COUNT CHECK-IN

FRONTS (EA): 12
SLEEVES (EA): 24 (26, 28, 36, 40, 44)
BACK: 48 (54, 60, 66, 68, 74)

ROW 21 (RS): As row 15.

ROW 23, 25 (RS): K to 1 st before mA, M1R, k1, smA, k1, M1L, k to 1 st before mB, M1R, k1, smB, k1, M1L, k to 1 st before mC, M1R, k1, smC, k1, M1L, k to 1 st before mD, M1R, k1, smD, k1, M1L, k to end (8 st inc).

ROW 27 (RS): As row 15.

STITCH COUNT CHECK-IN

FRONTS (EA): 18
SLEEVES (EA): 32 (34, 36, 44, 48, 52)
BACK: 56 (62, 68, 74, 76, 82)

ROWS 29, 31 (RS): K to 1 st before mA, M1R, k1, smA, k1, M1L, k to 1 st before mB, M1R, k1, smB, k1, M1L, k to 1 st before mC, M1R, k1, smC, k1, M1L, k to 1 st before mD, M1R, k1, smD, k1, M1L, k to end (8 st inc).

ROW 33 (RS): As row 15.

STITCH COUNT CHECK-IN

FRONTS (EA): 22
SLEEVES (EA): 38 (40, 42, 50, 54, 58)
BACK: 62 (68, 74, 80, 82, 88)

ROWS 35, 37 (RS): K to 1 st before mA, M1R, k1, smA, k1, M1L, k to 1 st before mB, M1R, k1, smB, k1, M1L, k to 1 st before mC, M1R, k1, smC, k1, M1L, k to 1 st before mD, M1R, k1, smD, k1, M1L, k to end (8 st inc).

ROW 39 (RS): As row 15.

STITCH COUNT CHECK-IN

FRONTS (EA): 26
SLEEVES (EA): 44 (46, 48, 56, 60, 64)
BACK: 68 (74, 80, 86, 88, 94)

ROWS 41, 43 (RS): K to 1 st before mA, M1R, k1, smA, k1, M1L, k to 1 st before mB, M1R, k1, smB, k1, M1L, k to 1 st before mC, M1R, k1, smC, k1, M1L, k to 1 st before mD, M1R, k1, smD, k1, M1L, k to end (8 st inc).

ROW 45 (RS): As row 15.

STITCH COUNT CHECK-IN

FRONTS (EA): 30
SLEEVES (EA): 50 (52, 54, 62, 66, 70)
BACK: 74 (80, 86, 92, 94, 100)

ROWS 47, 49 (RS): K to 1 st before mA, M1R, k1, smA, k1, M1L, k to 1 st before mB, M1R, k1, smB, k1, M1L, k to 1 st before mC, M1R, k1, smC, k1, M1L, k to 1 st before mD, M1R, k1, smD, k1, M1L, k to end (8 st inc).

Seaside back view.

SIZES 30/32, 34/36, 38/40, 42/44 ROW 51 (RS): Rep row 49 (8 st inc).

SIZES 46/48, 50/52 ROW 51 (RS): K to 3 st before mA, M1R, k2, M1R, k1, smA, k1, M1L, k to 1 st before mB, M1R, k1, smB, k1, M1L, k2, M1L, k to 3 st before mC, M1R, k2, M1R, k1, smC, k1, M1L, k to 1 st before mD, M1R, k1, smD, k1, M1L, k2, M1L, k to end (12 st inc).

SIZES 30/32, 34/36, 38/40, 42/44, 46/48 ROW 53 (RS): K to 3 st before mA, M1R, k2, M1R, k1, smA, k1, M1L, k to 1 st before mB, M1R, k1, smB, k1, M1L, k2, M1L, k to 3 st before mC, M1R, k2, M1R, k1, smC, k1, M1L, k to 1 st before mD, M1R, k1, smD, k1, M1L, k2, M1L, k to end (12 st inc).

SIZE 50/52 ROW 53 (RS): K to 5 st before mA, M1R, k2, M1R, k2, M1R, k1, smA, k1, M1L, k to 1 st before mB, M1R, k1, smB, k1, M1L, k2, M1L, k2, M1L, k to 5 st before mC, M1R, k2, M1R, k2, M1R, k1, smC, k1, M1L, k to 1 st before mD, M1R, k1, smD, k1, M1L, k2, M1L, k2, M1L, k to end (16 st inc).

STITCH COUNT CHECK-IN

FRONTS (EA): 35 (35, 35, 35, 36, 37)
SLEEVES (EA): 58 (60, 62, 70, 74, 78)
BACK: 84 (90, 96, 102, 106, 114)

Seaside front view.

SIZE 30/32 Work one last ws row, then proceed to Divide for Sleeves.

SIZES 34/36, 38/40, 42/44, 46/48, 50/52 ROW 55 (RS): Rep row 53 (for your size).

SIZE 34/36 Work one last ws row, then proceed to Divide for Sleeves.

All other sizes continue.

SIZES 38/40, 42/44, 46/48, 50/52 ROW 57 (RS): K to 5 st before mA, M1R, k2, M1R, k2, M1R, k1, smA, k1, M1L, k to 1 st before mB, M1R, k1, smB, k1, M1L, k2, M1L, k2, M1L, k to 5 st before mC, M1R, k2, M1R, k2, M1R, k1, smC, k1, M1L, k to 1 st before mD, M1R, k1, smD, k1, M1L, k2, M1L, k2, M1L, k to end (16 st inc).

SIZES 38/40, 42/44 Work one last ws row, then proceed to Divide for Sleeves.

SIZES 46/48, 50/52 ROW 59 (RS): Rep row 57 (16 st inc).

SIZES 46/48, 50/52 Work one last ws row, then proceed to Divide for Sleeves.

STITCH COUNT CHECK-IN

FRONTS (EA): 35 (37, 40, 40, 44, 46)
SLEEVES (EA): 58 (62, 66, 74, 80, 84)
BACK: 84 (94, 106, 112, 122, 132)*

*Place a locking m on your needle at the center of the back st for later use.

DIVIDE FOR SLEEVES: Work in pattern to mA, rem mA and place sleeve stitches onto waste yarn (loosely, so you can try it on later). CO 1 (3, 6, 6, 6, 6) st at the underarm and join to back section, removing mB in the process and replacing it at the center of the underarm. K to mC and rem mC, then place sleeve stitches onto waste yarn (loosely, so you can try it on later). CO 1 (3, 6, 6, 6, 6) st at the underarm and join to front, removing mD in the process and replacing it at the center of the underarm (in the center of the newly cast-on st). K to end.

STITCH COUNT CHECK-IN

156 (174, 198, 204, 222, 236) stitches in lower body

LOWER BODY: Work lower body in stockinette stitch (k on the rs, p on the ws) for 1" (2.5 cm).

FOR ALL SIZES EXCEPT 50/52: On the last row, inc 1 st on each side near the underarm using kfb (it will be obvious at first but will disappear into the texture as it's formed) 158 (176, 200, 206, 224, 236).

All sizes begin slipped st band as follows:

(RS): k2,[k4, sl2wyif] rep bet brackets to last six st, k6.

(WS): P2, k1, sl2wyif, k1 [k3, sl2wyif, k1] rep bet brackets to last two st, p2.

REP the slipped st band series three times in all (for a total of 6 rows).

On the next rs row, return to stockinette st and k to 2 st before the center m at the back, bind off 2 st, rem m, bind off 2 more st (4 st bound-off), then k to end of row.

(WS): P to first bound-off st and cast on 24 st (to become the pleat), then p across remainder of row.

WORK the lower body back and forth in stockinette st (the pleat will be tacked-down later) until body measures 11" (28 cm) from sleeve divide at underarm, ending after finishing a rs row.

TRANSITION to U.S. size 6/4 mm (32" [80 cm]) circular needle (or one size smaller than that used for body) and work one last ws row. At the same time inc 0 (2, 2, 0, 2, 2) st evenly using M1L and M1R, then begin lower ribbing as follows: [k2, p2] rep bet brackets across, ending k2. Continue ribbing for 2.25" (6 cm) and bind off in pattern with medium tension. Lower edge should not feel restrictive. If it does, bind off more loosely.

SLEEVES: With U.S. size 7/4.5 mm (12" [30 cm]) circular needle or DPN (or the same size as used for the body), pick up sleeve stitches from waste yarn (including st cast-on under the arm where applicable) plus an extra st as needed to reach the following count 60 (66, 72, 80, 86, 90) st. Pm at center of underarm to mark BOR. Knit in the round in stockinette st for 1" (2.5 cm).

NEXT ROUND: K2, k2tog, k to 4 st before m, ssk, k2 (2 st dec).

CONTINUE in stockinette stitch in the round, working a decrease round as indicated above approximately every 2" (5 cm) until sleeve measures approximately 13–15" (30–37.5 cm) from underarm, and you have the following number of stitches: 48 (52, 56, 68, 72, 80). On the last row, transition to U.S. size 5/3.75 mm (12" [30 cm]) circular needle or DPN (or two sizes smaller than used for sleeve/ body) for cuff and begin ribbing as follows: [k2, p2] rep between brackets to end of round. Continue in established ribbing (repeating [k2, p2] on every round) until cuff measures 3" (7.6 cm). Bind off in pattern with medium tension.

REP for second sleeve.

Using a U.S. size 5/3.75 mm (40" [100 cm]) circular needle, pick up stitch around the front/neck (approximately 5 of every 6 stitches, to end with a multiple of 6 + 2) to begin slipped st front band as follows:

SLIPPED-STITCH FRONT BAND (RS): K2, [k4, sl2wyif] rep bet brackets to last six st, k6.

(WS): P2, k1, sl2wyif, k1 [k3, sl2wyif, k1] rep bet brackets to last two st, p2.

WORK front band in slipped st pattern for 3.5" (8.75 cm). Bind off on the rs in pattern (but instead of sl2wyif, bind these off in p, instead).

PLEAT: From the ws, fold the pleat so that it lays flat and is evenly placed at the center of the back. Use matching wool and a yarn needle to tack the layers down and secure the pleat in place. The pleat should lay flat and the excess fabric should be arranged evenly underneath.

WEAVE-IN ends and wet block flat, taking care to smooth and pin down the pleat and the slipped st band on the body. Let dry.

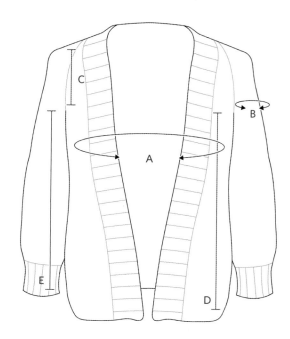

FINISHED MEASUREMENTS

A) BUST:
35.2" (38.8, 43.6, 44.8, 48.4, 51.2) (88 cm [97, 109, 112, 121, 128])*

B) SLEEVE AT WIDEST POINT:
11.8" (13, 14.4, 16, 17.2, 18) (29.5 cm [32.5, 36, 40, 43, 45])

C) TOP OF SHOULDER TO UNDERARM:
8.8" (9.2, 9.7, 10.3, 10.9, 11.2) (22.27 cm [23.45, 24.62, 26.18, 27.74, 28.53])

D) LENGTH OF BODY FROM UNDERARM:
13.25" (33.66 cm) prior to blocking

E) LENGTH OF SLEEVE FROM UNDERARM:
16–18" (40.64–45.72 cm) prior to blocking

*NOTE: This sweater does not close in front; this measurement is actual sweater coverage including front bands.

Abbey Pier Eyelet Pullover

Bold eyelet texture and twisted rib stand out against a backdrop of neutral speckles in this breezy pullover. Unlike other designs in this chapter, Abbey Pier's textural details begin early, but are so simple to work that they don't require much concentration. Designed to be layered over a solid tank top or tee, Abbey Pier features versatile sleeves and a relaxed fit with simple lace details and a strategic cable just under the bust. This creative marriage of texture and speckled color makes for an exciting wardrobe addition that is sure to attract notice.

TIMELINE

Abbey Pier is such a fun knit that it seems to fly off the needles, so anticipate a speedy project that will keep you moving from cast-on to bind-off. Most knitters will find this an easy project fo finish in about 7 to 10 days.

MATERIALS

Yarn	• DK | Three Irish Girls Springvale DK | 100% superwash Merino | 270 yards (247 m) per 115 g | 905 yards (1005, 1117, 1229, 1376, 1541) (828 m [919, 1021, 1124, 1258, 1409])
Yarn Notes	• Knit in a superwash Merino yarn, Abbey Pier's detail really shines after blocking, especially the center lace panel which won't lay flat until you block. Subtle speckled tones against a light background share the stage with dramatic lace and a strategically placed set of cables. This sweater would also shine in a solid, heather or tonal color.
Needles	• U.S. size 6/4 mm (24-32" [60-80 cm]) circular needle (body) • U.S. size 5/3.75 mm (24-32" [60-80 cm]) circular needle (lower body ribbing) • U.S. size 6/4 mm (12" [30 cm]) circular needle or DPN (sleeve) • U.S. size 4/3.5 mm (12" [30 cm]) circular needle or DPN (sleeve cuff) • U.S. size 4/3.5 mm (16-24" [40-60 cm]) circular needle (neck ribbing) • Note: Use needle size necessary to obtain gauge.

Gauge	• 20 st and 26 rows with larger needle over 4" (10 cm) in stockinette stitch
Notions	• Yarn needle • Stitch markers • Waste yarn

STITCH GLOSSARY

2/2lc	Slip 2 st to cn, hold to front, k2, then k2 from cn
2/2rc	Slip 2 st to cn, hold to back, k2, then k2 from cn
bet	between
BOR	beginning of round/row
CO	cast on
cn	cable needle
dec	decrease
ea	each
inc	increase
k	knit
k2tog	knit 2 st at once (dec 1)
kfb	knit into front and back of same st (inc 1)
ktbl	knit through the back loop (twisted st)
m	marker/markers

(continued)

mX	marker "X" indicates which marker (i.e, mA, mB, mC, etc.)
M1L	make one st that leans left (inc 1)
M1R	make one st that leans right (inc 1)
p	purl
pmX	place marker, "X" indicates which marker (i.e, mA, mB, mC, etc.)
ptbl	purl through the back loop (twisted st)
rem m	remove marker
rep	repeat
rs	right side
sm	slip marker/markers
smX	slip marker, "X" indicates which marker (i.e, smA, smB, smC, etc.)
ssk	slip, slip, knit together (dec 1)
st	stitch/stitches
ws	wrong side
yo	yarn over (inc 1)
[ ]	brackets always indicate a repeat

SIZES

Bust sizes 30/32" (34/36, 38/40, 42/44, 46/48, 50/52) (76/81 cm [86/91, 97/102, 107/112, 117/122, 127/132])

RECOMMENDED EASE

Positive ease is included for a comfortable fit. See finished measurements for final ease as compared to your actual bust measurement. If you are between sizes, refer to the final measurements to determine which size to choose. In many cases you'll find that the smaller of the two sizes will be the best choice.

CONSTRUCTION

Abbey Pier is worked flat until the neckline shaping is complete, then joined and worked in the round from that point down. The Eyelet Panel is established just after the neckline join and is worked down the front of the body, with a little double cable interruption that draws the garment in just a bit under the bust.

NOTE: Rows and rounds apply to all sizes unless otherwise indicated. Be sure to read ahead and mark sections that are specific to your size before you begin.

CABLE TIP: Strategically position the cable just under your bust by working an additional repeat (or more) of the Eyelet Panel.

ABBEY PIER PATTERN

With U.S. size 6/4 mm (24-32" [60-80 cm]) circular needle, cast on 36 (52, 78, 86, 94, 104) st using cable cast-on method. Do not join yet.

ROW 1 - SET UP (RS): K2, pmA, kfb, k0 (4, 12, 14, 18, 20), kfb, pmB, kfb, k26 (34, 44, 48, 48, 54), kfb, pmC, kfb, k0 (4, 12, 14, 18, 20), kfb, pmD, k2 (6 st inc).

ROW 2 (WS): P across, slipping m as you go.

ROW 3 (RS): K2, smA, k1, M1L, k to 1 st before mB, M1R, k1, smB, k1, M1L, k to 1 st before mC, M1R, k1, smC, k1, M1L, k to 1 st before mD, M1R, k1, smD, k2 (6 st inc).

ROW 4 (WS): As row 2.

ROW 5 (RS): K to 1 st before m, M1R, k1, smA, k1, M1L, k to 1 st before mB, M1R, k1, smB, k1, M1L, k to 1 st before mC, M1R, k1, smC, k1, M1L, k to 1 st before mD, M1R, k1, smD, k1, M1L, k to end (8 st inc).

ROW 6 (WS): As row 2.

REP these two rows 3 (2, 1, 1, 1, 1) time/s more.

STITCH COUNT CHECK-IN

FRONTS (EA): 6 (5, 4, 4, 4, 4)
SLEEVES (EA): 14 (16, 22, 24, 28, 30)
BACK: 40 (46, 54, 58, 58, 64)

NEXT ROW (RS): CO 2 st using knitted cast-on worked tightly*, then k to 1 st before m, M1R, k1, smA, k1, M1L, k to 1 st before mB, M1R, k1, smB, k1, M1L, k to 1 st before mC, M1R, k1, smC, k1, M1L, k to 1 st before mD, M1R, k1, smD, k1, M1L, k to end (8 st inc + CO).

NEXT ROW (WS): CO 2 st using knitted cast-on worked purlwise*, then p across, slipping m as you go.

*GOING FORWARD, all stitches cast-on on the right side will be worked using the knitted cast-on method, and all stitches cast-on on the wrong side will be worked using the knitted cast-on worked purlwise. Always knit the new stitch/es on the right side and purl the new stitch/es on the wrong side as you work through the rows.

REP these two rows once more.

STITCH COUNT CHECK-IN

FRONTS (EA): 12 (11, 10, 10, 10, 10)
SLEEVES (EA): 18 (20, 26, 28, 32, 34)
BACK: 44 (50, 58, 62, 62, 68)

NEXT ROW (RS): CO 4 st, then k to 1 st before m, M1R, k1, smA, k1, M1L, k to 1 st before mB, M1R, k1, smB, k1, M1L, k to 1 st before mC, M1R, k1, smC, k1, M1L, k to 1 st before mD, M1R, k1, smD, k1, M1L, k to end (8 st inc + CO).

NEXT ROW (WS): CO 4 st, then p across, slipping m as you go.

REP these two rows 0 (1, 2, 1, 1, 0) time/s more.

SIZES 30/32, 34/36, 38/40 Move ahead to Neckline Join.

SIZES 42/44, 46/48, 50/52 NEXT ROW (RS): CO 6 st, then k to 1 st before m, M1R, k1, smA, k1, M1L, k to 1 st before mB, M1R, k1, smB, k1, M1L, k to 1 st before mC, M1R, k1, smC, k1, M1L, k to 1 st before mD, M1R, k1, smD, k1, M1L, k to end (8 st inc + CO).

SIZES 42/44, 46/48, 50/52 NEXT ROW (WS): CO 6 st, then p across, slipping m as you go.

SIZES 42/44, 46/48 Move ahead to Neckline Join.

SIZE 50/52 NEXT ROW (RS): CO 6 st, then k to 1 st before m, M1R, k1, smA, k1, M1L, k to 1 st before mB, M1R, k1, smB, k1, M1L, k to 1 st before mC, M1R, k1, smC, k1, M1L, k to 1 st before mD, M1R, k1, smD, k1, M1L, k to end (8 st inc + CO).

SIZE 50/52 NEXT ROW (WS): CO 6 st, then p across, slipping m as you go.

STITCH COUNT CHECK-IN

FRONTS (EA): 17 (21, 25, 27, 27, 29)
SLEEVES (EA): 20 (24, 32, 34, 38, 40)
BACK: 46 (54, 64, 68, 68, 74)

NECKLINE JOIN: NEXT ROW (RS): CO 10 (10, 12, 12, 12, 14), then k to 1 st before m, M1R, k1, smA, k1, M1L, k to 1 st before mB, M1R, k1, smB, k1, M1L, k to 1 st before mC, M1R, k1, smC, k1, M1L, k to 1 st before mD, M1R, k1, smD, k1, M1L, k to end (8 st inc + CO). Cut yarn, leaving a tail.

REJOIN yarn just after mD, leaving a tail to weave in later. This marks the new BOR. Slide the stitches after mD to the left needle so they "meet" with the other stitches on the front section (all stitches between mD and mA are now the "front"). K across, joining the front stitches as you reach the gap (be careful not to twist stitches) and knit to end of round (no inc).

STITCH COUNT CHECK-IN

FRONT: 46 (54, 64, 68, 68, 74)
SLEEVES (EA): 22 (26, 34, 36, 40, 42)
BACK: 48 (56, 66, 70, 70, 76)

NEXT ROUND (INC): K1, M1L, k11 (15, 20, 22, 22, 25), pm1, k22, pm1, k11 (15, 20, 22, 22, 25), M1R, k1, smA, k1, M1L, k to 1 st before mB, M1R, k1, smB, k1, M1L, k to 1 st before mC, M1R, k1, smC, k1, M1L, k to 1 st before mD, M1R, k1 (8 st inc).

NEXT ROUND (NO INC): K across, slipping m as you go.

NEXT ROUND (INC): K1, M1L, k to mE, sm1, begin Center Panel starting with round 1 (written directions or chart)*, sm2, k to 1 st before mA, M1R, k1, smA, k1, M1L, k to 1 st before mB, M1R, k1, smB, k1, M1L, k to 1 st before mC, M1R, k1, smC, k1, M1L, k to 1 st before mD, M1R, k1 (8 st inc).

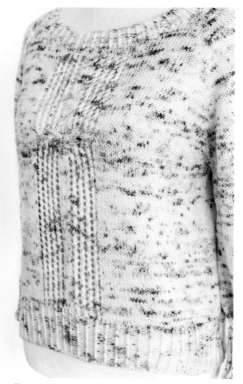

Abbey Pier front detail.

NEXT ROUND (NO INC): K across, slipping m as you go and maintaining Center Panel next row between mE and mF.

> ***PLEASE NOTE:** You will work two full repeats of the Center Eyelet Panel Chart (Part 1), then one full repeat of the Center Eyelet Panel Transition Chart (Part 2), then continue the remainder of the front in the Center Eyelet Panel Chart (Part 1) repeats. If you would like to move the placement of the cables further down, work an additional repeat of the Center Eyelet Panel Chart (Part 1) before moving to the Center Eyelet Panel Transition Chart (Part 2). This is what the pattern means when it indicates to work the "Center Panel."

REP these two rounds until you reach the following:

STITCH COUNT CHECK-IN

FRONT: 78 (88, 98, 102, 98, 104)
SLEEVES (EA): 54 (60, 68, 70, 70, 72)
BACK: 80 (90, 100, 104, 100, 106)

NEXT ROUND (EXTRA INC): K1, M1L, k2, M1L, k to mE, sm1, work Center Panel next round, sm2, k to 3 st before mA, M1R, k2, M1R, k1, smA, k1, M1L, k to 1 st before mB, M1R, k1, smB, k1, M1L, k2, M1L, k to 3 st before mC, M1R, K2, M1R, k1, smC, k1, M1L, k to 1 st before mD, M1R, k1 (12 st inc).

NEXT ROUND (NO INC): K across, slipping m as you go and maintaining Center Panel next row between mE and mF.

SIZES 30/32, 34/36, 38/40 Move ahead to next Stitch Count Check-In.

SIZES 42/44, 46/48, 50/52 Rep these two rounds - (-, -, 0, 2, 1) time/s more.

STITCH COUNT CHECK-IN

FRONT: 82 (92, 102, 106, 110, 112)
SLEEVES (EA): 56 (62, 70, 72, 76, 76)
BACK: 84 (94, 104, 108, 112, 114)

SIZES 30/32, 34/36, 38/40 Move ahead to Divide for Sleeves.

SIZES 42/44, 46/48, 50/52 NEXT ROUND (DOUBLE EXTRA INC): K1, M1L, k2, M1L, k2, M1L, k to mE, sm1, work Center Panel next round, sm2, k to 5 st before mA, M1R, k2, M1R, k2, M1R, k1, smA, k1, M1L, k to 1 st before mB, M1R, k1, smB, k1, M1L, k2, M1L, k2, M1L, k to 5 st before mC, M1R, K2, M1R, k2, M1R, k1, smC, k1, M1L, k to 1 st before mD, M1R, k1 (16 st inc).

SIZES 42/44, 46/48, 50/52 NEXT ROUND (NO INC): K across, slipping m as you go and maintaining Center Panel next row between mE and mF.

SIZE 42/44 Move ahead to Divide for Sleeves.

SIZES 46/48, 50/52 Rep these two rounds - (-, -, -, 1, 2) time/s more, then move ahead to Divide for Sleeves.

STITCH COUNT CHECK-IN

FRONT: 82 (92, 102, 112, 122, 130)
SLEEVES (EA): 56 (62, 70, 74, 80, 82)
BACK: 84 (94, 104, 114, 124, 132)

DIVIDE FOR SLEEVES: Work in pattern across front (maintaining Center Panel as established) to mA, rem mA and place sleeve stitches onto waste yarn (loosely, so you can try it on later). CO 4 (4, 4, 4, 4, 6) st at the underarm and join to back section, removing mB in the process. K to mC and rem mC, place sleeve stitches onto waste yarn (loosely, so you can try it on later). CO 4 (4, 4, 4, 4, 6) st at the underarm and join to front, removing mD in the process and replacing it at the center of the underarm (in the center of the newly cast-on st). K to end.

STITCH COUNT CHECK-IN

174 (194, 214, 234, 254, 274) st in lower body

LOWER BODY: K to mE, sm1, work Center Panel next round, sm2, k to end of round, slipping m as you go. Rep this round until lower body measures 11" (28 cm). Transition to U.S. size 5/3.75 mm (24-32" [60-80 cm]) circular needle (or one size smaller than that used for body) and work one round in stockinette (there are no further repeats of the Center Panel). At the same time, dec 0 (2, 1, 0, 2, 1) st evenly using k2tog to end with a multiple of 3 for lower ribbing. On the next round, begin lower ribbing as follows: [p2, ktbl] rep bet brackets to end of round. Continue in [p2, ktbl] ribbing until ribbing measures 2.5" (6.25 cm) and lower body measures 13.5" (34.25 cm) from underarm (at sleeve divide). Keep in mind that the body will grow in length with blocking.

SLEEVES: With U.S. size 6/4 mm (12" [30 cm]) circular needle or DPN (or same size as used for body), pick up stitches from waste yarn (including st cast-on under the arm, where applicable)— 60 (66, 70, 78, 84, 88) st. Pm at center of underarm to mark BOR. Knit sleeve in the round in stockinette st for 1" (2.5 cm).

NEXT ROUND: K2, k2tog, k to 4 st before m, ssk, k2 (2 st dec).

CONTINUE sleeve in stockinette st in the round, working a decrease round as indicated above approximately every 1.5-2" (3.8-5 cm) until sleeve measures approximately 11" (27.5 cm) from underarm and you have 48 (54, 60, 66, 72, 72) st, working an additional dec or so as needed on the last round to end with a multiple of 3 for twisted rib. On the next round transition to U.S. size 4/3.5 mm (12" [30 cm]) circular needle (or DPN) and knit one more round. On the next round begin twisted rib as follows: [k2, ptbl] rep bet brackets to end of round. (Note that this is opposite the other ribbing sections. This is intentional so that—when folded—it coordinates with the rest of the sweater. If you do not want to fold your cuff, work the cuff ribbing as [p2, ktbl], instead.) Continue working each round in this rib pattern (as established) until cuff measures 5" (12.5 cm). Bind off in pattern with medium/loose tension (not too loose, not too tight—cuff should be able to be folded once in half and sit comfortably on the arm).

REP for second sleeve.

NECKLINE: With U.S. size 4/3.5 mm (16-24" [40-60 cm]) circular needle, pick up nearly every st around the neckline (adjusting as needed for best results) to end with a multiple of 3. Work in [p2, ktbl] ribbing for 1.5" (3.8 cm). Bind off in pattern with medium tension.

WEAVE-IN ends and wet block, soaking thoroughly, and press out excess water. Pin flat, drawing the Center Eyelet Panel flat widthwise so it lays flat (you'll be inclined to want to draw it lengthwise, but in order to encourage the panel to dry where it belongs, you'll need to flatten it widthwise, as well). Allow to dry completely, turning as needed for even drying.

Abbey Pier front view.

CENTER EYELET PANEL DIRECTIONS

CENTER EYELET PANEL (PART 1): Work rounds 1–8 twice, then work one repeat of the Center Eyelet Panel Transition (Part 2), then return to the Center Eyelet Panel (Part 1) and repeat rounds 1–8 down the remainder of the body. To move the cable further down the bust, work an additional repeat of the Center Eyelet Panel (Part 1) before working the Transition (Part 2).

ROUND 1: [Yo, k2tog] four times, yo, ssk, k2, k2tog, [yo, ssk] four times, yo.

ROUND 2: K9, ktbl, k4, ktbl, k1, ktbl, k1, ktbl, k1, ktbl, k1.

ROUND 3: As round 1.

ROUND 4: As round 2.

ROUND 5: As round 1.

ROUND 6: As round 2.

ROUND 7: As round 1.

ROUND 8: As round 2.

CENTER EYELET PANEL TRANSITION (PART 2) (Work only once through)

ROUND 1: [Yo, k2tog] four times, yo, ssk, k2, k2tog, [yo, ssk] four times, yo.

ROUND 2: 22lc, k1, 22lc, k4, 22rc, k1, 22rc.

ROUND 3: K22.

ROUND 4: K2, 22lc, k1, 22lc, 22rc, k1, 22rc, k2.

ROUND 5: K22.

ROUND 6: Yo, k2tog, k2, 22lc, k6, 22rc, k2, ssk, yo.

ROUND 7: K20, ktbl, k1.

ROUND 8: Yo, k2tog, yo, k2tog, k2, 22lc, k2, 22rc, k2, ssk, yo, ssk, yo.

ROUND 9: K18, ktbl, k1, ktbl, k1.

ROUND 10: Yo, k2tog, yo, k2tog, yo, k2tog, k1, 22lc, 22rc, k1, ssk, yo, ssk, yo, ssk, yo.

ROUND 11: K16, [ktbl, k1] rep bet brackets four times.

CENTER EYELET PANEL CHART (PART 1)

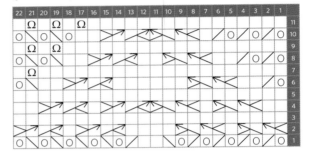

CENTER EYELET PANEL TRANSITION CHART (PART 2)

KEY		
2/2 LC	2/2 LC	(rs) Sl 2 to cn, hold to front, k2, k2 from cn
2/2 RC	2/2 RC	(rs) Sl 2 to cn, hold to back, k2, k2 from cn
☐	k	Knit (rs)
Ω	ktbl	Knit one stitch through the back loop
⧄	k2tog	Knit 2 stitches together
⧅	ssk	Slip, slip, knit slipped sts together
O	yo	(rs) Yarn over

FINISHED MEASUREMENTS

A) BUST:
34.8" (38.8, 42.8, 46.8, 50.8, 54.8) (87 cm [97, 107, 117, 127, 137])

B) SLEEVE AT WIDEST POINT:
12" (13, 14, 16, 17, 18) (30 cm [33, 35, 39, 42, 44])

C) TOP OF SHOULDER TO UNDERARM:
8.6" (9.2, 9.8, 10.3, 10.9, 11.1) (21.88 cm [23.45, 25.01, 26.18, 27.74, 28.14])

D) LENGTH OF BODY FROM UNDERARM:
13.5" (34.29 cm) prior to blocking

E) LENGTH OF SLEEVE FROM UNDERARM:
16" (40.64 cm) prior to blocking

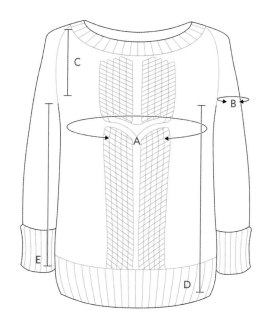

Stowaway Chevron Pullover

A beloved sweater is so much more than the individual parts: it's the way the different elements work together to create a garment we reach for often. Stowaway is the sweater we wear until it's threadbare, and then some. The chevrons down the side create visual interest without taking away from the efficiency of the overall project. A timeless, goes-with-everything heirloom design with twisted rib detail and a relaxed fit, this comfortable, stylish look can work for everyone.

TIMELINE

Like other designs in this section, Stowaway is an approachable project for a 7- to 10-day timeline regardless of size.

MATERIALS

Yarn	• Worsted | Brooklyn Tweed Shelter | 100% Targhee-Columbia wool | 140 yards (128 m) per 50 g | 850 yards (945, 1050, 1155, 1270, 1400) (777 m [864, 960, 1056, 1161, 1280])
Yarn Notes	• Woolen-spun fiber with tweed flecks create an earthy, natural background for this classic pullover.
Needles	• U.S. size 6/4 mm (24-32" [60-80 cm]) circular needle (body) • U.S. size 6/4 mm (12" [30 cm]) circular needle or DPN (sleeves) • U.S. size 4/3.5 mm (12" [30 cm]) circular needle or DPN (sleeve cuffs) • U.S. size 4/3.5 mm (16-24" [40-60 cm]) circular needle (neckline) • Note: Use needle size necessary to obtain gauge.
Gauge	• 20 st and 26 rows with larger needle over 4" (10 cm) in stockinette stitch
Notions	• Yarn needle • Stitch markers • Waste yarn

STITCH GLOSSARY

bet	between
BOR	beginning of round/row
CO	cast on
dec	decrease
ea	each
inc	increase
k	knit
k2tog	knit 2 st at once (dec 1)
ktbl	knit st through back loop (twisted knit st)
m	marker/markers
mX	marker "X" indicates which marker (i.e, mA, mB, mC, etc.)
M1	make one stitch by knitting into the bar between st to inc 1
M1L	make one st that leans left (inc 1)
M1R	make one st that leans right (inc 1)
p	purl
pmX	place marker, "X" indicates which marker (i.e, pmA, pmB, pmC, etc.)
rem m	remove marker
rep	repeat
rs	right side

(continued)

STITCH GLOSSARY

sm	slip marker/markers
smX	slip marker, "X" indicates which marker (i.e, smA, smB, smC, etc.)
ssk	slip, slip, knit together (dec 1)
st	stitch/stitches
ws	wrong side
[ ]	brackets always indicate a repeat

SIZES

Bust sizes 30/32" (34/36, 38/40, 42/44, 46/48, 50/52) (76/81 cm [86/91, 97/102, 107/112, 117/122, 127/132])

RECOMMENDED EASE

Positive ease is included for a comfortable fit. See finished measurements for final ease as compared to your actual bust measurement. If you are between sizes, refer to the final measurements to determine which size to choose. In many cases you'll find that the smaller of the two sizes will be the best choice.

CONSTRUCTION

Stowaway is cast-on at the neckline and worked flat until neckline shaping is complete. It's then joined in the round and worked top-down to the hem with subtle chevron detail at the sides.

NOTE: Rows and rounds apply to all sizes unless otherwise indicated. Be sure to read ahead and mark sections that are specific to your size before you begin.

ALSO: Markers with letters (mA, mB, etc.) denote the location of seams/increases in this design. Markers with numbers (m1, m2, etc.) denote the location of texture panels.

STOWAWAY PATTERN

With U.S. size 6/4 mm (24-32" [60-80 cm]) circular needle, cast on 65 (75, 81, 91, 111, 117) st using cable cast-on method. Do not join yet.

ROW 1 – SET UP (RS): K2, pmA, k13 (15, 15, 20, 25, 25), pmB, k1, M1L, k33 (39, 45, 45, 55, 61), M1R, k1, pmC, k13 (15, 15, 20, 25, 25), pmD, k2 (2 st inc).

ROW 2 (WS): P across, slipping m as you go.

ROW 3 (RS): K2, smA, k to mB, smB, k1, M1L, k to 1 st before mC, M1R, k1, smC, k to mD, smD, k2 (2 st inc).

ROW 4 (WS): As row 2.

ROW 5 (RS): As row 3.

ROW 6 (WS): As row 2.

ROW 7 (RS): CO 1 st using knitted cast-on worked tightly*, k to 1 st before mA, M1R, k1, smA, [k1, M1] rep bet brackets 2 (2, 2, 3, 3, 3) times total, k to 2 (2, 2, 3, 3, 3) st before mB, [M1, k1] rep bet brackets 2 (2, 2, 3, 3, 3) times, k to mB, smB, k1, M1L, k to 1 st before mC, M1R, k1, smC, [k1, M1] rep bet brackets 2 (2, 2, 3, 3, 3) times total, k to 2 (2, 2, 3, 3, 3) st before mD, [M1, k1] rep bet brackets 2 (2, 2, 3, 3, 3) times, k to mD, smD, k1, M1L, k to end = 13 (13, 13, 17, 17, 17) st inc + CO.

ROW 8 (WS): CO 1 st using knitted cast-on worked purlwise*, p across remainder of row, slipping m as you go.

***GOING FORWARD,** all stitches cast-on on the right side will be worked using the knitted cast-on method, and all stitches cast-on on the wrong side will be worked using the knitted cast-on worked purlwise. Always knit the new stitch/es on the right side and purl the new stitch/es on the wrong side as you work through the row.

STITCH COUNT CHECK-IN
FRONTS (EA): 4
SLEEVES (EA): 17 (19, 19, 26, 31, 31)
BACK: 43 (49, 55, 55, 65, 71)

Stowaway side view.

ROW 12 (WS): CO 1 (1, 2, 2, 2, 2) st, then p across row, slipping m as you go.

ROW 13 (RS): CO 1 (1, 2, 2, 4, 4) st, then k to 1 st before mA, M1R, k1, smA, k1, M1L, k to 1 st before mB, M1R, k1, smB, k1, M1L, k to 1 st before mC, M1R, k1, smC, k1, M1L, k to 1 st before mD, M1R, k1, smD, k1, M1L, k to end (8 st inc + CO).

ROW 14 (WS): CO 1 (1, 2, 2, 4, 4), then p across row, slipping m as you go.

STITCH COUNT CHECK-IN

FRONTS (EA): 10 (10, 12, 12, 14, 14)
SLEEVES (EA): 23 (25, 25, 32, 37, 37)
BACK: 49 (55, 61, 61, 71, 77)

ROW 15 (RS): CO 2 (2, 2, 2, 4, 4) st, then k to 1 st before mA, M1R, k1, smA, k1, M1L, k to 1 st before mB, M1R, k1, smB, k1, M1L, k to 1 st before mC, M1R, k1, smC, k1, M1L, k to 1 st before mD, M1R, k1, smD, k1, M1L, k to end (8 st inc + CO).

ROW 16 (WS): CO 2 (2, 2, 2, 4, 4) st, then p across, slipping m as you go.

ROW 17 (RS): CO 4 (4, 4, 4, 4, 6) st, then k to 1 st before mA, M1R, k1, smA, k1, M1L, k to 1 st before mB, M1R, k1, smB, k1, M1L, k to 1 st before mC, M1R, k1, smC, k1, M1L, k to 1 st before mD, M1R, k1, smD, k1, M1L, k to end (8 st inc + CO).

ROW 18 (WS): CO 4 (4, 4, 4, 4, 6), then p across, slipping m as you go.

STITCH COUNT CHECK-IN

FRONTS (EA): 18 (18, 20, 20, 24, 26)
SLEEVES (EA): 27 (29, 29, 36, 41, 41)
BACK: 53 (59, 65, 65, 75, 81)

ROW 19 (RS): CO 15 (21, 23, 23, 25, 27) st, then k to 1 st before mA, M1R, k1, smA, k1, M1L, k to 1 st before mB, M1R, k1, smB, k to mC, smC, k1, M1L, k to 1 st before mD, M1R, k1, smD, k1, M1L, k to end (6 st inc + CO).

CUT yarn, leaving a tail.

ROW 9 (RS): CO 1 st, then k to 1 st before mA, M1R, k1, smA, k1, M1L, k to 1 st before mB, M1R, k1, smB, k1, M1L, k to 1 st before mC, M1R, k1, smC, k1, M1L, k to 1 st before mD, M1R, k1, smD, k1, M1L, k to end (8 st inc + CO).

ROW 10 (WS): CO 1 st, then p across row, slipping m as you go.

ROW 11 (RS): CO 1 (1, 2, 2, 2, 2) st, then k to 1 st before mA, M1R, k1, smA, k1, M1L, k to 1 st before mB, M1R, k1, smB, k1, M1L, k to 1 st before mC, M1R, k1, smC, k1, M1L, k to 1 st before mD, M1R, k1, smD, k1, M1L, k to end (8 st inc + CO).

Stowaway back view.

STITCH COUNT CHECK-IN

FRONT: 53 (59, 65, 65, 75, 81)
SLEEVES (EA): 29 (31, 31, 38, 43, 43)
BACK: 53 (59, 65, 65, 75, 81)

NECKLINE JOIN: Rejoin yarn just after mD, leaving a tail to weave in later. This marks the new BOR. Slide the stitches after mD to the left needle so they "meet" with the other stitches on the front section (all stitches between mD and mA are now the "front")—53 (59, 65, 65, 75, 81) st between mD and mA. K this round, joining at the front stitches when you reach the gap (be careful not to twist stitches) and knit to end of round (no inc).

NEXT ROUND: At new BOR (just after mD) k to mA, smA, k1, M1L, k to 1 st before mB, M1R, k1, smB, k to mC, smC, k1, M1L, k to 1 st before mD, M1R, k1 (4 st inc).

NEXT ROUND (NO INC): K, slipping m as you go.

NEXT ROUND (INC): K to mA, smA, k1, M1L, k to 1 st before mB, M1R, k1, smB, k to mC, smC, k1, M1L, k to 1 st before mD, M1R, k1 (4 st inc).

STITCH COUNT CHECK-IN

FRONT: 53 (59, 65, 65, 75, 81)
SLEEVES (EA): 33 (35, 35, 42, 47, 47)
BACK: 53 (59, 65, 65, 75, 81)

REP the last two rounds, working increases only on the sleeves until you reach the following stitch count on the sleeves: 49 (51, 53, 60, 65, 65).

WORK one round without increases, then move ahead to the next increase round as follows.

NOTE: Increases on the front/back sections begin again on the next round to establish armscye and bust shaping.

NEXT ROUND (EXTRA INC): K1, M1L, k2, M1L, k to 3 st before mA, M1R, k2, M1R, k1, smA, k1, M1L, k to 1 st before mB, M1R, k1, smB, k1, M1L, k2, M1L, k to 3 st before mC, M1R, k2, M1R, k1, smC, k1, M1L, k to 1 st before mD, M1R, k1 (12 st inc).

NEXT ROUND (NO INC): K, slipping m as you go.

REP these two rounds 2 (3, 2, 3, 3, 4) times more.

STITCH COUNT CHECK-IN

FRONT: 65 (75, 77, 81, 91, 101)
SLEEVES (EA): 55 (59, 59, 68, 73, 75)
BACK: 65 (75, 77, 81, 91, 101)

NEXT ROUND (DOUBLE EXTRA INC): K1, M1L, k2, M1L, k2, M1L, k to 5 st before mA, M1R, k2, M1R, k2, M1R, k1, smA, k1, M1L, k to 1 st before mB, M1R, k1, smB, k1, M1L, k2, M1L, k2, M1L, k to 5 st before mC, M1R, k2, M1R, k2, M1R, k1, smC, k1, M1L, k to 1 st before mD, M1R, k1 (16 st inc).

NEXT ROUND (NO INC): K, slipping m as you go.

REP these two rounds 2 (2, 3, 4, 4, 4) times more.

STITCH COUNT CHECK-IN

FRONT: 83 (93, 101, 111, 121, 131)
SLEEVES (EA): 61 (65, 67, 78, 83, 85)
BACK: 83 (93, 101, 111, 121, 131)

DIVIDE FOR SLEEVES: K across front to mA, rem mA and place sleeve st onto waste yarn (loosely, so you can try it on later), then CO 2 (2, 4, 4, 4, 6) st underarm and join to back section, removing mB and replacing it at the center of the underarm to denote the side, k to mC, rem mC and place sleeve st on waste yarn (loosely), CO 2 (2, 4, 4, 4, 6) st underarm and join to front, replacing mD in the center of the underarm st.

STITCH COUNT CHECK-IN

170 (190, 210, 230, 250, 274) st in lower body

LOWER BODY: K7, pm1 (this will be the new BOR), k to 7 st before mB, pm2, k7, rem mB, k7 (the Chevron Rib panel will begin in this 14 st section on the next round), pm3, k to 7 st before mD, pm4, k7, rem mD.

NEXT ROUND: K to new BOR marker (m1) and work the next round as follows: K to m2, work Chevron Rib round 1, sm2, k to m3, sm3, work Chevron Rib round 1 to m4, sm4, k to end.

CONTINUE lower body in stockinette st in the round, working the Chevron Rib and repeating rounds 1–14 of the pattern until body measures 11″ (27.5 cm) from underarm. Discontinue the Chevron Rib (regardless of where you are in the repeat) and work one full round in stockinette st (size 50–52 will need to inc 1 st on this round using any subtle inc method near the side seam to end with a multiple of 5). Begin lower ribbing with the same needle as follows: [p3, k2tbl] rep bet brackets to end of round. Rep lower ribbing for 3″ (7.6 cm) and bind off in pattern (but do not twist the k st when you bind off—it will be too restrictive).

Stowaway side detail.

SLEEVES: With U.S. size 6/4 mm (12″ [30 cm]) circular needle or DPN, pick up sleeve st from waste yarn as well as st that were cast-on under the arm— 63 (67, 71, 82, 87, 91) st. Pm at the center of the underarm to denote BOR. Work the sleeves in stockinette st in the round for 2″ (5 cm).

DEC ROUND: K2, k2tog, work in pattern as established to 4 st before m, ssk, k2 (2 st dec).

CONTINUE in stockinette st, working a dec round approximately every 1–1.5″ (2.5–3.8 cm) until sleeve measures 19″ (48.25 cm) and you have 45 (45, 50, 50, 55, 65) st. Note: You may need to work one more or one less dec to reach these counts so you end with a multiple of 5.

TRANSITION to U.S. size 4/3.5 mm needle, work one more round in stockinette. On the next round begin ribbing as follows: [p3, k2tbl] rep bet brackets to end of round. Continue in established [p3, k2tbl] ribbing until cuff measures 2" (5 cm). Bind off in pattern with medium tension (but do not twist the k st when binding off or it will be too restrictive).

NECKLINE: With U.S. size 4/3.5 mm (16-24" [40-60 cm]) circular needle, pick up nearly every st around the neckline (or as needed for best results) to achieve a multiple of 5. Work in [p3, k2tbl] ribbing, rep bet brackets every round, until neckline measures 1.5" (3.8 cm). Bind off in pattern with medium tension (but do not twist the k st when binding off or it will be too restrictive).

WEAVE-IN ends and wet block flat, turning as needed for even drying.

CHEVRON RIB DIRECTIONS

ROUND 1: K1, p4, k4, p4, k1.
ROUND 2 (AND ALL EVEN ROUNDS 2-14): K the knits, p the purls.
ROUND 3: K1, p3, k6, p3, k1.
ROUND 5: K1, p2, k2, p1, k2, p1, k2, p2, k1.
ROUND 7: K1, p1, k2, p2, k2, p2, k2, p1, k1.
ROUND 9: K3, p3, k2, p3, k3.
ROUND 11: K2, p4, k2, p4, k2.
ROUND 13: K1, p5, k2, p5, k1.

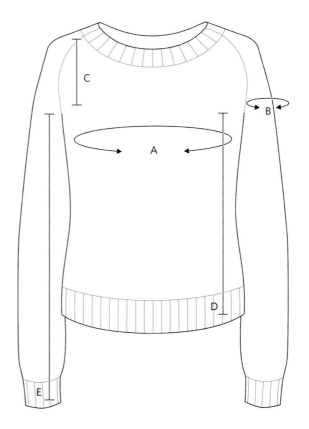

FINISHED MEASUREMENTS

A) BUST:
34" (38, 42, 46, 50, 54.8) (85 cm [95, 105, 115, 125, 137])

B) SLEEVE AT WIDEST POINT:
12.6" (13.4, 14, 16, 17, 18) (31 cm [33, 35, 41, 43, 45])

C) TOP OF SHOULDER TO UNDERARM:
9.2" (9.6, 9.9, 10.9, 11.3, 11.6) (23.25 cm [24.42, 25.2, 27.74, 28.72, 29.5])

D) LENGTH OF BODY FROM UNDERARM:
14" (35.5 cm)

E) LENGTH OF SLEEVE FROM UNDERARM:
21" (53.34 cm)

Tidepool Baby Doll Tee

A lightweight tee with twisted rib and an offset geometric lace insert, Tidepool is an elegant knit for warm weather. This darling sweater is perfect for the spring or summer season, and it pairs beautifully with a summer dress, shorts or capris. Try it partially tucked, as well! The length can be easily adjusted for a change in style—or you might swap out the unadorned lower edge for ribbing to give it a completely new look. This perfect staycation knit will give you quick results with minimal effort.

TIMELINE

Tidepool is a naturally speedy garment because the surface area is relatively small in comparison to other sweaters. Motivated knitters could finish this garment in 5 to 7 days with enough knitting time at their disposal.

MATERIALS

Yarn	• DK | Shoppel-Wolle Cashmere Queen | 35% cashmere, 45% Merino wool, 20% silk | 153 yards (140 m) per 50 g | 605 yards (670, 744, 818, 916, 1026) (553 m [613, 680, 748, 838, 938])
Yarn Notes	• Stockinette stitch is often underrated, but its versatility is unsurpassed. The fabric of this design should be soft and flexible with medium density and structured drape. The recommended yarn has an unusual single ply that resists the pilling often associated with cashmere. Thanks to the slightly lower neckline and cap sleeves (resulting in less yardage required), it's a bit easier to splurge on a luxury yarn.
Needles	• U.S. size 5/3.75 mm (24-32" [60-80 cm]) circular needle (body) • U.S. size 5/3.75 mm (12" [30 cm]) circular needle or DPN (sleeve) • U.S. size 3/3.25 mm (12" [30 cm]) circular needle or DPN (sleeve cuff) • U.S. size 3/3.25 mm (16-24" [40-60 cm]) circular needle (neckline) • Note: Use needle size necessary to obtain gauge.
Gauge	• 20 st and 26 rows with larger needle over 4" (10 cm) in stockinette stitch
Notions	• Yarn needle • Stitch markers (including a locking marker) • Waste yarn

STITCH GLOSSARY

bet	between
BOR	beginning of round/row
CO	cast on
dec	decrease
ea	each
inc	increase
k	knit
k2tog	knit 2 st at once (dec 1)
m	marker/markers
mX	marker "X" indicates which marker (i.e, mA, mB, mC, etc.)
M1L	make one st that leans left (inc 1)
M1R	make one st that leans right (inc 1)
p	purl
pmX	place marker, "X" indicates which marker (i.e, pmA, pmB, pmC, etc.)
psso	pass slipped st over
rem m	remove marker
rep	repeat
rs	right side
sl	slip
sm	slip marker/markers

(continued)

SIZES

Bust sizes 30/32" (34/36, 38/40, 42/44, 46/48, 50/52) (76/81 cm [86/91, 97/102, 107/112, 117/122, 127/132])

RECOMMENDED EASE

Positive ease is included for a comfortable fit. See finished measurements for final ease as compared to your actual bust measurement. If you are between sizes, refer to the final measurements to determine which size to choose. In many cases you'll find that the smaller of the two sizes will be the best choice.

CONSTRUCTION

With a wide neckline and short cap sleeves, this flirty cashmere tee is practical luxury at its finest. The neckline shaping is worked flat, then joined and worked in the round from that point forward. The body is worked in the round and features offset chevron lace detail. The picot bind-off at the neckline gives it a feminine, delicate finish.

NOTE: Rows and rounds apply to all sizes unless otherwise indicated. Be sure to read ahead and mark sections that are specific to your size before you begin.

TIP: The recommended yarn will roll at the bottom prior to blocking, but the blocking/pinning process will smooth it and it will lay flat. If you use a yarn substitution or find that your lower edge doesn't lay properly, you may consider ending with ribbing or a garter stitch, instead.

Tidepool detail.

TIDEPOOL PATTERN

With U.S. size 5/3.75 mm (24-32" [60-80 cm]) circular needle, cast on 34 (38, 56, 76, 80, 94) st using cable cast-on method. Do not join yet.

ROW 1 - SET UP (RS): K2, pmA, kfb, k0 (0, 6, 14, 16, 20), kfb, pmB, kfb, k24 (28, 34, 38, 38, 44), kfb, pmC, kfb, k0 (0, 6, 14, 16, 20), kfb, pmD, k2 (6 st inc).

ROW 2 (WS): P across, slipping m as you go.

ROW 3 (RS): K2, smA, k1, M1L, k to 1 st before mB, M1R, k1, smB, k1, M1L, k to 1 st before mC, M1R, k1, smC, k1, M1L, k to 1 st before mD, M1R, k1, smD, k2 (6 st inc).

ROW 4 (WS): As row 2.

ROW 5 (RS): As row 3.

ROW 6 (WS): As row 2.

ROW 7 (RS): K1, M1R, k1, smA, k1, M1L, k to 1 st before mB, M1R, k1, smB, k1, M1L, k to 1 st before mC, M1R, k1, smC, k1, M1L, k to 1 st before mD, M1R, k1, smD, k1, M1L, k1 (8 st inc).

ROW 8 (WS): As row 2.

STITCH COUNT CHECK-IN
FRONTS (EA): 3
SLEEVES (EA): 10 (10, 16, 24, 26, 30)
BACK: 34 (38, 44, 48, 48, 54)

ROW 9 (RS): As row 7.

ROW 10 (WS): As row 2.

ROW 11 (RS): CO 0 (2, 2, 2, 2, 2) st using knitted cast-on worked tightly*, k to 1 st before mA, M1R, k1, smA, k1, M1L, k to 1 st before mB, M1R, k1, smB, k1, M1L, k to 1 st before mC, M1R, k1, smC, k1, M1L, k to 1 st before mD, M1R, k1, smD, k1, M1L, k to end (8 st inc + CO).

ROW 12 (WS): CO 0 (2, 2, 2, 2, 2) st using knitted cast-on worked purlwise*, p across remainder of row, slipping m as you go.

*GOING FORWARD, all stitches cast-on on the right side will be worked using the knitted cast-on method, and all stitches cast-on on the wrong side will be worked using the knitted cast-on worked purlwise. Always knit the new stitch/es on the right side and purl the new stitch/es on the wrong side as you work through the row.

ROW 13 (RS): CO 2 (2, 4, 4, 4, 4) st, k to 1 st before mA, M1R, k1, smA, k1, M1L, k to 1 st before mB, M1R, k1, smB, k1, M1L, k to 1 st before mC, M1R, k1, smC, k1, M1L, k to 1 st before mD, M1R, k1, smD, k1, M1L, k to end (8 st inc + CO).

ROW 14 (WS): CO 2 (2, 4, 4, 4, 4) st, p across remainder of row, slipping m as you go.

STITCH COUNT CHECK-IN
FRONTS (EA): 8 (10, 12, 12, 12, 12)
SLEEVES (EA): 16 (16, 22, 30, 32, 36)
BACK: 40 (44, 50, 54, 54, 60)

ROW 15 (RS): CO 4 st, k to 1 st before mA, M1R, k1, smA, k1, M1L, k to 1 st before mB, M1R, k1, smB, k1, M1L, k to 1 st before mC, M1R, k1, smC, k1, M1L, k to 1 st before mD, M1R, k1, smD, k1, M1L, k to end (8 st inc + CO).

ROW 16 (WS): CO 4 st, p across remainder of row, slipping m as you go.

ROW 17 (RS): CO 4 (4, 4, 6, 6, 8) st, k to 1 st before mA, M1R, k1, smA, k1, M1L, k to 1 st before mB, M1R, k1, smB, k1, M1L, k to 1 st before mC, M1R, k1, smC, k1, M1L, k to 1 st before mD, M1R, k1, smD, k1, M1L, k to end (8 st inc + CO).

ROW 18 (WS): CO 4 (4, 4, 6, 6, 8) st, p across remainder of row, slipping m as you go.

ROW 19 (RS): CO 28 (28, 30, 30, 30, 32) st, k to 1 st before mA, M1R, k1, smA, k1, M1L, k to 1 st before mB, M1R, k1, smB, k1, M1L, k to 1 st before mC, M1R, k1, smC, k1, M1L, k to 1 st before mD, M1R, k1, smD, k1, M1L, k to end (8 st inc + CO). Cut yarn, leaving a tail.

NECKLINE JOIN: Rejoin yarn just after mD, leaving a tail to weave in later. This marks the new BOR. Slide the stitches after mD to the left needle so they "meet" with the other stitches on the front section (all stitches between mD and mA are now the "front"). K across, joining the front stitches as you reach the gap (be careful not to twist stitches) and knit to end of round (no inc). Note that the center 10 st on the front will become the pleat and will draw the neckline in slightly.

STITCH COUNT CHECK-IN
FRONT: 66 (70, 76, 80, 80, 86)
SLEEVES (EA): 22 (22, 28, 36, 38, 42)
BACK: 46 (50, 56, 60, 60, 66)

NEXT ROUND (INC): K1, M1L, k27 (29, 32, 34, 34, 37), place locking marker here at the neckline to mark the pleat for later, k10, place another locking marker here to mark the other edge of the pleat, k10, pmE to mark the placement of the zigzag texture for later, k17 (19, 22, 24, 24, 27), M1R, k1, smA, k1, M1L, k to 1 st before mB, M1R, k1, smB, k1, M1L, k to 1 st before mC, M1R, k1, smC, k1, M1L, k to 1 st before mD, M1R, k1 (8 st inc).

NEXT ROUND (NO INC): K the round, slipping m as you go.

NEXT ROUND (INC): K1, M1L, k across front (slipping mE when you reach it) to 1 st before mA, M1R, k1, smA, k1, M1L, k to 1 st before mB, M1R, k1, smB, k1, M1L, k to 1 st before mC, M1R, k1, smC, k1, M1L, k to 1 st before mD, M1R, k1 (8 st inc).

NEXT ROUND (NO INC): K the round, slipping m as you go.

REP these two rounds until you reach the following:

STITCH COUNT CHECK-IN

FRONT: 102 (108, 112, 114, 114, 118)
SLEEVES (EA): 58 (60, 64, 70, 72, 74)
BACK: 82 (88, 92, 94, 94, 98)

SIZE 30/32 Move ahead to Divide for Sleeves.

SIZES 34/36, 38/40, 42/44, 46/48, 50/52 NEXT ROUND (INC): K1, M1L, k2, M1L, k across front (slipping mE) to 3 st before mA, M1R, k2, M1R, k1, smA, k1, M1L, k to 1 st before mB, M1R, k1, smB, k1, M1L, k2, M1L, k to 3 st before mC, M1R, k2, M1R, k1, smC, k1, M1L, k to 1 st before mD, M1R, k1 (12 st inc).

NEXT ROUND (NO INC): K the round, slipping m as you go.

REP these two rounds - (0, 1, 2, 1, 2) time/s more.

STITCH COUNT CHECK-IN

FRONT: - (112, 120, 126, 122, 130)
SLEEVES (EA): - (62, 68, 76, 76, 80)
BACK: - (92, 100, 106, 102, 110)

SIZES 34/36, 38/40 Move ahead to Divide for Sleeves.

SIZES 42/44, 46/48, 50/52 NEXT ROUND (INC): K1, M1L, k2, M1L, k2, M1L, k across front (slipping mE) to 5 st before mA, M1R, k2, M1R, k2, M1R, k1, smA, k1, M1L, k to 1 st before mB, M1R, k1, smB, k1, M1L, k2, M1L, k2, M1L, k to 5 st before mC, M1R, k2, M1R, k2, M1R, k1, smC, k1, M1L, k to 1 st before mD, M1R, k1 (16 st inc).

NEXT ROUND (NO INC): K the round, slipping m as you go.

REP these two rounds - (-, -, 0, 2, 2) time/s more.

ALL SIZES continue.

Tidepool detail.

STITCH COUNT CHECK-IN

FRONT: 102 (112, 120, 132, 140, 148)
SLEEVES (EA): 58 (62, 68, 78, 82, 86)
BACK: 82 (92, 100, 112, 120, 128)

DIVIDE FOR SLEEVES: K to mA, rem mA and place sleeve stitches onto waste yarn (loosely, so you can try it on later). CO 2 (4, 4, 4, 4, 6) st underarm and join to back section, removing mB in the process. K to mC and rem mC, placing sleeve stitches onto waste yarn (loosely, so you can try it on later). CO 2 (4, 4, 4, 4, 6) st underarm and join to front, removing mD in the process and replacing it at the center of the underarm (in the center of the newly cast-on st) to mark BOR. K to end.

STITCH COUNT CHECK-IN

188 (212, 228, 252, 268, 288) st in lower body

Tidepool neck and arm detail.

CONTINUE lower body in stockinette stitch (knitting every round) until lower body measures 7–9" (17.5–22.5 cm) from underarm (sweater is meant to be cropped for summer, but those with longer torsos will want to work the longer length). On the next round, k to mE, smE and begin Triple Chevron (chart or written) working 7 (7, 7, 9, 9, 11) repeats in all, then pmF to mark the end of the panel and k to end of round.

WORK Triple Chevron rounds 1–18 once.

At the completion of the Triple Chevron pattern, work the remainder of the lower body in stockinette st in the round until the body measures 12–14" (30.5–35.5 cm) from underarm. On the next round, bind off with medium/loose tension (not sloppy, but not restrictive) in pattern.

SLEEVES: Using U.S. size 5/3.75 mm (12" [30 cm]) circular needle or DPN (or same size as used for body), pick up sleeve st from waste yarn, plus additional st cast-on under the arm at the sleeve divide 60 (66, 72, 82, 86, 92) st. Work ten rounds in stockinette st. On the next round transition to U.S. size 3/3.25 mm (16–24" [40–60 cm]) needle and

k one more round. On the next round begin [k1, p1] ribbing, repeating bet brackets to end of round. Work three more rounds in [k1, p1] ribbing, then k four rounds and bind off in pattern with medium/loose tension. Rep for second sleeve.

NECKLINE: With a U.S. size 3/3.25 mm (16–24" [40–60 cm]) circular needle, pick up approximately 5 of every 6 available st around the neckline, and join to work in the round. K three rounds. Note: If you prefer a slightly narrower neckline, work a series of 10 dec (evenly spaced) using k2tog on the final round before you continue. Work a picot bind-off as follows: [Cast on two st using knitted cast on method. Bind off four stitches (including the two you just cast on). Slide the final st from the right needle back to the left needle.] Rep bet brackets to end of round and tack down the final st. Adjust as needed for your st count.

WET block flat, turning as needed.

TRIPLE CHEVRON DIRECTIONS

ROUND 1: [K1, yo, ssk, k7, k2tog, yo] rep bet brackets 7 (7, 7, 9, 9, 11) times total.

ROUND 2 AND ALL EVEN CHART ROUNDS: K.

ROUND 3: [K2, yo, ssk, k5, k2tog, yo, k1] rep bet brackets 7 (7, 7, 9, 9, 11) times total.

ROUND 5: [K1, (yo, ssk) twice, k3, (k2tog, yo) twice] rep bet brackets 7 (7, 7, 9, 9, 11) times total.

ROUND 7: [K2, (yo, ssk) twice, k1, (k2tog, yo) twice, k1] rep bet brackets 7 (7, 7, 9, 9, 11) times total.

ROUND 9: [K1, (yo, ssk) twice, yo, sl2-k1-p2sso, yo, (k2tog, yo) twice] rep bet brackets 7 (7, 7, 9, 9, 11) times total.

ROUND 11: Rep round 7.

ROUND 13: [K3, yo, ssk, yo, sl2-k1-p2sso, yo, k2tog, yo, k2] rep bet brackets 7 (7, 7, 9, 9, 11) times total.

ROUND 15: [K4, yo, ssk, k1, k2tog, yo, k3] rep bet brackets 7 (7, 7, 9, 9, 11) times total.

ROUND 17: [K5, yo, sl2-k1-p2sso, yo, k4] rep bet brackets 7 (7, 7, 9, 9, 11) times total.

TRIPLE CHEVRON CHART

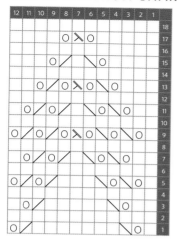

KEY

□	k	(rs) Knit	
◿	k2tog	(rs) Knit 2 stitches together	
◺	ssk	(rs) Slip, slip, knit slipped sts together	
⬓	s12-k1-p2sso	Slip 2 st knitwise, k the next st, pass two st over the k st (2 st dec)	
◻	yo	(rs) Yarn Over	

FINISHED MEASUREMENTS

A) BUST:
37.6" (42.4, 45.6, 50.4 53.6, 57.6) (94 cm [106, 114, 126, 134, 144])

B) SLEEVE AT WIDEST POINT:
12" (13, 14, 16, 17, 18) (30 cm [33, 36, 41, 43, 46])

C) TOP OF SHOULDER TO UNDERARM:
8.6" (8.9, 9.3, 10.1, 10.6, 11.0) (21.77 cm [22.5, 23.59, 25.76, 26.85, 27.94])

D) LENGTH OF BODY FROM UNDERARM:
12–14" (30–35 cm)

E) LENGTH OF SLEEVE FROM UNDERARM:
3" (7.62 cm)

Vacation Knits

MINDLESS & TRAVEL-FRIENDLY PROJECTS

The most important part of travel is narrowing down projects and deciding how much yarn to bring. No one wants to run short partway through their vacation and have to scramble desperately for a local yarn shop. Over the years I've had it both ways and here's what I've learned: I'd rather take too much and have leftovers than end up without a project. The sweaters in this chapter are essential pieces that you'll wear often, and they're perfect for distracted knitting time. Whether you're knitting on a tour bus, at a campsite, sitting on a boat or visiting with friends, you'll have something steady to knit so you can focus on having fun.

Pebble Bay Simple Pullover

Simplicity can be the ultimate luxury. Marled two-tone wool and miles of stockinette stitch unite in a timeless pullover with a comfortable fit. Sometimes a traditional, vanilla pullover is exactly what you need. Whether it's a canvas to showcase remarkable yarn, or it's employed to create visual balance in an otherwise busy outfit, I cannot say enough about the value of a basic sweater. Pebble Bay is perfect in its sparse detail, and ideal for on-the-go knitting thanks to its intuitive design and the absence of fussy details. This is one of my favorites for everyday wear!

TIMELINE

This simple sweater will practically fly off your needles, and can realistically be completed in 5 to 7 days for knitters on a mission. If you're looking for almost instant results, Pebble Bay is a perfect choice.

MATERIALS

Yarn
- DK | HiKoo Trenzado | 50% superwash Merino wool, 50% Merino wool | 109 yards (100 m) per 50 g | 935 yards (1035, 1150, 1265, 1395, 1535) (855 m [946, 1052, 1157, 1276, 1404])

Yarn Notes
- Worked in a swirled two-ply yarn with a bouncy twist, the two different types of Merino (superwash vs. non-superwash) take the dye differently to create a unique tonal yarn.

Needles
- U.S. size 5/3.75 mm (24-32" [60-80 cm]) circular needle (body)
- U.S. size 5/3.75 mm (12" [30 cm]) circular needle or DPN (sleeves)
- U.S. size 3/3.25 mm (12" [30 cm]) circular needle or DPN (sleeve cuffs)
- U.S. size 3/3.25 mm (16-24" [40-60 cm]) circular needle (neck ribbing)
- U.S. size 4/3.5 mm (24-32" [60-80 cm]) circular needle (lower body ribbing)
- Note: Use needle size necessary to obtain gauge.

Gauge
- 21 st and 26 rows with larger needle over 4" (10 cm) in stockinette stitch

Notions
- Yarn needle
- Stitch markers
- Waste yarn

STITCH GLOSSARY

bet	between
BOR	beginning of round/row
CO	cast on
dec	decrease
ea	each
inc	increase
k	knit
k2tog	knit 2 st at once (dec 1)
kfb	knit into the front and back of same st (inc 1)
m	marker/markers
mX	marker "X" indicates which marker (i.e, mA, mB, mC, etc.)
M1L	make one st that leans left (inc 1)
M1R	make one st that leans right (inc 1)
p	purl
pmX	place marker, "X" indicates which marker (i.e, pmA, pmB, pmC, etc.)
rem m	remove marker
rep	repeat
rs	right side
sm	slip marker/markers

(continued)

STITCH GLOSSARY

smX	slip marker, "X" indicates which marker (i.e, smA, smB, smC, etc.)
ssk	slip, slip, knit together (dec 1)
st	stitch/stitches
ws	wrong side
[ ]	brackets always indicate a repeat

SIZES

Bust sizes 30/32" (34/36, 38/40, 42/44, 46/48, 50/52) (76/81 cm [86/91, 97/102, 107/112, 117/122, 127/132])

RECOMMENDED EASE

Positive ease is included for a comfortable fit. See finished measurements for final ease as compared to your actual bust measurement. If you are between sizes, refer to the final measurements to determine which size to choose. In many cases you'll find that the smaller of the two sizes will be the best choice.

CONSTRUCTION

Pebble Bay is worked flat until neck shaping is complete, then joined and worked in the round from that point forward. Sleeves and neckline are worked last. This mindless project is perfect for knitting on-the-go.

NOTE: Rows and rounds apply to all sizes unless otherwise indicated. Be sure to read ahead and mark sections that are specific to your size before you begin.

TIP: If you prefer the neckline a little higher, work a bit of extra ribbing until you achieve the fit you like.

PEBBLE BAY PATTERN

With U.S. size 5/3.75 mm (24–32" [60–80 cm]) circular needle (or size to obtain gauge), cast on 30 (46, 72, 88, 98, 108) st using cable cast-on method. Do not join.

ROW 1 – SET UP (RS): K2, pmA, kfb, k0 (4, 12, 18, 22, 24), kfb, pmB, kfb, k20 (28, 38, 42, 44, 50), kfb, pmC, kfb, k0 (4, 12, 18, 22, 24), kfb, pmD, k2 (6 st inc).

ROW 2 (WS): P across, slipping m as you go.

SIZE 30/32 ONLY ROW 3 (RS): K2, smA, K1, M1L, k2, M1R, k1, smB, k3, M1L, k to 3 st before mC, M1R, k3, smC, k1, M1L, k 2, M1R, k1, smD, k2 (6 st inc).

SIZES 34/36, 38/40, 42/44, 46/48, 50/52 ROW 3 (RS): K2, smA, k3, M1L, k to 3 st before mB, M1R, k3, smB, k3, M1L, k to 3 st before mC, M1R, k3, smC, k3, M1L, k to 3 st before mD, M1R, k3, smD, k2 (6 st inc).

ALL SIZES continue.

ROW 4 (WS): P across, slipping m as you go.

ROW 5 (RS): K to 1 st before mA, M1R, k1, smA, k3, M1L, k to 3 st before mB, M1R, k3, smB, k3, M1L, k to 3 st before mC, M1R, k3, smC, k3, M1L, k to 3 st before mD, M1R, k3, smD, k1, M1L, k to end (8 st inc).

ROW 6 AND ALL WS ROWS (UNLESS OTHERWISE INDICATED): P across, slipping m as you go.

STITCH COUNT CHECK-IN

FRONTS (EA): 3
SLEEVES (EA): 8 (12, 20, 26, 30, 32)
BACK: 28 (36, 46, 50, 52, 58)

ROW 7 (RS): Rep row 5.

SIZES 30/32, 34/36 ROW 9 (RS): K to 3 st before mA, M1R, k3, smA, k3, M1L, k to 3 st before mB, M1R, k3, smB, k3, M1L, k to 3 st before mC, M1R, k3, smC, k3, M1L, k to 3 st before mD, M1R, k3, smD, k3, M1L, k to end (8 st inc).

SIZES 38/40, 42/44, 46/48, 50/52 ROW 9 (RS): CO 1 st using knitted cast-on method worked tightly*, k to 3 st before mA, M1R, k3, smA, k3, M1L, k to 3 st before mB, M1R, k3, smB, k3, M1L, k to 3 st before mC, M1R, k3, smC, k3, M1L, k to 3 st before mD, M1R, k3, smD, k3, M1R, k to end (8 st inc + CO).

SIZES 30/32, 34/36 ROW 10 (WS): Rep row 6.

SIZES 38/40, 42/44, 46/48, 50/52 ROW 10 (WS): CO 1 st using knitted cast-on worked purlwise*, p to end of row, slipping m as you go.

*GOING FORWARD, all stitches cast-on on the right side will be worked using the knitted cast-on method, and all stitches cast-on on the wrong side will be worked using the knitted cast-on worked purlwise. Always knit the new stitch/es on the right side and purl the new stitch/es on the wrong side as you work through the rows.

ALL SIZES continue.

ROW 11 (RS): CO 1 st, k to 3 st before mA, M1R, k3, smA, k3, M1L, k to 3 st before mB, M1R, k3, smB, k3, M1L, k to 3 st before mC, M1R, k3, smC, k3, M1L, k to 3 st before mD, M1R, k3, smD, k3, M1R, k to end (8 st inc + CO).

ROW 12 (WS): CO 1 st, p to end of row, slipping m as you go.

ROW 13 (RS): CO 1 (1, 1, 1, 2, 2) st, k to 3 st before mA, M1R, k3, smA, k3, M1L, k to 3 st before mB, M1R, k3, smB, k3, M1L, k to 3 st before mC, M1R, k3, smC, k3, M1L, k to 3 st before mD, M1R, k3, smD, k3, M1R, k to end (8 st inc + CO).

ROW 14 (WS): CO 1 (1, 1, 1, 2, 2) st, then p to end of row, slipping m as you go.

ROW 15 (RS): CO 1 (1, 2, 2, 2, 2) st, k to 1 st before mA, M1R, k3, smA, k3, M1L, k to 3 st before mB, M1R, k3, smB, k3, M1L, k to 3 st before mC, M1R, k3, smC, k3, M1L, k to 3 st before mD, M1R, k3, smD, k3, M1R, k to end (8 st inc + CO).

ROW 16 (WS): CO 1 (1, 2, 2, 2, 2) st, then p to end of row, slipping m as you go.

STITCH COUNT CHECK-IN

FRONTS (EA): 11 (11, 13, 13, 14, 14)
SLEEVES (EA): 18 (22, 30, 36, 40, 42)
BACK: 38 (46, 56, 60, 62, 68)

ROW 17 (RS): CO 1 (2, 2, 2, 2, 4) st, k to 3 st before mA, M1R, k3, smA, k3, M1L, k to 3 st before mB, M1R, k3, smB, k3, M1L, k to 3 st before mC, M1R, k3, smC, k3, M1L, k to 3 st before mD, M1R, k3, smD, k3, M1R, k to end (8 st inc + CO).

Pebble Bay front view.

ROW 18 (WS): CO 1 (2, 2, 2, 2, 4) st, then p to end of row, slipping m as you go.

ROW 19 (RS): CO 2 (2, 2, 4, 4, 4) st, then k to 3 st before mA, M1R, k3, smA, k3, M1L, k to 3 st before mB, M1R, k3, smB, k3, M1L, k to 3 st before mC, M1R, k3, smC, k3, M1L, k to 3 st before mD, M1R, k3, smD, k3, M1R, k to end (8 st inc + CO).

ROW 20 (WS): CO 2 (2, 2, 4, 4, 4) st, then p to end of row, slipping m as you go.

ROW 21 (RS): CO 2 (4, 4, 4, 4, 4) st, then k to 3 st before mA, M1R, k3, smA, k3, M1L, k to 3 st before mB, M1R, k3, smB, k3, M1L, k to 3 st before mC, M1R, k3, smC, k3, M1L, k to 3 st before mD, M1R, k3, smD, k3, M1R, k to end (8 st inc + CO).

ROW 22 (WS): CO 2 (4, 4, 4, 4, 4) st, then p to end of row, slipping m as you go.

ROW 23 (RS): CO 6 (8, 14, 14, 14, 16) st, then k to 3 st before mA, M1R, k3, smA, k3, M1L, k to 3 st before mB, M1R, k3, smB, k3, M1L, k to 3 st before mC, M1R, k3, smC, k3, M1L, k to 3 st before mD, M1R, k3, smD, k3, M1R, k to end (8 st inc + CO).

Pebble Bay arm detail.

CUT yarn, leaving a tail long enough to weave in later.

NECKLINE JOIN: Rejoin yarn just after mD, leaving a tail to weave in later. This marks the new BOR. Slide the stitches after mD to the left needle so they "meet" with the other stitches on the front section (all stitches between mD and mA are now the "front"). K across, joining the front stitches as you reach the gap (be careful not to twist stitches) and knit to end of round.

STITCH COUNT CHECK-IN

FRONT: 46 (54, 64, 68, 70, 76)
SLEEVES (EA): 26 (30, 38, 44, 48, 50)
BACK: 46 (54, 64, 68, 70, 76)

NEXT ROUND (INC): At BOR, k3, M1L, k to 3 st before mA, M1R, k3, smA, k3, M1L, k to 3 st before mB, M1R, k3, smB, k3, M1L, k to 3 st before mC, M1R, k3, smC, k3, M1L, k to 3 st before mD, M1R, k3, smD (8 st inc).

NEXT ROUND (NO INC): K the round, slipping m as you go.

REP these two rounds until you have the following number of stitches:

STITCH COUNT CHECK-IN

FRONT: 74 (82, 92, 96, 96, 100)
SLEEVES (EA): 54 (58, 66, 72, 74, 74)
BACK: 74 (82, 92, 96, 96, 100)

NEXT ROUND (EXTRA INC): K3, M1L, k2, M1L, k to 5 st before mA, M1R, k2, M1R, k3, smA, k3, M1L, k to 3 st before mB, M1R, k3, smB, k3, M1L, k2, M1L, k to 5 st before mC, M1R, k2, M1R, k3, smC, k3, M1L, k to 3 st before mD, M1R, k3, smD (12 st inc).

NEXT ROUND (NO INC): K the round, slipping m as you go.

REP these two rounds 2 (1, 1, 1, 2, 2) more times.

SIZE 30/32 Move ahead to Divide for Sleeves.

SIZES 34/36, 38/40, 42/44, 46/48, 50/52 NEXT ROUND (DOUBLE EXTRA INC): K3, M1L, k2, M1L, k2, M1L, k to 7 st before mA, M1R, k2, M1R, k2, M1R, k3, smA, k3, M1L, k to 3 st before mB, M1R, k3, smB, k3, M1L, k2, M1L, k2, M1L, k to 7 st before mC, M1R, k2, M1R, k2, M1R, k3, smC, k3, M1L, k to 3 st before mD, M1R, k3, smD (16 st inc).

NEXT ROUND (NO INC): K the round, slipping m as you go.

REP these two rounds - (0, 0, 1, 2, 3) more times, then move ahead to Divide for Sleeves.

STITCH COUNT CHECK-IN

FRONT: 86 (96, 106, 116, 126, 136)
SLEEVES (EA): 60 (64, 72, 80, 86, 88)
BACK: 86 (96, 106, 116, 126, 136)

DIVIDE FOR SLEEVES: K across front to mA, rem mA and place sleeve stitches onto waste yarn (loosely, so you can try it on later). CO 4 (4, 4, 4, 4, 6) st underarm and join to back section, removing mB in the process. K to mC and rem mC, place sleeve stitches onto waste yarn (loosely, so you can try it on later). CO 4 (4, 4, 4, 4, 6) st underarm and join to front, removing mD in the process and replacing it at the center of the underarm (in the center of the newly cast-on st)—mD now denotes BOR.

STITCH COUNT CHECK-IN

180 (200, 220, 240, 260, 284) st in lower body

LOWER BODY: Knit the lower body in stockinette stitch in the round until body measures 12" (30 cm) from underarm. Transition to U.S. size 4/3.5 mm (24–32" [60–80 cm]) circular needle (or needle one size smaller than that used for the body) on next round and knit one round. On this round inc 0 (0, 0, 0, 0, 1) st, using kfb, near the side to end with a multiple of 5. Begin lower ribbing as follows: [k3, p2] repeat between brackets to end of round. Rep this round until ribbing measures 2.5" (6.4 cm). Bind off with medium tension in pattern. Note: Bottom edge should not feel restrictive. If it does, bind off more loosely.

SLEEVES: With U.S. size 5/3.75 mm (12" [30 cm]) circular needle or DPN (or the same size as used for the body), pick up sleeve st from waste yarn (including st cast-on under the arm)—64 (68, 76, 84, 90, 94) st. Pm at center of underarm to mark BOR. Knit in the round in stockinette st for 2" (5 cm).

NEXT ROUND: K2, k2tog, k to 4 st before m, ssk, k2 (2 st dec).

CONTINUE sleeve in the round in stockinette st, working a decrease round as indicated above approximately every 1.5" (3.8 cm) until sleeve measures approximately 18" (45.75 cm) from underarm, and you have the following: 45 (50, 55, 65, 70, 75) st. Note: You may need to work one more or one less dec to reach these counts so you end with a multiple of 5. On the last round, transition to U.S. size 3/3.25 mm (12" [30 cm]) circular needle or DPN (or two sizes smaller than used for sleeve/body) for cuff and begin ribbing as follows: [k3, p2] rep between brackets to end of round. Continue in established ribbing until cuff measures 2.5" (6.4 cm). Bind off in pattern with medium tension (cuff should not feel restrictive).

REP for second sleeve.

NECKLINE: With U.S. size 3/3.25 mm (16–24" [40–60 cm]) circular needle (or needle two sizes smaller than used for the body), pick up approximately 8 of every 9 available st around the neckline to end with a multiple of 5. Begin [k3, p2] ribbing and rep bet brackets in the round until neck ribbing measures 1.5" (3.8 cm). Bind off in pattern with medium tension.

WEAVE-IN ends and wet block. Pin flat and allow to dry completely, turning as needed.

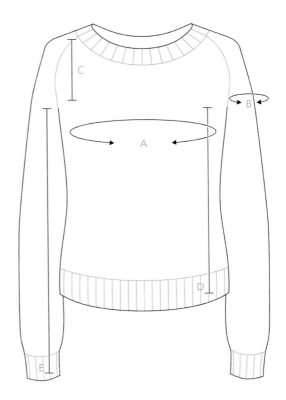

FINISHED MEASUREMENTS

A) BUST:
34.3" (38, 42, 45.7, 49.5, 54) (85.7 cm [95.2, 104.8, 114.3, 123.8, 135.2])

B) SLEEVE AT WIDEST POINT:
12.2" (13, 14.5, 16, 17, 17.9) (30.5 cm [32.4, 36.2, 40, 43, 44.8])

C) TOP OF SHOULDER TO UNDERARM:
9.2" (9.5, 10.2, 10.9, 11.5, 11.7) (23.45 cm [24.23, 25.79, 27.74, 29. 31, 29.7])

D) LENGTH OF BODY FROM UNDERARM:
14.5" (36.83 cm) prior to blocking

E) LENGTH OF SLEEVE FROM UNDERARM:
20.5" (52.07 cm) prior to blocking

Blue Heron Drop-Stitch Tee

This beautiful spring pullover features a stockinette bodice that expands into a charming drop-stitch lace. The empire waist creates a flattering silhouette with delicate drape. Designed for quick knitting on-the-go, the drop-stitch lace becomes second nature and requires little attention to the instructions once established.

TIMELINE

While it may look complicated, Blue Heron is a quick project that average-speed knitters can finish in about 7 to 10 days.

MATERIALS

Yarn	• DK | The Fibre Co. Acadia | 60% Merino, 20% baby alpaca, 20% silk | 145 yards (133 m) per 50 g | 900 yards (1000, 1100, 1210, 1335, 1464) (823 m [914, 1006, 1106, 1221, 1339])
Yarn Notes	• A soft, flowing blend of silk, alpaca and wool, the fabric should be light and loose with delicate drape.
Needles	• U.S. size 6/4 mm (24-32" [60-80 cm]) circular needle (body) • U.S. size 6/4 mm (12" [30 cm]) circular needle (sleeves) • U.S. size 4/3.5 mm (16-24" [40-60 cm]) circular needle (neckline) • Note: Use needle size necessary to obtain gauge.
Gauge	• 20 st and 30 rows with larger needle over 4" (10 cm) in stockinette stitch
Notions	• Yarn needle • Stitch markers • Waste yarn

STITCH GLOSSARY

bet	between
BOR	beginning of round/row
CO	cast on
dec	decrease
ea	each
inc	increase
k	knit
k2tog	knit 2 st at once (dec 1)
kfb	knit into the front and back of same st (inc 1)
m	marker/markers
mX	marker "X" indicates which marker (i.e, mA, mB, mC, etc.)
M1	make one stitch by knitting into the bar between st (inc 1)
M1L	make one st that leans left (inc 1)
M1R	make one st that leans right (inc 1)
p	purl
pmX	place marker, "X" indicates which marker (i.e, pmA, pmB, pmC, etc.)
rem m	remove marker
rep	repeat
rs	right side
sm	slip marker/markers

(continued)

STITCH GLOSSARY

smX	slip marker, "X" indicates which marker (i.e, smA, smB, smC, etc.)
ssk	slip, slip, knit together (dec 1)
st	stitch/stitches
ws	wrong side
yo	yarn over
[ ]	brackets always indicate a repeat

SIZES

Bust sizes 30/32" (34/36, 38/40, 42/44, 46/48, 50/52) (76/81 cm [86/91, 97/102, 107/112, 117/122, 127/132])

RECOMMENDED EASE

Positive ease is included for a comfortable fit. See finished measurements for final ease as compared to your actual bust measurement. If you are between sizes, refer to the final measurements to determine which size to choose. In many cases you'll find that the smaller of the two sizes will be the best choice.

CONSTRUCTION

Blue Heron is worked flat until neckline shaping is complete, then joined to work in the round from there. Garter stitch under the bust marks the transition to waves of seafoam lace, and the neckline is finished with a tidy rolled edge.

NOTE: Rows and rounds apply to all sizes unless otherwise indicated. Be sure to read ahead and mark sections that are specific to your size before you begin.

ALSO: Markers with letters (mA, mB, etc.) denote the location of seams/increases in this design. Markers with numbers (m1, m2, etc.) denote the location of texture panels.

TIP: Don't fret over your yarn-overs in the lace section; even if they seem a bit wonky along the way, blocking will even things out.

BLUE HERON PATTERN

With U.S. size 6/4 mm (24–32" [60–80 cm]) circular needle (or size needed to obtain gauge), cast on 65 (75, 81, 91, 111, 117) st using cable cast-on method. Do not join yet.

ROW 1 – SET UP (RS): K2, pmA, k13 (15, 15, 20, 25, 25), pmB, k1, M1L, k33 (39, 45, 45, 55, 61), M1R, k1, pmC, k13 (15, 15, 20, 25, 25), pmD, k2 (2 st inc).

ROW 2 (WS): P across, slipping m as you go.

ROW 3 (RS): K2, smA, k to mB, smB, k1, M1L, k to 1 st before mC, M1R, k1, smC, k to mD, smD, k2 (2 st inc).

ROW 4 (WS): As row 2.

ROW 5 (RS): As row 3.

ROW 6 (WS): As row 2.

ROW 7 (RS): K to 1 st before mA, M1R, k1, smA, [k1, M1] rep bet brackets 2 (2, 2, 3, 3, 3) times total, k to 2 (2, 2, 3, 3, 3) st before mB, [M1, k1] rep bet brackets 2 (2, 2, 3, 3, 3) times total, k to mB, smB, k1, M1L, k to 1 st before mC, M1R, k1, smC, [k1, M1] rep bet brackets 2 (2, 2, 3, 3, 3) times total, k to 2 (2, 2, 3, 3, 3) st before mD, [M1, k1] rep bet brackets 2 (2, 2, 3, 3, 3) times total, k to mD, smD, k1, M1L, k to end = 12 (12, 12, 16, 16, 16) st inc.

ROW 8 (WS): As row 2.

*GOING FORWARD, all stitches cast-on on the right side will be worked using the knitted cast-on method, and all stitches cast-on on the wrong side will be worked using the knitted cast-on worked purlwise. Always knit the new stitch/es on the right side and purl the new stitch/es on the wrong side as you work through the row.

STITCH COUNT CHECK-IN

FRONTS (EA): 3
SLEEVES (EA): 17 (19, 19, 26, 31, 31)
BACK: 43 (49, 55, 55, 65, 71)

ROW 9 (RS): K to 1 st before mA, M1R, k1, smA, k1, M1L, k to 1 st before mB, M1R, k1, smB, k1, M1L, k to 1 st before mC, M1R, k1, smC, k1, M1L, k to 1 st before mD, M1R, k1, smD, k1, M1L, k to end (8 st inc).

ROW 10 (WS): Rep row 2.

SIZES 30/32, 34/36 ROW 11 (RS): Rep row 9.

SIZES 38/40, 42/44, 46/48, 50/52 ROW 11 (RS): CO - (-, 1, 1, 1, 1) st, then k to 1 st before mA, M1R, k1, smA, k1, M1L, k to 1 st before mB, M1R, k1, smB, k1, M1L, k to 1 st before mC, M1R, k1, smC, k1, M1L, k to 1 st before mD, M1R, k1, smD, k1, M1L, k to end (8 st inc + CO).

SIZES 30/32, 34/36 ROW 12 (WS): Rep row 2.

SIZES 38/40, 42/44, 46/48, 50/52 ROW 12 (WS): CO - (-, 1, 1, 1, 1) st, then p across row, slipping m as you go.

ROW 13 (RS): Rep row 11 for your size.

ROW 14 (WS): Rep row 12 for your size.

STITCH COUNT CHECK-IN
FRONTS (EA): 6 (6, 8, 8, 8, 8)
SLEEVES (EA): 23 (25, 25, 32, 37, 37)
BACK: 49 (55, 61, 61, 71, 77)

ROW 15 (RS): CO 1 (1, 1, 1, 2, 2) st, then k to 1 st before mA, M1R, k1, smA, k1, M1L, k to 1 st before mB, M1R, k1, smB, k1, M1L, k to 1 st before mC, M1R, k1, smC, k1, M1L, k to 1 st before mD, M1R, k1, smD, k1, M1L, k to end (8 st inc + CO).

ROW 16 (WS): CO 1 (1, 1, 1, 2, 2) st, then p across row, slipping m as you go.

ROW 17 (RS): Rep row 15.

ROW 18 (WS): Rep row 16.

STITCH COUNT CHECK-IN
FRONTS (EA): 10 (10, 12, 12, 14, 14)
SLEEVES (EA): 27 (29, 29, 36, 41, 41)
BACK: 53 (59, 65, 65, 75, 81)

ROW 19 (RS): CO 1 (2, 2, 2, 2, 2) st, then k to 1 st before mA, M1R, k1, smA, k1, M1L, k to 1 st before mB, M1R, k1, smB, k to mC, smC, k1, M1L, k to 1 st before mD, M1R, k1, smD, k1, M1L, k to end (6 st inc + CO).

Blue Heron lace detail.

ROW 20 (WS): CO 1 (2, 2, 2, 2, 2) st, then p across row, slipping m as you go.

ROW 21 (RS): CO 2 (2, 4, 4, 4, 4) st, then k to 1 st before mA, M1R, k1, smA, k1, M1L, k to 1 st before mB, M1R, k1, smB, k to mC, smC, k1, M1L, k to 1 st before mD, M1R, k1, smD, k1, M1L, k to end (6 st inc + CO).

ROW 22 (WS): CO 2 (2, 4, 4, 4, 4) st, then p across row, slipping m as you go.

ROW 23 (RS): CO 4 (4, 4, 4, 4, 6) st, then k to 1 st before mA, M1R, k1, smA, k1, M1L, k to 1 st before mB, M1R, k1, smB, k to mC, smC, k1, M1L, k to 1 st before mD, M1R, k1, smD, k1, M1L, k to end (6 st inc + CO).

ROW 24 (WS): CO 4 (4, 4, 4, 4, 6) st, then p across row, slipping m as you go.

ROW 25 (RS): CO 12 (16, 14, 14, 20, 22) st, then k to 1 st before mA, M1R, k1, smA, k1, M1L, k to 1 st before mB, M1R, k1, smB, k to mC, smC, k1, M1L, k to 1 st before mD, M1R, k1, smD, k1, M1L, k to end (6 st inc + CO).

CUT yarn, leaving a tail.

REJOIN yarn just after mD, leaving a tail to weave in later. This marks the new BOR. Slide the stitches after mD to the left needle so they "meet" with the other stitches on the front section (all stitches between mD and mA are now the "front")—54 (60, 66, 66, 76, 82) st between mD and mA. K this round, joining at the front stitches when you reach the gap (be careful not to twist stitches) and knit to end of round (no inc).

NEXT ROUND (INC): At new BOR (just after mD), k to mA, smA, k1, M1L, k to m1, k to 1 st before mB, M1R, k1, smB, k to mC, smC, k1, M1L, k to 1 st before mD, M1R, k1 (4 st inc).

NEXT ROUND (NO INC): K, slipping m as you go.

NEXT ROUND (INC): K to mA, smA, k1, M1L, k to 1 st before mB, M1R, k1, smB, k to mC, smC, k1, M1L, k to 1 st before mD, M1R, k1 (4 st inc).

NEXT ROUND (NO INC): K, slipping m as you go.

REP the last two rounds, working inc only on the sleeves until you reach the following stitch count on the sleeves: 49 (51, 53, 60, 65, 65), ending after a non-inc round.

NOTE: Increases on the front/back sections begin again on the next round to establish armscye and bust shaping.

NEXT ROUND (EXTRA INC): K1, M1L, k2, M1L, k to 3 st before mA, M1R, k2, M1R, k1, smA, k1, M1L, k to 1 st before mB, M1R, k1, smB, k1, M1L, k2, M1L, k to 3 st before mC, M1R, k2, M1R, k1, smC, k1, M1L, k to 1 st before mD, M1R, k1 (12 st inc).

NEXT ROUND (NO INC): K, slipping m as you go.

REP these two rounds 2 (3, 2, 3, 3, 4) times more.

NEXT ROUND (DOUBLE EXTRA INC): K1, M1L, k2, M1L, k2, M1L, k to 5 st before mA, M1R, k2, M1R, k2, M1R, k1, smA, k1, M1L, k to 1 st before mB, M1R, k1, smB, k1, M1L, k2, M1L, k2, M1L, k to 5 st before mC, M1R, k2, M1R, k2, M1R, k1, smC, k1, M1L, k to 1 st before mD, M1R, k1 (16 st inc).

NEXT ROUND (NO INC): K, slipping m as you go.

REP these two rounds 2 (2, 3, 4, 4, 4) times more.

DIVIDE FOR SLEEVES: K to mA, rem mA and place sleeve st on waste yarn (loosely, so you can try it on later). CO 2 (2, 4, 4, 4, 6) st underarm and join to next section, placing a m in the center of the underarm to denote the side, removing mB in the process. K to mC and place sleeve st on waste yarn (loosely, so you can try it on later). CO 2 (2, 4, 4, 4, 5) st underarm and join to next section, replacing mD in the center of the underarm st—mD now marks the BOR.

171 (191, 211, 231, 251, 273) st in lower body

LOWER BODY: K in the round for approximately 4" (10 cm) or until sweater reaches your lower bra line (try it on as you go, if necessary).

SEAFOAM LACE SET-UP: [P one round, k one round] to create garter ridges—rep bet brackets 3 times total. On the next round inc 19 (19, 19, 19, 19, 17) st somewhat evenly on the round using kfb method (this will seem noticeable at first, but will disappear into the texture on the next round)— 190 (210, 230, 250, 270, 290) st.

SEAFOAM LACE (OVER A MULTIPLE OF 10 ST) ROUND 1: [K6, (yo) twice, k1, (yo) three times, k1, (yo) four times, k1, (yo) three times, k1, (yo) twice] rep bet brackets to end of round.

ROUND 2: P the round, dropping the yo's off the needles as you pass them.

ROUND 3: K the round.

ROUND 4: P the round.

ROUND 5: K1, [(yo) twice, k1, (yo) three times, k1, (yo) four times, k1, (yo) three times, k1, (yo) twice, k6] rep bet brackets to end of round, with last rep ending k5 instead of k6.

ROUND 6: As round 2.

ROUND 7: K the round.

ROUND 8: P the round.

REP rounds 1–8 to establish pattern.

CONTINUE lower body in Seafoam Lace pattern (rep rounds 1–8 as established) until body measures approximately 11" (28 cm) from underarm, ending after a round 8 in pattern. Work 2" (5 cm) in garter stitch (k one round, p one round) and bind off in pattern with medium tension.

TIP: Remember that the recommended yarn will grow due to the addition of both baby alpaca and silk in the fiber content. This will add at least 2" (5 cm) to the length of both body and sleeves, if not more. Yarn substitutions may create different results.

SLEEVES: With U.S. size 6/4 mm (12" [30 cm]) circular needles or DPN (or same size as used for body), pick up sleeve st from waste yarn as well as st that were cast-on under the arm. Pm at the center of the underarm to denote BOR and join to work in the round. Work the sleeves in stockinette st in the round for 2" (5 cm).

DEC ROUND: K2, k2tog, work in pattern as established to 4 st before m, ssk, k2.

CONTINUE in stockinette st, working a dec round approximately every 1.5" (3.8 cm) until sleeve measures 16" (40 cm) and you have approximately 43 (47, 51, 62, 67, 70) st. Work 18 rows in garter stitch (k one row, p one row) and bind off on a k row with medium tension.

REP for second sleeve.

NECKLINE: With U.S. size 4/3.5 mm (16–24" [40–60 cm]) circular needle (or two sizes smaller than that used for body), pick up nearly every st around the neckline (or as needed for best results). Join to work in the round and k three rows. Bind off in pattern with medium tension for a slight rolled edge. For a narrower neckline, work a set of 8 evenly spaced decreases on the second to last round before binding off.

WEAVE-IN ends and wet block flat, turning as needed for even drying.

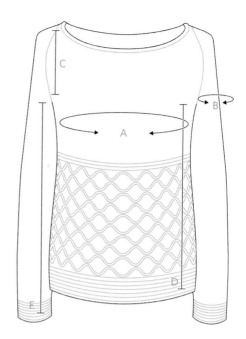

FINISHED MEASUREMENTS

A) BUST:
34" (38, 42, 46, 50, 54) (85 cm [95, 105, 115, 125, 135])

B) SLEEVE AT WIDEST POINT:
12" (13, 14, 16, 17, 18) (30 cm [33, 35, 41, 43, 45])

C) TOP OF SHOULDER TO UNDERARM:
8" (8.6, 9.1, 10, 10.3, 10.7) (20.32 cm [21.84, 23.20, 25.40, 26.25, 27.26])

D) LENGTH OF BODY FROM UNDERARM:
13" (33.02 cm) prior to blocking

E) LENGTH OF SLEEVE FROM UNDERARM:
18" (45.72 cm) prior to blocking

Newport Classic Turtleneck

My first knitting projects came from vintage books and magazines ranging from 1940 to the 1970s. Styles certainly change from decade to decade, but one thing has remained consistent: the turtleneck. As someone who is nearly always cold, I consider a turtleneck to be an essential part of a sweater collection. Newport has a classic shape—without being clingy—and a modern neckline for an updated look. Designed to be timeless, Newport is an approachable, cool-weather knit that you'll wear for years to come.

TIMELINE

Those with social knitting opportunities or long stretches of travel time will find this sweater manageable to finish in 10 to 12 days at a steady pace.

MATERIALS

Yarn
- DK | HiKoo Sueno | 80% superwash Merino, 20% bamboo viscose| 255 yards (233 m) per 100 g | 1114 yards (1238, 1375, 1513, 1664, 1830) (1019 m [1132, 1257, 1383, 1522, 1673])

Yarn Notes
- Worked in a bouncy superwash Merino/bamboo blend, the fiber has drape and sheen with excellent stitch definition.

Needles
- U.S. size 5/3.75 mm (24-32" [60-80 cm]) circular needle (body)
- U.S. size 5/3.75 mm (12" [30 cm]) circular needle or DPN (sleeves)
- U.S. size 4/3.5 mm (24-32" [60-80 cm]) circular needle (lower body ribbing)
- U.S. size 4/3.5 mm (12" [30 cm]) circular needle or DPN (sleeve cuff)
- U.S. size 3/3.25 mm (16-24" [40-60 cm]) circular needle (neckline)
- Note: Use needle size necessary to obtain gauge.

Gauge
- 22 st and 32 rows with larger needle over 4" (10 cm) in stockinette stitch

Notions
- Yarn needle
- Stitch markers
- Waste yarn

STITCH GLOSSARY

bet	between
BOR	beginning of round/row
CO	cast on
dec	decrease
ea	each
inc	increase
k	knit
k2tog	knit 2 st at once (dec 1)
kfb	knit into the front and back of same st (inc 1)
m	marker/markers
mX	marker "X" indicates which marker (i.e, mA, mB, mC, etc.)
M1L	make one st that leans left (inc 1)
M1R	make one st that leans right (inc 1)
p	purl
pmX	place marker, "X" indicates which marker (i.e, pmA, pmB, pmC, etc.)
rem m	remove marker
rep	repeat
rs	right side
sm	slip marker/markers

(continued)

STITCH GLOSSARY

smX	slip marker, "X" indicates which marker (i.e. smA, smB, smC, etc.)
ssk	slip, slip, knit together (dec 1)
st	stitch/stitches
ws	wrong side
[ ]	brackets always indicate a repeat

SIZES

Bust sizes 30/32" (34/36, 38/40, 42/44, 46/48, 50/52) (76/81 cm [86/91, 97/102, 107/112, 117/122, 127/132])

RECOMMENDED EASE

Positive ease is included for a comfortable fit. See finished measurements for final ease as compared to your actual bust measurement. If you are between sizes, refer to the final measurements to determine which size to choose. In many cases you'll find that the smaller of the two sizes will be the best choice.

CONSTRUCTION

Newport is worked flat at first until the front neck shaping is complete, then joined and worked in the round from there. The sleeves and turtleneck are worked last. The body features exaggerated ribbing and a cropped length for a modern twist.

NOTE: Rows and rounds apply to all sizes unless otherwise indicated. Be sure to read ahead and mark sections that are specific to your size before you begin.

TIP: In a solid or slightly tonal yarn with good stitch definition, Newport has a crisp, nautical appearance. Transform the look from classic to statement piece by changing up the yarn and introducing a bold colorway or yarn with textural interest.

NEWPORT PATTERN

With U.S. size 5/3.75 mm (24-32" [60-80 cm]) circular needle, cast on 50 (66, 78, 96, 112, 120) st using cable cast-on method. Do not join.

ROW 1 – SET UP (RS): K2, pmA, kfb, k4 (8, 10, 18, 26, 26), kfb, pmB, kfb, k32 (40, 48, 50, 50, 58), kfb, pmC, kfb, k4 (8, 10, 18, 26, 26), kfb, pmD, k2 (6 st inc).

ROW 2 (WS): P across, slipping m as you go.

ROW 3 (RS): Kfb, k to m, smA, k3, M1L, k to 3 st before mB, M1R, k3, smB, k3, M1L, k to 3 st before mC, M1R, k3, smC, k3, M1L, k to 3 st before mD, M1R, k3, smD, k to last st, kfb (8 st inc).

ROW 4 (WS): P to m, sm, k3, p to 3 st before m, k3, sm, k3, p to 3 st before m, k3, sm, k3, p to 3 st before m, k3, sm, p to end.

ROW 5 (RS) AND 6 (WS): Rep rows 3 and 4 once more.

ROW 7 (RS): CO 1 st using knitted cast-on worked knitwise*, k the new st, then k to 3 st before m, M1R, k3, smA, k3, M1L, k to 3 st before mB, M1R, k3, smB, k3, M1L, k to 3 st before mC, M1R, k3, smC, k3, M1L, k to 3 st before mD, M1R, k3, smD, k3, M1L, k to end (8 st inc + CO).

ROW 8 (WS): CO 1 st using knitted cast-on worked purlwise*, p the new st, then p to 3 st before m, k3, sm, k3, p to 3 st before m, k3, sm, k3, p to 3 st before m, k3, sm, k3, p to end.

*GOING FORWARD, all stitches cast-on on the right side will be worked using the knitted cast-on method, and all stitches cast-on on the wrong side will be worked using the knitted cast-on worked purlwise. Always knit the new stitch/es on the right side and purl the new stitch/es on the wrong side as you work through the row.

ROW 9 (RS): CO 1 st, k to 3 st before mA, M1R, k3, smA, k3, M1L, k to 3 st before mB, M1R, k3, smB, k3, M1L, k to 3 st before mC, M1R, k3, smC, k3, M1L, k to 3 st before mD, M1R, k3, smD, k3, M1L, k to end (8 st inc + CO).

ROW 10 (WS): CO 1 st, p to 3 st before m, k3, sm, k3, p to 3 st before m, k3, sm, k3, p to 3 st before m, k3, sm, k3, p to 3 st before m, k3, sm, k3, p to end.

ROW 11 (RS): Rep row 9.

ROW 12 (WS): Rep row 10.

ROW 13 (RS): CO 2 st, k to 3 st before mA, M1R, k3, smA, k3, M1L, k to 3 st before mB, M1R, k3, smB, k3, M1L, k to 3 st before mC, M1R, k3, smC, k3, M1L, k to 3 st before mD, M1R, k3, smD, k3, M1L, k to end (8 st inc + CO).

ROW 14 (WS): CO 2 st, p to 3 st before m, k3, sm, k3, p to 3 st before m, k3, sm, k3, p to 3 st before m, k3, sm, k3, p to 3 st before m, k3, sm, k3, p to end.

STITCH COUNT CHECK-IN

FRONTS (EA): 13
SLEEVES (EA): 20 (24, 26, 34, 42, 42)
BACK: 48 (56, 64, 66, 66, 74)

ROW 15 (RS): CO 4 st, k to 3 st before mA, M1R, k3, smA, k3, M1L, k to 3 st before mB, M1R, k3, smB, k3, M1L, k to 3 st before mC, M1R, k3, smC, k3, M1L, k to 3 st before mD, M1R, k3, smD, k3, M1L, k to end (8 st inc + CO).

ROW 16 (WS): CO 4 st, p to 3 st before m, k3, sm, k3, p to 3 st before m, k3, sm, k3, p to 3 st before m, k3, sm, k3, p to 3 st before m, k3, sm, k3, p to end.

ROW 17 (RS): CO 4 (6, 4, 4, 4, 4) st, k to 3 st before mA, M1R, k3, smA, k3, M1L, k to 3 st before mB, M1R, k3, smB, k3, M1L, k to 3 st before mC, M1R, k3, smC, k3, M1L, k to 3 st before mD, M1R, k3, smD, k3, M1L, k to end (8 st inc + CO).

ROW 18 (WS): CO 4 (6, 4, 4, 4, 4) st, p to 3 st before m, k3, sm, k3, p to 3 st before m, k3, sm, k3, p to 3 st before m, k3, sm, k3, p to 3 st before m, k3, sm, k3, p to end.

STITCH COUNT CHECK-IN

FRONTS (EA): 23 (25, 23, 23, 23, 23)
SLEEVES (EA): 24 (28, 30, 38, 46, 46)
BACK: 52 (60, 68, 70, 70, 78)

The following rows have directions specific to certain sizes. Follow the rows for your size in order, moving ahead as directed.

SIZES 30/32, 34/36 ROW 19 (RS): CO 6 (10, -, -, -, -) st, k to 3 st before mA, M1R, k3, smA, k3, M1L, k to 3 st before mB, M1R, k3, smB, k3, M1L, k to 3 st before mC, M1R, k3, smC, k3, M1L, k to 3 st before mD, M1R, k3, smD, k3, M1L, k to end (8 st inc + CO). Cut yarn, leaving a tail. Move ahead to Neckline Join.

Newport side view.

SIZES 38/40, 42/44, 46/48, 50/52 ROW 19 (RS): CO - (-, 6, 6, 6, 4) st, k to 3 st before mA, M1R, k3, smA, k3, M1L, k to 3 st before mB, M1R, k3, smB, k3, M1L, k to 3 st before mC, M1R, k3, smC, k3, M1L, k to 3 st before mD, M1R, k3, smD, k3, M1L, k to end (8 st inc + CO).

SIZES 38/40, 42/44, 46/48, 50/52 ROW 20 (WS): CO - (-, 6, 6, 6, 4) st, p to 3 st before m, k3, sm, k3, p to 3 st before m, k3, sm, k3, p to 3 st before m, k3, sm, k3, p to 3 st before m, k3, sm, k3, p to end.

SIZES 38/40, 42/44, 46/48 ROW 21 (RS): CO - (-, 10, 12, 12, -) st, k to 3 st before mA, M1R, k3, smA, k3, M1L, k to 3 st before mB, M1R, k3, smB, k3, M1L, k to 3 st before mC, M1R, k3, smC, k3, M1L, k to 3 st before mD, M1R, k3, smD, k3, M1L, k to end (8 st inc + CO). Cut yarn, leaving a tail. Move ahead to Neckline Join.

Newport neck shaping detail.

NECKLINE JOIN: Rejoin yarn just after mD, leaving a tail to weave in later. This marks the new BOR. Slide the stitches after mD to the left needle so they "meet" with stitches on the other front section (all stitches between mD and mA are now the "front"). P3, k across, joining the front stitches as you reach the gap (be careful not to twist stitches), and continue to k to 3 st before mA, p3, smA, p3, k to 3 st before mB, p3, smB, p3, k to 3 st before mC, p3, smC, p3, k to 3 st before mD, p3.

STITCH COUNT CHECK-IN

FRONT: 54 (62, 72, 74, 74, 84)
SLEEVES (EA): 26 (30, 34, 42, 50, 52)
BACK: 54 (62, 72, 74, 74, 84)

NEXT ROUND (INC): K3, M1L, k to 3 st before mA, M1R, k3, smA, k3, M1L, k to 3 st before mB, M1R, k3, smB, k3, M1L, k to 3 st before mC, m1R, k3, smC, k3, M1L, k to 3 st before mD, m1R, k3 (8 st inc).

NEXT ROUND (NO INC): P3, k to 3 st before mA, p3, smA, p3, k to 3 st before mB, p3, smB, p3, k to 3 st before mC, p3, smC, p3, k to 3 st before mD, p3.

REP these two rounds until st count reaches:

FRONT: 92 (104, 112, 110, 108, 118)

SLEEVES: 64 (72, 74, 78, 84, 86)

BACK: 92 (104, 112, 110, 108, 118)

NEXT ROUND (EXTRA INC): K3, M1L, k2, M1L, k to 5 st before mA, M1R, k2, M1R, k3, smA, k3, M1L, k to 3 st before mB, M1R, k3, smB, k3, M1L, k2, M1L, k to 5 st before mC, M1R, k2, M1R, k3, smC, k3, M1L, k to 3 st before mD, m1R, k3 (12 st inc).

NEXT ROUND (NO INC): P3, k to 3 st before mA, p3, smA, p3, k to 3 st before mB, p3, smB, p3, k to 3 st before mC, p3, smC, p3, k to 3 st before mD, p3.

SIZE 30/32, 34/36 Move ahead to Divide for Sleeves.

SIZES 38/40, 42/44, 46/48, 50/52 NEXT ROUND (EXTRA INC): K3, M1L, k2, M1L, k to 5 st before mA, M1R, k2, M1R, k3, smA, k3, M1L, k to 3 st before mB, M1R, k3, smB, k3, M1L, k2, M1L, k to 5 st before mC, M1R, k2, M1R, k3, smC, k3, M1L, k to 3 st before mD, m1R, k3 (12 st inc).

SIZE 50/52 ROW 21 (RS): CO - (-, -, -, -, 6) st, k to 3 st before mA, M1R, k3, smA, k3, M1L, k to 3 st before mB, M1R, k3, smB, k3, M1L, k to 3 st before mC, M1R, k3, smC, k3, M1L, k to 3 st before mD, M1R, k3, smD, k3, M1L, k to end (8 st inc + CO).

SIZE 50/52 ROW 22 (WS): CO - (-, -, -, -, 6) st, p to 3 st before m, k3, sm, k3, p to 3 st before m, k3, sm, k3, p to 3 st before m, k3, sm, k3, p to 3 st before m, k3, sm, k3, p to end.

SIZE 50/52 ROW 23 (RS): CO - (-, -, -, -, 12) st, k to 3 st before mA, M1R, k3, smA, k3, M1L, k to 3 st before mB, M1R, k3, smB, k3, M1L, k to 3 st before mC, M1R, k3, smC, k3, M1L, k to 3 st before mD, M1R, k3, smD, k3, M1L, k to end (8 st inc + CO). Cut yarn, leaving a tail. Move ahead to Neckline Join.

NEXT ROUND (NO INC): P3, k to 3 st before mA, p3, smA, p3, k to 3 st before mB, p3, smB, p3, k to 3 st before mC, p3, smC, p3, k to 3 st before mD, p3.

SIZE 38/40 Move ahead to Divide for Sleeves.

SIZES 42/44, 46/48, 50/52 NEXT ROUND (EXTRA INC): K3, M1L, k2, M1L, k to 5 st before mA, M1R, k2, M1R, k3, smA, k3, M1L, k to 3 st before mB, M1R, k3, smB, k3, M1L, k2, M1L, k to 5 st before mC, M1R, k2, M1R, k3, smC, k3, M1L, k to 3 st before mD, m1R, k3 (12 st inc).

NEXT ROUND (NO INC): P3, k to 3 st before mA, p3, smA, p3, k to 3 st before mB, p3, smB, p3, k to 3 st before mC, p3, smC, p3, k to 3 st before mD, p3.

SIZES 42/44, 46/48, 50/52 NEXT ROUND (DOUBLE EXTRA INC): K3, M1L, k2, M1L, k2, M1L, k to 7 st before mA, M1R, k2, M1R, k2, M1R, k3, smA, k3, M1L, k to 3 st before mB, M1R, k3, smB, k3, M1L, k2, M1L, k2, M1L, k to 7 st before mC, M1R, k2, M1R, k2, M1R, k3, smC, k3, M1L, k to 3 st before mD, m1R, k3 (16 st inc).

NEXT ROUND (NO INC): P3, k to 3 st before mA, p3, smA, p3, k to 3 st before mB, p3, smB, p3, k to 3 st before mC, p3, smC, p3, k to 3 st before mD, p3.

SIZE 42/44 Move ahead to Divide for Sleeves.

SIZES 46/48, 50/52 NEXT ROUND (DOUBLE EXTRA INC): K3, M1L, k2, M1L, k2, M1L, k to 7 st before mA, M1R, k2, M1R, k2, M1R, k3, smA, k3, M1L, k to 3 st before mB, M1R, k3, smB, k3, M1L, k2, M1L, k2, M1L, k to 7 st before mC, M1R, k2, M1R, k2, M1R, k3, smC, k3, M1L, k to 3 st before mD, m1R, k3 (16 st inc).

NEXT ROUND (NO INC): P3, k to 3 st before mA, p3, smA, p3, k to 3 st before mB, p3, smB, p3, k to 3 st before mC, p3, smC, p3, k to 3 st before mD, p3.

SIZES 46/48, 50/52 Repeat the above two rounds, one more time. Then move ahead to Divide for Sleeves.

STITCH COUNT CHECK-IN

FRONT: 96 (108, 120, 128, 138, 148)
SLEEVES (EA): 66 (74, 78, 86, 96, 98)
BACK: 96 (108, 120, 128, 138, 148)

Newport shoulder and back view.

DIVIDE FOR SLEEVES: K across front to mA, rem mA and place sleeve stitches onto waste yarn (loosely, so you can try it on later), then CO 0 (0, 0, 3, 4, 6) st underarm and join to back section, removing mB in the process, k to mC and rem mC, place sleeve stitches onto waste yarn (loosely, so you can try it on later), then CO 0 (0, 0, 3, 4, 6) st underarm and join to front—mD now denotes BOR.

STITCH COUNT CHECK-IN

192 (216, 240, 262, 284, 308) st in lower body

LOWER BODY: Work lower body in the round in stockinette stitch until body measures 8" (20 cm) from sleeve divide. Transition to U.S. size 4/3.5 mm (24–32" [60–80 cm]) circular needle (or one size smaller than that used for the body) and knit one more row. At the same time inc 0 (0, 0, 2, 4, 4) st using M1R or M1L spaced evenly to end with a multiple of 8. At the next BOR, begin lower ribbing as follows: [k5, p3] rep bet brackets to end. Continue to work ribbing until it measures 4" (10 cm) and body measures 12" (30 cm) from underarm at sleeve divide. Bind off in pattern with medium/loose tension. Lower edge should not be restrictive. If it is, bind off more loosely.

SLEEVES: With U.S. size 5/3.75 mm (12" [30 cm]) circular needle or DPN (or the same size as used for the body), pick up sleeve stitches from waste yarn (including st cast-on under the arm where applicable)—66 (74, 78, 89, 100, 104) st. Pm at center of underarm to mark BOR. Knit sleeve in the round in stockinette st for 2" (5 cm).

NEXT ROUND: K2, k2tog, k to 4 st before m, ssk, k2 (2 st dec).

CONTINUE in stockinette stitch in the round, working a decrease round as indicated approximately every 1.5–2" (3.8–5 cm). Work a last dec or two as needed to end with the following number of stitches: 55 (60, 65, 70, 80, 85) and sleeve measures approximately 14" (35.5 cm) from underarm.

NEXT ROUND: With U.S. size 4/3.5 mm (12" [30 cm]) circular needle or DPN, begin cuff ribbing as follows: [k3, p2] rep between brackets to end of round. Continue in established ribbing (repeating [k3, p2] on every round) until cuff measures 5" (12.5 cm). Bind off in pattern with medium tension.

REP for second sleeve.

NECKLINE: With U.S. size 3/3.25 mm (16–24" [40–60 cm]) circular needle, pick up every stitch along the upper shoulders and back, and 7 of every 8 st (approx.) along the front, ending with a multiple of 5. Adjust as needed for best results. Join to work in the round and begin ribbing as follows: [k3, p2], rep bet brackets to end of round. Continue ribbing in the round until turtleneck measures 5" (12.5 cm). Bind off in pattern with medium tension.

WEAVE-IN ends and wet block, pinning flat until dry.

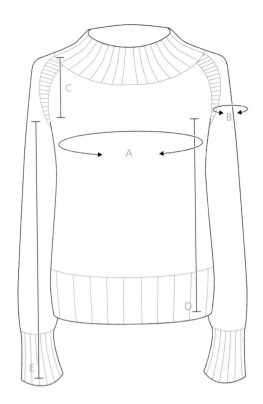

FINISHED MEASUREMENTS

A) BUST:
35" (39, 44, 48, 52, 56) (87 cm [98, 109, 119, 129, 140])

B) SLEEVE AT WIDEST POINT:
12.4" (13.8, 14.5, 15.6, 17.5, 17.8) (31 cm [35, 36, 40, 45, 47])

C) TOP OF SHOULDER TO UNDERARM:
9.1" (10, 10.4, 11.4, 12.4, 12.7) (23.22 cm [25.4, 26.49, 29.03, 31.57, 32.29])

D) LENGTH OF BODY FROM UNDERARM:
12" (30 cm) prior to blocking

E) LENGTH OF SLEEVE FROM UNDERARM:
19" (48.26 cm) prior to blocking

Offshore Eyelet Cardigan

While they may be a bit controversial, I love open-front sweaters. I rarely button my cardigans anyway, and appreciate the flattering vertical visual they create. Offshore is no exception; it drapes beautifully down the front in an A-line, and the wide front panels create the option of closure if you'd rather pin it. Simple eyelet details keep the project interesting while enabling you to move along at a swift pace.

TIMELINE

The most time-consuming part of this sweater is the surface area, but the pattern itself is relatively simple and makes for an easy travel project. Focused knitters should have no trouble finishing this sweater within the 2-week timeline, and may finish sooner if extended opportunities for knitting are available.

MATERIALS

Yarn
- DK | Lolodidit Wholotta DK | 85% Polwarth wool, 15% silk | 725 yards (663 m) in 250 g | 1000 yards (1080, 1200, 1320, 1452, 1597) (914 m [988, 1097, 1207, 1328, 1460])

Yarn Notes
- Tidy rows of eyelets glimmer in this blend of Polwarth wool and silk. Yarn should have medium body with structure and drape.

Needles
- U.S. size 6/4 mm (24-32" [60-80 cm]) circular needle (body)
- U.S. size 6/4 mm (12" [30 cm]) circular needle or DPN (sleeves)
- U.S. size 5/3.75 mm (24-32" [60-80 cm]) circular needle (lower body ribbing)
- U.S. size 4/3.5 mm (12" [30 cm]) circular needle or DPN (sleeve cuff)
- U.S. size 4/3.5 mm (24-32" [60-80 cm]) circular needle (neckline and front ribbing)
- Note: Use needle size necessary to obtain gauge.

Gauge
- 20 st and 28 rows with larger needle over 4" (10 cm) in stockinette

Notions
- Yarn needle
- Stitch markers
- Waist yarn

STITCH GLOSSARY

bet	between
BOR	beginning of round/row
CO	cast on
dec	decrease
DPN	double point needle/s
ea	each
inc	increase
k	knit
kfb	knit into the front and back of the same st (inc 1)
k2tog	knit two st together as one (dec 1)
m	marker/markers
mX	marker "X" indicates which marker (i.e, mA, mB, mC, etc.)
M1L	make one st that leans left (inc 1)
M1R	make one st that leans right (inc 1)
p	purl
pmX	place marker, "X" indicates which marker (i.e, pmA, pmB, pmC, etc.)
rem m	remove marker
rep	repeat
rs	right side
sm	slip marker/markers

(continued)

smX	slip marker, "X" indicates which marker (i.e, smA, smB, smC, etc.)
ssk	slip, slip, knit the two together (dec 1)
st	stitch/stitches
ws	wrong side
yo	yarn over (inc 1)
[ ]	brackets always indicate a repeat

SIZES

Bust sizes 30/32" (34/36, 38/40, 42/44, 46/48, 50/52) (76/81 cm [86/91, 97/102, 107/112, 117/122, 127/132])

RECOMMENDED EASE

The back and arms fit with slight positive ease for comfortable layering, but because the front has generous overlapping panels that don't close unless pinned, ease is flexible. Knitting the size that represents your actual bust measurement will result in a sweater that fits well in the back and arms, with generous front drape that can be worn open or overlapped and closed with a pin. If in doubt, choose the size with the arm fit that corresponds with the appropriate size for your arms. See Chapter 2 (page 11) for more information about size, fit and ease.

CONSTRUCTION

Offshore is worked top-down (flat) with a neckline that is shaped through a series of increases at the start of each row in the beginning. When the shaping is complete, the eyelet series begins. The eyelet panels will seem wide at first, but are meant to create attractive vertical waves down the front of the body; sleeves and ribbing are worked last. Predominantly knit in stockinette stitch with easy details, this rhythmic knit will be off your needles in no time.

NOTE: Rows and rounds apply to all sizes unless otherwise indicated. Be sure to read ahead and mark sections that are specific to your size before you begin.

ABOUT THE MARKERS: Marker A sits at the raglan seam on what will become your front left (if you are wearing the sweater). The left sleeve sits between marker A (mA) and marker B (mB). The back stitches sit between marker B (mB) and marker C (mC). The right sleeve sits between marker C (mC) and marker D (mD). The stitches after marker D will be the right front of the sweater. Differentiating the markers (at least in your mind) will make it easier to keep track of which section you're working on as the pattern begins to form. When markers are placed, slipped or removed, they'll be mentioned as they are assigned (pmA = place marker A, smA = slip marker A, rem mA = remove marker A).

QUICK TIP: There are no increases on the sleeve sections until after the first Stitch Count Check-In. This creates a slight saddle shoulder.

TIP: Drape is essential to the style of this sweater, so keep this in mind when making yarn substitutions. Choose a neutral or classic color so you can wear it often with a range of outfits.

OFFSHORE PATTERN

With U.S. size 6/4 mm (24–32" [60–80 cm]) circular needle or size to obtain gauge, cast on 42 (46, 60, 84, 92, 112) st using cable cast-on method.

ROW 1 - SET UP ROW (RS): Kfb, pmA, k9 (9, 15, 24, 26, 30), pmB, kfb, k20 (24, 26, 32, 36, 48), kfb, pmC, k9 (9, 15, 24, 26, 30), pmD, kfb (4 st inc).

ROW 2 AND ALL (WS) ROWS UNTIL OTHERWISE INDICATED: P across, slipping m as you go.

ROW 3 (RS): K1, M1R, k1, smA, k to mB, smB, k2, M1L, k to 2 st before mC, M1R, k2, smC, k to mD, smD, k1, M1L, k1 (4 st inc).

ROW 5 (RS): K1, M1R, k2, smA, k to mB, smB, k2, M1L, k to 2 st before mC, M1R, k2, smC, k to mD, smD, k2, M1L, k to end (4 st inc).

Offshore front panel detail.

STITCH COUNT CHECK-IN

FRONTS (EA): 4
SLEEVES (EA): 9 (9, 15, 24, 26, 30)
BACK: 28 (32, 34, 40, 44, 56)

ROW 7 (RS): K to 2 st before mA, M1R, k2, smA, k to mB, smB, k2, M1L, k to 2 st before mC, M1R, k2, smC, k to mD, smD, k2, M1L, k to end (4 st inc).

ROW 9 (RS): K1, M1R, k to 2 st before m, M1R, k2, smA, k2, M1L, k to 2 st before mB, M1R, k2, smB, k2, M1L, k to 2 st before mC, M1R, k2, smC, k2, M1L, k to 2 st before mD, M1R, k2, smD, k2, M1L, k to 1 st before end, M1L, k1 (10 st inc).

ROW 11 (RS): As row 9.

ROW 13 (RS): As row 9.

ROW 15 (RS): As row 9.

STITCH COUNT CHECK-IN

FRONTS (EA): 13
SLEEVES (EA): 17 (17, 23, 32, 34, 38)
BACK: 38 (42, 44, 50, 54, 66)

ROW 17 (RS): CO 2 (2, 2, 2, 2, 4) st using knitted cast-on worked knitwise*, k to 2 st before mA, M1R, k2, smA, k2, M1L, k to 2 st before mB, M1R, k2, smB, k2, M1L, k to 2 st before mC, M1R, k2, smC, k2, M1L, k to 2 st before mD, M1R, k2, smD, k2, M1L, k to end (8 st inc + CO).

ROW 18 (WS): CO 2 (2, 2, 2, 2, 4) st using knitted cast-on worked purlwise*, p to end of row, slipping m as you go.

ROW 19 (RS): As row 17.

ROW 20 (WS): As row 18.

ROW 21 (RS): CO 2 (2, 2, 2, 4, 4) st using knitted cast-on worked knitwise*, k to 2 st before mA, M1R, k2, smA, k2, M1L, k to 2 st before mB, M1R, k2, smB, k2, M1L, k to 2 st before mC, M1R, k2, smC, k2, M1L, k to 2 st before mD, M1R, k2, smD, k2, M1L, k to end (8 st inc + CO).

ROW 22 (WS): CO 2 (2, 2, 2, 4, 4) st using knitted cast-on worked purlwise*, p to end of row, slipping m as you go.

*GOING FORWARD, all stitches cast-on on the right side will be worked using the knitted cast-on method, and all stitches cast-on on the wrong side will be worked using the knitted cast-on worked purlwise. Always knit the new stitch/es on the right side and purl the new stitch/es on the wrong side as you work through the row.

ROW 23 (RS): As row 21.

ROW 24 (WS): As row 22.

STITCH COUNT CHECK-IN

FRONTS (EA): 25 (25, 25, 25, 29, 33)
SLEEVES (EA): 25 (25, 31, 40, 42, 46)
BACK: 46 (50, 52, 58, 62, 74)

ROW 25 (RS): CO 26 (30, 30, 30, 32, 32) st, k to 2 st before mA, M1R, k2, smA, k2, M1L, k to 2 st before mB, M1R, k2, smB, k2, M1L, k to 2 st before mC, M1R, k2, smC, k2, M1L, k to 2 st before mD, M1R, k2, smD, k2, M1L, k to end (8 st inc + co).

ROW 26 (WS): CO 26 (30, 30, 30, 32, 32) st, then p to end of row, slipping m as you go.

NECKLINE/FRONT panel shaping is now complete.

ROW 27 (RS): [K6, yo, k2tog] rep bet brackets a total of 4 times, pm1, then k to 2 st before mA, M1R, k2, smA, k2, M1L, k to 2 st before mB, M1R, k2, smB, k2, M1L, k to 2 st before mC, M1R, k2, smC, k2, M1L, k to 2 st before mD, M1R, k2, smD, k2, M1L, k to last 32 st, pm2, [k2tog, yo, k6] rep bet brackets to end (8 st inc).

ROW 28 (WS): P across, slipping m as you go.

ROW 29 (RS): K to 2 st before mA (passing m1 along the way), M1R, k2, smA, k2, M1L, k to 2 st before mB, M1R, k2, smB, k2, M1L, k to 2 st before mC, M1R, k2, smC, k2, M1L, k to 2 st before mD, M1R, k2, smD, k2, M1L, k to end (passing m2 along the way) (8 st inc).

ROW 30 (WS): As row 28.

ROW 31 (RS): K2, [yo, k2tog, k6] rep bet brackets to m1, ending last rep with k4 (instead of k6), sm1, k to 2 st before mA, M1R, k2, smA, k2, M1L, k to 2 st before mB, M1R, k2, smB, k2, M1L, k to 2 st before mC, M1R, k2, smC, k2, M1L, k to 2 st before mD, M1R, k2, smD, k2, M1L, k to m2, sm2, k4, [k2tog, yo, k6] rep bet brackets to end, ending last rep with k2 instead of k6 (8 st inc).

ROW 32 (WS): As row 28.

ROW 33 (RS): K to 2 st before mA (passing m1 along the way), M1R, k2, smA, k2, M1L, k to 2 st before mB, M1R, k2, smB, k2, M1L, k to 2 st before mC, M1R, k2, smC, k2, M1L, k to 2 st before mD, M1R, k2, smD, k2, M1L, k to end (passing m2 along the way) (8 st inc).

ROW 34 (WS): As row 28.

REP rows 27–34 until you reach the following:

Offshore side view.

STITCH COUNT CHECK-IN

FRONTS (EA): 67 (73, 72, 72, 77, 81)
SLEEVES (EA): 57 (61, 65, 74, 74, 78)
BACK: 78 (86, 86, 92, 94, 106)

SIZES 30/32, 34/36 Move ahead to Divide for Sleeves.

SIZES 38/40, 42/44, 46/48, 50/52 NEXT ROW (RS): Maintain eyelets in established pattern to m1, sm1, k to 4 st before mA, M1R, k2, M1R, k2, smA, k2, M1L, k to 2 st before mB, M1R, k2, smB, k2, M1L, k2, M1L, k to 4 st before mC, M1R, k2, M1R, k2, smC, k2, M1L, k to 2 st before mD, M1R, k2, smD, k2, M1L, k2, M1L, k to m2, sm2, work in eyelet pattern as established to end (12 st inc).

SIZES 38/40, 42/44, 46/48, 50/52 NEXT ROW (WS): P across, slipping m as you go.

Offshore back view.

DIVIDE FOR SLEEVES: Maintain eyelets as established to m1, sm1, and k to mA. Rem mA and place sleeve st on waste yarn (loosely, so you can try it on later). CO 1 (2, 2, 2, 4, 4) st at the underarm and join to back section, removing mB in the process. K to mC, rem mC, and place sleeve st on waste yarn (loosely). CO 1 (2, 2, 2, 4, 4) st and join to front, removing mD in the process. K to m2, and work eyelet pattern as established to end.

STITCH COUNT CHECK-IN

214 (236, 254, 272, 300, 320) st in lower body

NEXT ROW (RS): Work in established eyelet pattern to m1, sm1, k to m2, sm2, work in established eyelet pattern to end.

NEXT ROW (WS): P across, slipping m as you go.

REP these two rows (maintaining eyelet pattern as established) until lower body measures 10″ (25 cm). Transition to U.S. size 5/3.75 mm (24–32″ [60–80 cm]) circular needle (or one size smaller than that used for body), and work one last row in pattern. Inc 4 (2, 4, 1, 3, 3) st evenly using M1R or M1L. Rem m1 and m2 on this row to conclude the eyelet detail 218 (238, 258, 273, 303, 323) st.

LOWER RIBBING (RS): K3, [p2, k3] rep bet brackets to end.

LOWER RIBBING (WS): p3, [k2, p3] rep bet brackets to end.

WORK lower ribbing for 2″ (5 cm) and bind off in pattern with medium tension.

NECKLINE: With U.S. size 4/3.5 mm (24″ [60 cm]) circular needle, starting on the rs, pick up nearly every st along the neckline and top edge, ending with a multiple of 5 + 3 for the ribbing. On the rs, work in [k3, p2] ribbing, repeating bet brackets to end of row, ending k3. On the ws, p3, [k2, p3] rep bet brackets to end. Continue in ribbing for just over 1″ (2.5 cm). Bind off in pattern.

SIZES 38/40, 42/44, 46/48, 50/52 NEXT ROW (RS): Maintain eyelets in established pattern to m1, sm1, k to 6 st before mA, M1R, k2, M1R, k2, M1R, k2, smA, k2, M1L, k to 2 st before mB, M1R, k2, smB, k2, M1L, k2, M1L, k2, M1L, k to 6 st before mC, M1R, k2, M1R, k2, M1R, k2, smC, k2, M1L, k to 2 st before mD, M1R, k2, smD, k2, M1L, k2, M1L, k2, M1L, k to m2, sm2, work in eyelet pattern as established to end (16 st inc).

SIZES 38/40, 42/44, 46/48, 50/52 NEXT ROW (WS): P across, slipping m as you go.

REP the last two rows - (-, 0, 1, 2, 2) times more.

FRONT BAND: With U.S. size 4/3.5 mm (32" [80 cm]) circular needle (or two sizes smaller than that used for body), start at the right front of the sweater on the rs (starting at the bottom edge, working toward the top). Pick up roughly 6 of every 7 st along the front edge (or as needed for best results), ending up with a multiple of 5 + 3 for the ribbing. Work in [k3, p2] ribbing (rep bet brackets), ending k3 on the rs, and [p3, k2] ribbing (rep bet brackets), ending p3 on the ws for 1.5" (3.8 cm). Bind off in pattern with medium tension. Repeat for the left front, starting at the top of the sweater on the rs and working downward.

SLEEVES: With U.S. size 6/4 mm (12" [30 cm]) circular needle or DPN, pick up sleeve st from waste yarn as well as st cast-on under the arm—58 (63, 71, 82, 86, 90) st. Pm at center of underarm to denote BOR. Knit in the round for 2" (5 cm).

DEC ROUND: K1, k2tog, work in pattern to 3 st before m, ssk, k1 (2 st dec).

CONTINUE sleeve in stockinette st (knitting every round) and work a dec round as established every 1–1.5" (2.5–3.8 cm) until sleeve measures 17" (43 cm) and you have 42 (48, 54, 60, 63, 69) st— working a last dec as needed to obtain this count. Transition to U.S. size 4/3.5 mm (12" [30 cm]) circular or DPN and knit one last round, then begin cuff ribbing as follows: [k2, p1] rep bet brackets to end of round. Continue in ribbing as established for 2" (5 cm). Bind off in pattern. (Recommended yarn will grow several inches with blocking. Please keep this in mind before adding length.)

REP for second sleeve.

WEAVE-IN ends and wet block flat, turning as necessary for even drying.

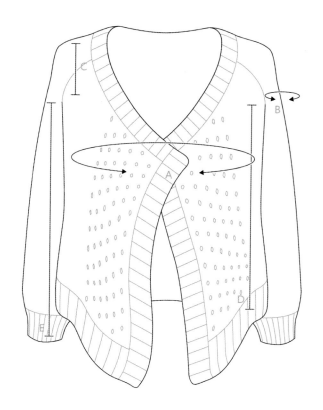

FINISHED SIZE

A) ACTUAL MEASUREMENT AROUND BUST, INCLUDING FRONT PANELS THAT OVERLAP:
42.8" (47.2, 50.8, 54.4, 60, 64) (107 cm [118, 127, 136, 150, 160])

B) SLEEVE AT WIDEST POINT:
11.6" (12.6, 14.2, 16.4, 17.2, 18) (29 cm [32, 36, 41, 43, 45])

C) TOP OF SHOULDER TO UNDERARM:
8.3" (9, 10.1, 11.7, 12.3, 12.9) (21.05 cm [22.86, 25.76, 29.75, 31.21, 32.66])

D) LENGTH OF BODY FROM UNDERARM (MEASURED AT BACK, NOT INCLUDING A-LINE):
12" (30 cm) prior to blocking

E) LENGTH OF SLEEVE FROM UNDERARM:
19" (48.26 cm) prior to blocking

Cape Creek Minimalist Pullover

In spite of my addiction to neutral colors, I find that a bright pop of color goes a long way in an otherwise muted wardrobe. Cape Creek is the perfect canvas to showcase a bright tonal; while it's primarily knit in stockinette stitch, it features strategic wildflower knot columns down both sides of the body for subtle visual interest. They create a very slight bit of shaping at the sides, as well. With extra length and positive ease for a comfortable fit, Cape Creek will be a quick favorite.

TIMELINE

There's nothing complex to slow down the process, but the long sleeves and long body length will require a little additional time. Estimate 8 to 10 days for the motivated knitter to finish.

MATERIALS

Yarn
- Worsted | Malabrigo Rios | 100% superwash Merino | 210 yards (192 m) per 100 g | 775 yards (860, 955, 1050, 1176, 1317) (709 m [786, 873, 960, 1075, 1204])

Yarn Notes
- Worked in hand-dyed, superwash Merino, you can expect a relaxed fit with some growth in length (body and sleeves) after blocking. Keep this in mind before adding extra length.

Needles
- U.S. size 7/4.5 mm (24-32" [60-80 cm]) circular needle (body)
- U.S. size 7/4.5 mm (12" [30 cm]) circular needle (sleeves)
- U.S. size 6/4 mm (24-32" [60-80 cm]) circular needle (lower body ribbing)
- U.S. size 5/3.75 mm (12" [30 cm]) circular needle (sleeve cuff)
- U.S. size 5/3.75 mm (16-24" [40-60 cm]) circular needle (neckline)
- Note: Use needle size necessary to obtain gauge.

Gauge
- 18 st and 25 rows with largest needle over 4" (10 cm) in stockinette stitch

Notions
- Yarn needle
- Stitch markers
- Waste yarn

STITCH GLOSSARY

bet	between
BOR	beginning of round/row
CO	cast on
dec	decrease
ea	each
inc	increase
k	knit
k2tog	knit 2 st at once (dec 1)
m	marker/markers
mX	marker "X" indicates which marker (i.e, mA, mB, mC, etc.)
M1L	make one st that leans left (inc 1)
M1R	make one st that leans right (inc 1)
p	purl
p3tog	purl three st together at once (dec 2)
pmX	place marker, "X" indicates which marker (i.e, pmA, pmB, pmC, etc.)
rem m	remove marker
rep	repeat
rs	right side
sm	slip marker/markers

(continued)

STITCH GLOSSARY

smX	slip marker, "X" indicates which marker (i.e, smA, smB, smC, etc.)
ssk	slip, slip, knit together (dec 1)
st	stitch/stitches
wfk	wildflower knot—p3tog and keep on needle, yo, p3tog again (the same three st), then slide from left needle. Do not work this stitch too tightly.
ws	wrong side
yo	yarn over (inc 1)
[ ]	brackets always indicate a repeat

SIZES

Bust sizes 30/32" (34/36, 38/40, 42/44, 46/48, 50/52) (76/81 cm [86/91, 97/102, 107/112, 117/122, 127/132])

RECOMMENDED EASE

Positive ease is included for a comfortable fit. See finished measurements for final ease as compared to your actual bust measurement. If you are between sizes, refer to the final measurements to determine which size to choose. In many cases you'll find that the smaller of the two sizes will be best.

CONSTRUCTION

Cape Creek is worked flat from the beginning until the neck shaping is complete, then joined to work in the round from there. Wildflower knot columns down the lower portion of the body offer visual interest throughout the project, and help to break up significant portions of stockinette stitch.

NOTE: Rows and rounds apply to all sizes unless otherwise indicated. Be sure to read ahead and mark sections that are specific to your size before you begin.

QUICK TIP: Be careful not to work the wildflower knots too tightly; they should not appear to noticeably stress the yarn around them. I recommend practicing the wildflower knot stitch on part of your swatch just to familiarize yourself with the process.

CAPE CREEK PATTERN

With U.S. size 7/4.5 mm (24–32" [60–80 cm]) circular needle, cast on 30 (40, 62, 66, 70, 80) st using cable cast-on method. Do not join.

ROW 1 – SET UP (RS): K2, pmA, kfb, k0 (2, 8, 8, 10, 12), kfb, pmB, kfb, k20 (26, 36, 40, 40, 46), kfb, pmC, kfb, k0 (2, 8, 8, 10, 12), kfb, pmD, k2 (6 st inc).

ROW 2 (WS): P across, slipping m as you go.

SIZE 30/32 ROW 3 (RS): K2, smA, K1, M1L, k2, M1R, k1, smB, k2, M1L, k to 2 st before mC, M1R, k2, smC, k1, M1L, k 2, M1R, k1, smD, k2 (6 st inc).

SIZES 34/36, 38/40, 42/44, 46/48, 50/52 ROW 3 (RS): K2, smA, k2, M1L, k to 2 st before mB, M1R, k2, smB, k2, M1L, k to 2 st before mC, M1R, k2, smC, k2, M1L, k to 2 st before mD, M1R, k2, smD, k2 (6 st inc).

ALL SIZES continue.

ROW 4 (WS): P across, slipping m as you go.

ROW 5 (RS): K1, M1R, k2, smA, k2, M1L, k to 2 st before mB, M1R, k2, smB, k2, M1L, k to 2 st before mC, M1R, k2, smC, k2, M1L, k to 2 st before mD, M1R, k2, smD, k2, M1L, k to end (8 st inc).

ROW 6 (WS): P across, slipping m as you go.

ROW 7 (RS): CO 0 (0, 0, 0, 0, 1) st using knitted cast-on worked tightly*, k to 2 st before mA, M1R, k2, smA, k2, M1L, k to 2 st before mB, M1R, k2, smB, k2, M1L, k to 2 st before mC, M1R, k2, smC, k2, M1L, k to 2 st before mD, M1R, k2, smD, k2, M1L, k to end (8 st inc + cast on).

ROW 8 (WS): CO 0 (0, 0, 0, 0, 1) st using knitted cast-on worked purlwise*, p across row (including newly cast-on st), slipping m as you go.

Cape Creek side view.

ROW 9 (RS): CO 0 (1, 1, 1, 1, 1) st using knitted cast-on worked tightly, k to 2 st before mA, M1R, k2, smA, k2, M1L, k to 2 st before mB, M1R, k2, smB, k2, M1L, k to 2 st before mC, M1R, k2, smC, k2, M1L, k to 2 st before mD, M1R, k2, smD, k2, M1L, k to end (8 st inc + cast on).

ROW 10 (WS): CO 0 (1, 1, 1, 1, 1) st using knitted cast-on worked purlwise, p across row (including newly cast-on st), slipping m as you go.

STITCH COUNT CHECK-IN

FRONTS (EA): 5 (6, 6, 6, 6, 7)
SLEEVES (EA): 12 (14, 20, 20, 22, 24)
BACK: 32 (38, 48, 52, 52, 58)

*GOING FORWARD, all stitches cast-on on the right side will be worked using the knitted cast-on method, and all stitches cast-on on the wrong side will be worked using the knitted cast-on worked purlwise. Always knit the new stitch/es on the right side and purl the new stitch/es on the wrong side as you work through the row.

ROW 11 (RS): CO 0 (1, 2, 2, 2, 2) st, k to 2 st before mA, M1R, k2, smA, k2, M1L, k to 2 st before mB, M1R, k2, smB, k2, M1L, k to 2 st before mC, M1R, k2, smC, k2, M1L, k to 2 st before mD, M1R, k2, smD, k2, M1L, k to end (8 st inc + cast on).

ROW 12 (WS): CO 0 (1, 2, 2, 2, 2) st and p across row, slipping m as you go.

ROW 13 (RS): CO 1 (1, 2, 2, 2, 4) st, k to 2 st before mA, M1R, k2, smA, k2, M1L, k to 2 st before mB, M1R, k2, smB, k2, M1L, k to 2 st before mC, M1R, k2, smC, k2, M1L, k to 2 st before mD, M1R, k2, smD, k2, M1L, k to end (8 st inc + cast on).

ROW 14 (WS): CO 1 (1, 2, 2, 2, 4) st and p across row, slipping m as you go.

ROW 15 (RS): CO 1 (2, 4, 4, 4, 4) st, k to 2 st before mA, M1R, k2, smA, k2, M1L, k to 2 st before mB, M1R, k2, smB, k2, M1L, k to 2 st before mC, M1R, k2, smC, k2, M1L, k to 2 st before mD, M1R, k2, smD, k2, M1L, k to end (8 st inc + cast on).

ROW 16 (WS): CO 1 (2, 4, 4, 4, 4) st and p across row, slipping m as you go.

ROW 17 (RS): CO 4 (4, 4, 6, 6, 6) st, k to 2 st before mA, M1R, k2, smA, k2, M1L, k to 2 st before mB, M1R, k2, smB, k2, M1L, k to 2 st before mC, M1R, k2, smC, k2, M1L, k to 2 st before mD, M1R, k2, smD, k2, M1L, k to end (8 st inc + cast on).

ROW 18 (WS): CO 4 (4, 4, 6, 6, 6) st and p across row, slipping m as you go.

ROW 19 (RS): CO 10 (10, 12, 12, 12, 12) st, k to 2 st before mA, M1R, k2, smA, k2, M1L, k to 2 st before mB, M1R, k2, smB, k2, M1L, k to 2 st before mC, M1R, k2, smC, k2, M1L, k to 2 st before mD, M1R, k2, smD, k2, M1L, k to end (8 st inc + cast on). Cut yarn, leaving a tail.

STITCH COUNT CHECK-IN

FRONTS (EA): 21 (24, 29, 31, 31, 34)
SLEEVES (EA): 22 (24, 30, 30, 32, 34)
BACK: 42 (48, 58, 62, 62, 68)

NECKLINE JOIN: Rejoin yarn just after mD, leaving a tail to weave in later. This marks the new BOR. Slide the stitches after mD to the left needle so they "meet" with the stitches on the other front section (all stitches between mD and mA are now the "front"). K across, joining the front stitches as you reach the gap (be careful not to twist stitches) and knit to end of round.

NEXT ROUND (INC): At BOR, k2, M1L, k to 2 st before mA, M1R, k2, smA, k2, M1L, k to 2 st before mB, M1R, k2, smB, k2, M1L, k to 2 st before mC, M1R, k2, smC, k2, M1L, k to 2 st before mD, M1R, k2 (8 st inc).

NEXT ROUND (NO INC): K the round, slipping m as you go.

REP these two rounds until you have the following number of stitches:

STITCH COUNT CHECK-IN
FRONT: 74 (82, 92, 96, 94, 100)
SLEEVES (EA): 54 (58, 64, 64, 64, 66)
BACK: 74 (82, 92, 96, 94, 100)

NEXT ROUND (EXTRA INC): K2, M1L, k2, M1L, k to 4 st before mA, M1R, k2, M1R, k2, smA, k2, M1L, k to 2 st before mB, M1R, k2, smB, k2, M1L, k2, M1L, k to 4 st before mC, M1R, k2, M1R, k2, smC, k2, M1L, k to 2 st before mD, M1R, k2 (12 st inc).

NEXT ROUND (NO INC): K the round, slipping m as you go.

REP these two rounds 0 (0, 0, 1, 3, 3) more times. You should have the following number of stitches:

STITCH COUNT CHECK-IN
FRONT: 78 (86, 96, 104, 110, 116)
SLEEVES (EA): 56 (60, 66, 68, 72, 74)
BACK: 78 (86, 96, 104, 110, 116)

DIVIDE FOR SLEEVES: K across front to mA, rem mA and place sleeve stitches onto waste yarn (loosely, so you can try it on later). CO 2 (2, 2, 2, 4, 6) st underarm and join to back section, removing mB in the process. Replace mB at the center of the underarm (in the center of the newly cast-on st). K to mC and remove mC, place sleeve stitches onto waste yarn (loosely, so you can try it on later), then CO 2 (2, 2, 2, 4, 6) st underarm and join to front, removing mD in the process. Replace mD at the center of the underarm (in the center of the newly cast-on st)—mD now denotes BOR. You should now have two markers: mD at the underarm on the right side and mB at the underarm on the left side.

STITCH COUNT CHECK-IN
160 (176, 196, 212, 228, 244) stitches in lower body

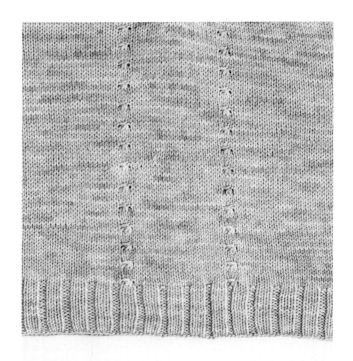

Cape Creek side detail.

LOWER BODY: Work the body in the stockinette st (knitting every round) for 1" (2.5 cm).

WILDFLOWER KNOTS: K10, pm1, wfk, k to 13 st before mB, wfk, pm2, k10, smB, k10, pm3, wfk, k to 13 st before mD, wfk, pm4, k10.

WILDFLOWER KNOT DETAIL: Knit four rounds.

REP these five rounds (one Wildflower Knot round plus four knit rounds) until body measures approximately 13" (25 cm) from underarm join and you have just completed a Wildflower Knot round. (This will be approximately 14-15 Wildflower Knot repeats.)

CONTINUE in the round, working 2" (5 cm) more in stockinette st. On the last round transition to U.S. size 6/4 mm (24-32" [60-80 cm]) circular needle (or one size smaller than that used for the body) to prepare to work lower ribbing. On the next round (with this smaller needle), inc 0 (4, 4, 3, 2, 1) somewhat evenly using M1R/M1L method—160 (180, 200, 215, 230, 245) st.

BEGIN LOWER RIBBING AS FOLLOWS: [K3, p2] rep bet brackets to end of round. Continue in established [k3, p2] ribbing until lower rib measures 2.5" (6.4 cm). Bind off with medium tension in pattern. Note: Bottom edge should not feel tight and restrictive. If it does, bind off more loosely.

SLEEVES: With U.S. size 7/4.5 mm (12" [30 cm]) circular needle or DPN (or the same size as used for the body), pick up sleeve stitches from waste yarn (including st cast-on under the arm where applicable)—58 (62, 68, 70, 76, 80) st. Pm at center of underarm to mark BOR. Knit sleeve in the round in stockinette st for 2" (5 cm).

NEXT ROUND: K2, k2tog, k to 4 st before m, ssk, k2 (2 st dec).

CONTINUE in stockinette stitch in the round, working a decrease round as indicated above approximately every 1.5" (3.8 cm) until you have the following number of stitches: 38 (42, 48, 50, 56, 60) and sleeve measures approximately 12" (30 cm) from underarm. Work 1" (2.5 cm) in stockinette, and on the next round transition to U.S. size 5/3.75 mm (12" [30 cm]) circular needle or DPN—or two sizes smaller than that used for sleeve—and decrease 3 (2, 3, 0, 1, 0) st evenly using k2tog.

NEXT ROUND: Begin cuff ribbing as follows: [k3, p2] rep between brackets to end of round. Continue in established ribbing (repeating [k3, p2] on every round) until cuff measures 7" (17.8 cm). Bind off in pattern with medium tension.

REP for second sleeve.

NOTE: The recommended yarn is a superwash yarn that will grow at least 2" (5 cm) in length at the sleeves (maybe more). Keep this in mind when considering adding length to your sleeve.

NECKLINE: With U.S. size 5/3.75 mm (16–24" [40–60 cm]) circular needle (or needle two sizes smaller than used for the body), pick up every available stitch along the shoulders and back, and approximately 6 of every 7 st along the front, ending with a multiple of 5 (adjust as needed for best results). Begin ribbing as follows: [k3, p2] rep bet brackets to end of round. Work ribbing in the round as established until neck ribbing measures 2" (5 cm). Bind off in pattern with medium tension.

WEAVE-IN ends and wet block, soaking thoroughly, then rinse well to remove excess dye (if needed). Pin flat and allow to dry completely, turning as needed for even drying.

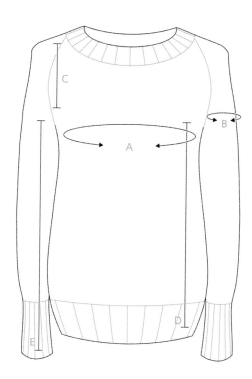

FINISHED MEASUREMENTS

A) BUST:
35.6" (39, 43.6, 47, 50.7, 54.2) (88.9 cm [110, 111.1, 119.4, 127.8, 136.1])

B) SLEEVE AT WIDEST POINT:
12.9" (13.8, 15, 15.6, 16.9, 17.8) (32.2 cm [34.4, 37.8, 38.9, 42.2, 44.4])

C) TOP OF SHOULDER TO UNDERARM:
9.1" (9.4, 9.4, 9.8, 10.4, 10.7) (23.2 cm [24, 24, 24.8, 26.4, 27.2])

D) LENGTH OF BODY FROM UNDERARM:
17.5" (44.45 cm) prior to blocking

E) LENGTH OF SLEEVE FROM UNDERARM:
19" (48.26 cm) prior to blocking

Binge Knits

RICH TEXTURE & VIBRANT DETAIL

If a 2-week sweater isn't challenge enough, may I tempt you by taking it up a notch? Binge-knitting isn't much different than binge-watching your favorite show; it involves focused time and long stretches without deviating to other things. The result is significant progress in a short period of time. And surely I'm not the only knitter who likes to binge-knit while I'm binge-watching my favorite moody crime series?

If you know you'll have a little extra time for binge-knitting, you'll love the rich texture and vibrant details in the sweaters on the following pages. These elegant, graphic designs, like Shoreline (page 123), are so easy to memorize so you can knit them anywhere.

Shoreline Textured Cardigan

Shoreline's graphic structure comes from a unique—and highly addictive!—stitch pattern called granite stitch. I love what this interesting texture does to reinforce the fabric, making it ideal for an open-front cardigan. Even in this wool/cotton/silk blend—which might otherwise grow beyond your expectations over time—granite stitch keeps your stitches where you want them. Perfect for walks along the coastline or curling up with a good book—I've done both in this sweater with much success.

TIMELINE

All-over texture and wide ribbing add a little extra time to this project, but if you have an opportunity to hunker down and knit, you can complete Shoreline in approximately 12 to 14 days.

MATERIALS

Yarn	• DK | Magpie Fibers Solstice | 50% domestic superwash Merino, 25% domestic cotton, 25% silk | 300 yards (274 m) per 100 g | 1034 yards (1149, 1276, 1404, 1572, 1761) (945 m [1051, 1167, 1284, 1437, 1610])
Yarn Notes	• Worked in a highly textured blend of wool, cotton and silk, the fabric feel should be soft and slubby with gentle drape.
Needles	• U.S. size 6/4 mm (24–32" [60–80 cm]) circular needle (body) • U.S. size 5/3.75 mm (24–32" [60–80 cm]) circular needle (lower body ribbing) • U.S. size 6/4 mm (12" [30 cm]) circular needle or DPN (sleeves) • U.S. size 4/3.5 mm (24–32" [60–80 cm]) circular needle (front band/neck ribbing) • U.S. size 4/3.5 mm (12" [30 cm]) circular needle or DPN (sleeve cuff) • Note: Use needle size necessary to obtain gauge.
Gauge	• 20 st and 25 rows with larger needle over 4" (10 cm) in stockinette stitch
Notions	• Yarn needle • Stitch markers • Waste yarn

STITCH GLOSSARY

bet	between
BOR	beginning of round/row
CO	cast on
dec	decrease
ea	each
inc	increase
k	knit
k2tog	knit 2 st at once (dec 1)
m	marker/markers
mX	marker "X" indicates which marker (i.e, mA, mB, mC, etc.)
M1L	make one st that leans left (inc 1)
M1R	make one st that leans right (inc 1)
p	purl
p2tog	purl two st together at once (dec 1)
pmX	place marker, "X" indicates which marker (i.e, pmA, pmB, pmC, etc.)
rem m	remove marker
rep	repeat
rs	right side
sm	slip marker/markers

(continued)

STITCH GLOSSARY

smX	slip marker, "X" indicates which marker (i.e, smA, smB, smC, etc.)
ssk	slip, slip, knit together (dec 1)
st	stitch/stitches
ws	wrong side
[ ]	brackets always indicate a repeat

SIZES

Bust sizes 30/32" (34/36, 38/40, 42/44, 46/48, 50/52) (76/81 cm [86/91, 97/102, 107/112, 117/122, 127/132])

RECOMMENDED EASE

Shoreline can run a bit small depending on your granite stitch rows. The front panels have extra width as they overlap in the front, so don't let the finished measurements of the bust confuse you. Either choose the size range that most closely fits your actual bust measurement, or refer to the measurements for the sleeves at the widest point to select that size closest to your own arm measurement. Ideally your sleeve should measure just slightly larger than your arm measurement at the widest point. Unlike other designs in this book, I don't recommend going down a size. Refer to pages 14–16 for additional information about sizing, fit and ease.

CONSTRUCTION

Shoreline is an open-front cardigan that alternates versatile stockinette with nubby horizontal lines of granite stitch. It is worked flat from top to bottom, with the wide front band/neckline picked up and worked afterward for stability and structure.

NOTE: Rows and rounds apply to all sizes unless otherwise indicated. Be sure to read ahead and mark sections that are specific to your size before you begin.

TEXTURE NOTE: Shoreline features granite stitch texture, which is worked over two rows as part of an 8-row repeat. One row you will work a significant number of decreases across, and on the next row these decreases will be recovered with the same number of increases across. You will not count these decreases or increases in your overall stitch count as they should always balance out evenly after the two rows are worked; no stitches will have been lost or gained when the texture rows are completed (at least not as a result of the texture).

Oops! Did you miss an increase? If you miss an increase somewhere in the pattern, you'll discover it when you go to work the first row of granite stitch because you'll have a single stitch left that doesn't have a partner to work the k2tog. If this happens, don't fear! Simply knit that single stitch, and on the next row (rs) work a kfb into this stitch so that it mirrors the other stitches in the texture pattern. This will help you recover the missing stitch without tinking and no one will ever know.

QUICK TIP: Remember that adding length anywhere on the sweater (sleeves or body) adds time to the overall project. Keep this in mind and adjust accordingly.

SHORELINE PATTERN

With U.S. size 6/4 mm (24-32" [60-80 cm]) circular needle (or size to obtain gauge), cast on 32 (50, 76, 84, 92, 102) st using cable cast-on method. Do not join—pattern is worked flat.

ROW 1 – SET UP (RS): K2, pmA, kfb, k0 (4, 12, 14, 18, 20), kfb, pmB, kfb, k22 (32, 42, 46, 46, 52), kfb, pmC, kfb, k0 (4, 12, 14, 18, 20), kfb, pmD, k2 (6 st inc).

ROW 2 (WS): P across, slipping m as you go.

SIZE 30/32 ROW 3 (RS): K2, smA, K1, M1L, k2, M1R, k1, smB, k2, M1L, k to 2 st before mC, M1R, k2, smC, k1, M1L, k 2, M1R, k1, smD, k2 (6 st inc).

SIZES 34/36, 38/40, 42/44, 46/48, 50/52 ROW 3 (RS): K2, smA, k1, M1L, k to 1 st before mB, M1R, k1, smB, k1, M1L, k to 1 st before mC, M1R, k1, smC, k1, M1L, k to 1 st before mD, M1R, k1, smD, k2 (6 st inc).

ALL SIZES continue.

ROW 4 (WS): P2, sm, p2, [k2tog] rep bet brackets to 2 st before m, p2, sm, p2, [k2tog] rep bet brackets to 2 st before m, p2, sm, p2, [k2tog] rep bet brackets to 2 st before m, p2, sm, p2.

ROW 5 (RS): K to 1 st before mA, M1R, k1, smA, k1, M1L, k1, [kfb] rep bet brackets to 2 st before mB, k1, M1R, k1, smB, k1, M1L, k1, [kfb] rep bet brackets to 2 st before mC, k1, M1R, k1, smC, k1, M1L, k1, [kfb] rep bet brackets to 2 st before mD, k1, M1R, k1, smD, k1, M1L, k to end (8 st inc—do not count granite stitch increases because they merely bring your stitch count back to where it belongs).

ROW 6 (WS): P across, slipping m as you go.

ROW 7 (RS): K to 1 st before mA, M1R, k1, smA, k1, M1L, k to 1 st before mB, M1R, k1, smB, k1, M1L, k to 1 st before mC, M1R, k1, smC, k1, M1L, k to 1 st before mD, M1R, k1, smD, k1, M1L, k to end (8 st inc).

ROW 8 (WS): P across, slipping m as you go.

REP rows 7 and 8 once more.

STITCH COUNT CHECK-IN
FRONTS (EA): 5
SLEEVES (EA): 12 (16, 24, 26, 30, 32)
BACK: 34 (44, 54, 58, 58, 64)

ROW 11 (RS): K to 1 st before mA, M1R, k1, smA, k1, M1L, k to 1 st before mB, M1R, k1, smB, k1, M1L, k to 1 st before mC, M1R, k1, smC, k1, M1L, k to 1 st before mD, M1R, k1, smD, k1, M1L, k to end (8 st inc).

ROW 12 (WS): P2, k2tog, p2, sm, p2, [k2tog] rep bet brackets to 2 st before m, p2, sm, p2, [k2tog] rep bet brackets to 2 st before m, p2, sm, p2, [k2tog] rep bet brackets to 2 st before m, p2, sm, p2, p2tog, p2.

ROW 13 (RS): K2, kfb, k1, M1R, k1, smA, k1, M1L, k1, [kfb] rep bet brackets to 2 st before mB, k1, M1R, k1, smB, k1, M1L, k1, [kfb] rep bet brackets to 2 st before mC, k1, M1R, k1, smC, k1, M1L, k1, [kfb] rep bet brackets to 2 st before mD, k1, M1R, k1, smD, k1, M1L, k1, kfb, k to end (8 st inc + granite stitch).

ROW 14 (WS): P across, slipping m as you go.

ROW 15 (RS): K to 1 st before mA, M1R, k1, smA, k1, M1L, k to 1 st before mB, M1R, k1, smB, k1, M1L, k to 1 st before mC, M1R, k1, smC, k1, M1L, k to 1 st before mD, M1R, k1, smD, k1, M1L, k to end (8 st inc).

ROW 16 (WS): P across, slipping m as you go.

Shoreline front view.

STITCH COUNT CHECK-IN
FRONTS (EA): 8
SLEEVES (EA): 18 (22, 30, 32, 36, 38)
BACK: 40 (50, 60, 64, 64, 70)

REP rows 15 and 16 once more.

ROW 19 (RS): K to 1 st before mA, M1R, k1, smA, k1, M1L, k to 1 st before mB, M1R, k1, smB, k1, M1L, k to 1 st before mC, M1R, k1, smC, k1, M1L, k to 1 st before mD, M1R, k1, smD, k1, M1L, k to end (8 st inc).

ROW 20 (WS): P2, [k2tog] rep bet brackets to 2 st before m, p2, sm, p2, [k2tog] rep bet brackets to 2 st before m, p2, sm, p2, [k2tog] rep bet brackets to 2 st before m, p2, sm, p2, [k2tog] rep bet brackets to last two st, p2.

ROW 21 (RS): K2, [kfb] rep bet brackets to 2 st before mA, k1, M1R, k1, smA, k1, M1L, k1, [kfb] rep bet brackets to 2 st before mB, k1, M1R, k1, smB, k1, M1L, k1, [kfb] rep bet brackets to 2 st before mC, k1, M1R, k1, smC, k1, M1L, k1, [kfb] rep bet brackets to 2 st before mD, k1, M1R, k1, smD, k1, M1L, k1, [kfb] rep bet brackets to last two st, k2 (8 st inc + granite stitch).

ROW 22 (WS): P across, slipping m as you go.

ROW 23 (RS): K to 1 st before mA, M1R, k1, smA, k1, M1L, k to 1 st before mB, M1R, k1, smB, k1, M1L, k to 1 st before mC, M1R, k1, smC, k1, M1L, k to 1 st before mD, M1R, k1, smD, k1, M1L, k to end (8 st inc).

ROW 24 (WS): P across, slipping m as you go.

REP rows 23 and 24 once more.

STITCH COUNT CHECK-IN

FRONTS (EA): 13
SLEEVES (EA): 28 (32, 40, 42, 46, 48)
BACK: 50 (60, 70, 74, 74, 80)

ROW 27 (RS): K to 1 st before mA, M1R, k1, smA, k1, M1L, k to 1 st before mB, M1R, k1, smB, k1, M1L, k to 1 st before mC, M1R, k1, smC, k1, M1L, k to 1 st before mD, M1R, k1, smD, k1, M1L, k to end (8 st inc).

ROW 28 (WS): P2, [k2tog] rep bet brackets to 2 st before m, p2, sm, p2, [k2tog] rep bet brackets to 2 st before m, p2, sm, p2, [k2tog] rep bet brackets to 2 st before m, p2, sm, p2, [k2tog] rep bet brackets to 2 st before m, p2, sm, p2, [k2tog] rep bet brackets to last two st, p2.

ROW 29 (RS): K2, [kfb] rep bet brackets to 2 st before mA, k1, M1R, k1, smA, k1, M1L, k1, [kfb] rep bet brackets to 2 st before mB, k1, M1R, k1, smB, k1, M1L, k1, [kfb] rep bet brackets to 2 st before mC, k1, M1R, k1, smC, k1, M1L, k1, [kfb] rep bet brackets to 2 st before mD, k1, M1R, k1, smD, k1, M1L, k1, [kfb] rep bet brackets to last two st, k2 (8 st inc + granite stitch).

ROW 30 (WS): P across, slipping m as you go.

STITCH COUNT CHECK-IN

FRONTS (EA): 15
SLEEVES (EA): 32 (36, 44, 46, 50, 52)
BACK: 54 (64, 74, 78, 78, 84)

ROW 31 (RS): K1, M1R, k to 1 st before mA, M1R, k1, smA, k1, M1L, k to 1 st before mB, M1R, k1, smB, k1, M1L, k to 1 st before mC, M1R, k1, smC, k1, M1L, k to 1 st before mD, M1R, k1, smD, k1, M1L, k to last st, M1L, k1 (10 st inc).

ROW 32 (WS): P across, slipping m as you go.

REP rows 31 and 32 once more.

ROW 35 (RS): K1, M1R, k to 1 st before mA, M1R, k1, smA, k1, M1L, k to 1 st before mB, M1R, k1, smB, k1, M1L, k to 1 st before mC, M1R, k1, smC, k1, M1L, k to 1 st before mD, M1R, k1, smD, k1, M1L, k to last st, M1L, k1 (10 st inc).

ROW 36 (WS): P3, [k2tog] rep bet brackets to 2 st before m, p2, sm, p2, [k2tog] rep bet brackets to 2 st before m, p2, sm, p2, [k2tog] rep bet brackets to 2 st before m, p2, sm, p2, [k2tog] rep bet brackets to 2 st before m, p2, sm, p2, [k2tog] rep bet brackets to last three st, p3.

ROW 37 (RS): K1, M1R, k2, [kfb] rep bet brackets to 2 st before mA, k1, M1R, k1, smA, k1, M1L, k1, [kfb] rep bet brackets to 2 st before mB, k1, M1R, k1, smB, k1, M1L, k1, [kfb] rep bet brackets to 2 st before mC, k1, M1R, k1, smC, k1, M1L, k1, [kfb] rep bet brackets to 2 st before mD, k1, M1R, k1, smD, k1, M1L, k1, [kfb] rep bet brackets to last three st, k2, M1L, k1 (10 st inc + granite st).

ROW 38 (WS): P across, slipping m as you go.

STITCH COUNT CHECK-IN

FRONTS (EA): 23
SLEEVES (EA): 40 (44, 52, 54, 58, 60)
BACK: 62 (72, 82, 86, 86, 92)

REP rows 31–38 until you reach the following:

STITCH COUNT CHECK-IN

FRONTS (EA): 37 (39, 39, 39, 37, 37)
SLEEVES (EA): 54 (60, 68, 70, 72, 74)
BACK: 76 (88, 98, 102, 100, 106)

NEXT ROW (EXTRA INC) RS: K1, M1R, k to 3 st before mA, M1R, k2, M1R, k1, smA, k1, M1L, k to 1 st before mB, M1R, k1, smB, k1, M1L, k2, M1L, k to 3 st before mC, M1R, k2, M1R, k1, smC, k1, M1L, k to 1 st before mD, M1R, k1, smD, k1, M1L, k2, M1L, k to last st, M1L, k1 (14 st inc).

NEXT ROW (WS): P across, slipping m as you go.

SIZES 30/32, 34/36, 38/40 Move ahead to Divide for Sleeves.

SIZE 42/44 Move to next instructions for your size below.

SIZES 46/48, 50/52 Rep the last two rows once more.

SIZES 42/44, 46/48, 50/52 NEXT ROW (DOUBLE EXTRA INC) RS: K1, M1R, k to 5 st before mA, M1R, k2, M1R, k2, M1R, k1, smA, k1, M1L, k to 1 st before mB, M1R, k1, smB, k1, M1L, k2, M1L, k2, M1L, k to 5 st before mC, M1R, k2, M1R, k2, M1R, k1, smC, k1, M1L, k to 1 st before mD, M1R, k1, smD, k1, M1L, k2, M1L, k2, M1L, k to last st, M1L, k1 (18 st inc).

SIZES 42/44, 46/48, 50/52 NEXT ROW (WS): P across, slipping m as you go.

SIZE 42/44 Move ahead to Divide for Sleeves.

SIZES 46/48, 50/52 NEXT ROW (DOUBLE EXTRA INC) RS: K1, M1R, k to 5 st before mA, M1R, k2, M1R, k2, M1R, k1, smA, k1, M1L, k to 1 st before mB, M1R, k1, smB, k1, M1L, k2, M1L, k2, M1L, k to 5 st before mC, M1R, k2, M1R, k2, M1R, k1, smC, k1, M1L, k to 1 st before mD, M1R, k1, smD, k1, M1L, k2, M1L, k2, M1L, k to last st, M1L, k1 (18 st inc).

SIZES 46/48, 50/52 NEXT ROW (WS): P3, [k2tog] rep bet brackets to 2 st before m, p2, sm, p2, [k2tog] rep bet brackets to 2 st before m, p2, sm, p2, [k2tog] rep bet brackets to 2 st before m, p2, sm, p2, [k2tog] rep bet brackets to 2 st before m, p2, sm, p2, [k2tog] rep bet brackets to last three st, p3.

STITCH COUNT CHECK-IN
FRONTS (EA): 40 (42, 42, 46, 51, 51)
SLEEVES (EA): 56 (62, 66, 74, 80, 82)
BACK: 80 (92, 102, 112, 120, 126)

DIVIDE FOR SLEEVES: Work across front in pattern to mA, rem mA and place sleeve stitches onto waste yarn (loosely, so you can try it on later). CO 4 (4, 4, 4, 4, 6) st underarm and join to back section, removing mA and mB in the process. K to mC and place sleeve stitches onto waste yarn (loosely), removing mC in the process. CO 4 (4, 4, 4, 4, 6) st at the underarm and join to front section, removing mD in the process.

Shoreline back detail.

STITCH COUNT CHECK-IN
168 (184, 194, 212, 230, 240) st in lower body

LOWER BODY: Knit the lower body back and forth flat (no additional increases), maintaining the 8-row granite stitch texture as established until body measures 13" (33 cm) from underarm, ending just before or just after a granite stitch series on ws row. Transition to U.S. size 5/3.75 mm (24–32" [60–80 cm]) circular needle (or needle one size smaller than that used for body) and k the row. At the same time, dec 0 (1, 1, 0*, 2, 2), st using k2tog, somewhat evenly spaced as applicable *(size 42/44 inc 1 st using kfb). At the conclusion of this row, you should have the following number of stitches: 168 (183, 193, 213, 228, 238). On the next row (ws) begin lower ribbing as follows: p3 [k2, p3] rep bet brackets to end of row. On the rs work ribbing as k3 [p2, k3] rep bet brackets to end of row.

REP these two rows until ribbing measures 2.5" (6.4 cm). Bind off with medium tension in pattern. Note: Bottom edge should not feel tight and restrictive. If it does, bind off more loosely.

SLEEVE NOTE: Granite stitch texture continues on the sleeves in the 8-row series (two rounds of granite stitch plus six rounds of stockinette), as established on the body. It is worked in the same manner as when working flat—on the first row work the [p2tog] repeat, and on the second row work the [kfb] repeat into the p2tog from the previous row. Continue to follow this pattern, while working the decreases as written below. To make things simpler, do not work your dec rounds on the same rounds as the granite stitch texture.

SLEEVES: With U.S. size 6/4 mm (12" [30 cm]) circular needle or DPN (or the same size as used for the body), pick up sleeve stitches from waste yarn (including st cast-on under the arm)—60 (66, 74, 78, 84, 88) st. Pm at center of underarm to mark BOR. Knit sleeve in the round in 8-row granite stitch repeat for 2" (5 cm).

NEXT ROUND: K2, k2tog, k to 4 st before m, ssk, k2 (2 st dec).

CONTINUE sleeve in pattern as established, working a dec round approximately every 1.5" (3.8 cm) until sleeve measures 18" (46 cm) and you have 40 (46, 50, 58, 64, 68) stitches. You will not work any additional granite stitch texture after this point; if you are in the middle of a granite stitch series, complete the series before you continue.

TRANSITION to U.S. size 4/3.5 mm (12" [30 cm]) circular needle or DPN (or two sizes smaller than that used for sleeves). Work one round in stockinette st, dec 0 (1, 0, 3, 4, 3) st evenly using k2tog to end with a multiple of 5. Begin cuff ribbing as follows: [k3, p2] rep bet brackets to end of round.

CONTINUE ribbing as established until cuff measures 2.5" (6.4 cm). Bind off in pattern with medium tension.

REP for second sleeve.

NECKLINE & FRONT BAND: With U.S. size 4/3.5 mm (16–24" [40–60 cm]) circular needle (or needle two sizes smaller than used for the body), pick up stitches around the fronts and neckline in the following manner: Starting at the bottom right front (on the rs), pick up approximately 6 of every 7 stitches along front band, up around the neckline and back down the left side, ending with a multiple of 6 + 3 (see page 161). Work in ribbing as follows: [k3, p3] rep between brackets across, ending k3 (on the rs), and work as [p3, k3] ending p3 on the ws. Work ribbing back and forth in this manner (k3 [p2, k3] on the rs and p3 [k2, p3] on the wrong side) until front ribbing measures 5" (12.5 cm). Bind off in pattern with medium tension.

WEAVE-IN ends and wet block. Pin flat, drawing the granite stitch horizontally more than vertically, folding the collar down at the neckline partway through the drying process to create shaping. Allow to dry completely, turning as needed.

FINISHED MEASUREMENTS

A) BUST (INCLUDES OVERLAPPING WIDE RIBBING AT FRONT):
43.6" (46.8, 48.8, 52.4, 56, 58) (109.4 cm [117.4, 122.4, 131.4, 140.4, 145.4])

B) MEASUREMENT ACROSS BACK FROM UNDERARM TO UNDERARM:
16.8" (19.2, 21.2, 23.2, 24.8, 26.4) (42 cm [48, 53, 58, 62, 66])

C) SLEEVE AT WIDEST POINT:
12" (13.2, 14.8, 15.6, 16.8, 17.6) (30 cm [33, 37, 39, 42, 44])

D) TOP OF SHOULDER TO UNDERARM:
9.1" (10, 11.5, 11.8, 12.8, 13.4) (23.06 cm [25.4, 29.31, 30.09, 32.43, 34])

E) LENGTH OF LOWER BODY FROM UNDERARM:
15.5" (39.37 cm) prior to blocking

F) LENGTH OF SLEEVE FROM UNDERARM:
20.5" (52.07 cm) prior to blocking

Sandscape Slipped-Stitch Pullover

Understated, with monochromatic embossed texture and clean lines, Sandscape is a little slice of perfection in its intentional simplicity. Sometimes when I design a sweater, I find myself saying "less is more" over and over in my head as I strip away excess and pare the concept down to the right balance of details. Sandscape required no extra fiddling; the idea arrived in my head almost exactly as you see it here. Slipped stitches against a landscape of stockinette maintain interest without requiring a lot of fuss or concentration. Once you've established the slipped-stitch formation, the sweater flows beautifully and easily from the needles.

TIMELINE

Long sleeves and a long body plus slipped-stitch texture on all sections (front, back and sleeves) can add a little time to this project. Estimate 10 to 14 days for eager knitters with time to knit.

Gauge	• 20 st and 26 rows with larger needle over 4" (10 cm) in stockinette stitch
Notions	• Yarn needle • Stitch markers • Waste yarn

MATERIALS

Yarn	• Worsted | Woolfolk Far | 100% Ovis 21 ultimate Merino wool | 142 yards (130 m) per 50 g | 997 yards (1108, 1231, 1354, 1516, 1698) (912 m [1013, 1126, 1238, 1386, 1553])
Yarn Notes	• Linear, architectural details through slipped stitches create a bit of structure down the sleeves and body of the sweater. The fabric of this sweater should be soft and flexible with medium density and comfortable drape. The recommended yarn is a deliciously soft, airy chained merino that blooms slightly when blocked.
Needles	• U.S. size 7/4.5 mm (24-32" [60-80 cm]) circular needle (body) • U.S. size 7/4.5 mm (12" [30 cm]) circular needle or DPN (sleeves) • U.S. size 6/4 mm (24-32" [60-80 cm]) circular needle (lower body ribbing) • U.S. size 5/3.75 mm (12" [30 cm]) circular needle or DPN (sleeve cuff) • U.S. size 5/3.75 mm (16-24" [40-60 cm]) circular needle (neckline) • Note: Use needle size necessary to obtain gauge.

STITCH GLOSSARY

bet	between
BOR	beginning of round/row
CO	cast on
dec	decrease
ea	each
inc	increase
k	knit
k2tog	knit 2 st at once (dec 1)
m	marker/markers
mX	marker "X" indicates which marker (i.e, mA, mB, mC, etc.)
M1	make one stitch by knitting into the bar between st to inc 1
M1L	make one st that leans left (inc 1)
M1R	make one st that leans right (inc 1)
p	purl

(continued)

STITCH GLOSSARY

pmX	place marker, "X" indicates which marker (i.e, pmA, pmB, pmC, etc.)
rem m	remove marker
rep	repeat
rs	right side
sm	slip marker/markers
smX	slip marker, "X" indicates which marker (i.e, smA, smB, smC, etc.)
ssk	slip, slip, knit together (dec 1)
st	stitch/stitches
swyib	slip st with yarn in back (where you can't see it)
swyif	slip st with yarn in front (where you can see it)
ws	wrong side
[ ]	brackets always indicate a repeat

SIZES

Bust sizes 30/32" (34/36, 38/40, 42/44, 46/48, 50/52) (76/81 cm [86/91, 97/102, 107/112, 117/122, 127/132])

RECOMMENDED EASE

Positive ease is included for a comfortable fit. See finished measurements for final ease as compared to your actual bust measurement. If you are between sizes, refer to the final measurements to determine which size to choose. In many cases you'll find that the smaller of the two sizes will be best.

CONSTRUCTION

Sandscape is worked flat until neckline shaping is complete, then joined and worked in the round from there. Slipped-stitch details down the front, back and sleeves create an embossed effect against the monochrome of a solid color. The sleeves and neckline are worked last.

NOTE: Rows and rounds apply to all sizes unless otherwise indicated. Be sure to read ahead and mark sections that are specific to your size before you begin.

ALSO: Markers with letters (mA, mB, etc.) denote the location of seams/increases in this design. Markers with numbers (m1, m2, etc.) denote the location of texture panels.

QUICK TIP: Pay special attention to the increases which are worked at a different pace than a traditional top-down sweater and are not always worked in all sections as you might expect. This syncopated increase structure creates an almost set-in sleeve shape with a hint of saddle shoulder.

SANDSCAPE PATTERN

With U.S. size 7/4.5 mm (24-32" [60-80 cm]) circular needle, cast on 65 (75, 81, 91, 111, 117) st using cable cast-on method. Do not join yet.

ROW 1 - SET UP (RS): K2, pmA, k13 (15, 15, 20, 25, 25), pmB, k1, M1L, k 33 (39, 45, 45, 55, 61), M1R, k1, pmC, k13 (15, 15, 20, 25, 25), pmD, k2 (2 st inc).

ROW 2 (WS): P across, slipping m as you go.

ROW 3 (RS): K2, smA, k to mB, smB, k1, M1L, k to 1 st before mC, M1R, k1, smC, k to mD, smD, k2.

ROW 4 (WS): As row 2.

NOTE: Placement for embossed texture on sleeves and back begins on row 5. Please follow the specific row for your size.

SIZES 30/32, 34/36, 38/40 ROW 5 (RS): K2, smA, k3 (4, 4, -, -, -), pm1, slwyib, k5, slwyib, pm2, k3 (4, 4,-, -, -), smB, k1, M1L, k 3 (6, 6, -, -, -), pm3, [slwyib, k5] rep bet brackets 5 (5, 6, -, -, -) times total, slwyib, pm4, k3 (6, 6, -, -, -), M1R, k1, smC, k3 (4, 4, -, -, -), pm5, slwyib, k5, slwyib, pm6, k3 (4, 4,-, -, -), smD, k2 (2 st inc).

Seascape sleeve detail.

Embossed texture panels have now been established at the center of the sleeves and back, and will be worked between the numbered markers (m1, m2, m3, m4, etc.) going forward. The texture panels on the front will begin later. Keep in mind: The slipped stitches you've established will be slipped for three rows as written (rs, ws, rs) then purled across a ws row, then the 4-row sequence is repeated. You will always be slipping the same stitches that had been slipped before (no more, no less) so that the trails of slipped stitches run in straight lines down the sleeves and body.

ROW 6 (WS): P across, BUT when you reach the slipped st from the previous row, swyif, slipping all m as you work across the row.

ROW 7 (RS): CO 1 st using knitted cast-on worked tightly*, k to 1 st before mA, M1R, k1, smA, [k1, M1] rep bet brackets 2 (2, 2, 3, 3, 3) times total, k to m1, sm1, work the slipped st pattern as established to m2, sm2, k to 2 (2, 2, 3, 3, 3) st before mB, [M1, k1] rep bet brackets 2 (2, 2, 3, 3, 3) times, k to mB, smB, k1, M1L, k to m3, sm3, work the slipped st pattern as established on row 5 to m4, sm4, k to 1 st before mC, M1R, k1, smC, [k1, M1] rep bet brackets 2 (2, 2, 3, 3, 3) times total, k to m4, sm4, work the slipped st pattern as established to m5, sm5, k to 2 (2, 2, 3, 3, 3) st before mD, [M1, k1] rep bet brackets 2 (2, 2, 3, 3, 3) times, k to mD, smD, k1, M1L, k to end = 13 (13, 13, 17, 17, 17) st inc + CO.

ROW 8 (WS): CO 1 st using knitted cast-on worked purlwise*, p across remainder of row, slipping m as you go (no slipped st this row).

SIZE 42/44 ROW 5 (RS): K2, smA, k - (-, -, 4, -, -), pm1, slwyib, k5, slwyib, k5, slwyib, pm2, k4, smB, k1, M1L, k - (-, -, 6, -, -), pm3, [slwyib, k5] rep bet brackets - (-, -, 6, -, -) times total, slwyib, pm4, k - (-, -, 6, -, -), M1R, k1, smC, k4, pm5, slwyib, k5, slwyib, k5, slwyib, pm6, k4 (2 st inc).

SIZES 46/48, 50/52 ROW 5 (RS): K2, smA, k - (-, -, -, 3, 3), pm1, slwyib, [k5, slwyib] three times, pm2, k -(-, -, -, 3, 3), smB, k1, M1L, k - (-, -, -, 8, 11), pm3, [slwyib, k5] rep bet brackets - (-, -, -, 7, 7) times total, slwyib, pm4, k - (-, -, -, 8, 11), M1R, k1, smC, k - (-, -, -, 3, 3), pm5, slwyib, [k5, slwyib] three times, pm6, k - (-, -, -, 3, 3), smD, k2 (2 st inc).

***GOING FORWARD,** all stitches cast-on on the right side will be worked using the knitted cast-on method, and all stitches cast-on on the wrong side will be worked using the knitted cast-on worked purlwise. Always knit the new stitch/es on the right side and purl the new stitch/es on the wrong side as you work through the row.

STITCH COUNT CHECK-IN

FRONTS (EA): 4
SLEEVES (EA): 17 (19, 19, 26, 31, 31)
BACK: 43 (49, 55, 55, 65, 71)

ROW 9 (RS): CO 1 st, k to 1 st before mA, M1R, k1, smA, k1, M1L, k to m1, sm1, work the slipped st pattern as established to m2, sm2, k to 1 st before mB, M1R, k1, smB, k1, M1L, k to m3, sm3, work the slipped st pattern as established to m4, sm4, k to 1 st before mC, M1R, k1, smC, k1, M1L, k to m5, sm5, work the slipped st pattern as established to m6, sm6, k to 1 st before mD, M1R, k1, smD, k1, M1L, k to end (8 st inc + CO).

ROW 10 (WS): CO 2 st, then p across, but when you reach the slipped st from the previous row, swyif, slipping all m as you work across the row.

ROW 11 (RS): CO 1 (1, 2, 2, 2, 2) st, k to 1 st before mA, M1R, k1, smA, k1, M1L, k to m1, sm1, work the slipped st pattern as established to m2, sm2, k to 1 st before mB, M1R, k1, smB, k1, M1L, k to m3, sm3, work the slipped st pattern as established to m4, sm4, k to 1 st before mC, M1R, k1, smC, k1, M1L, k to m5, sm5, work the slipped st pattern as established to m6, sm6, k to 1 st before mD, M1R, k1, smD, k1, M1L, k to end (8 st inc + CO).

ROW 12 (WS): CO 1 (1, 2, 2, 2, 2) st, p across remainder of row, slipping m as you go (no slipped st this row).

ROW 13 (RS): CO 1 (1, 2, 2, 4, 4) st, to 1 st before mA, M1R, k1, smA, k1, M1L, k to m1, sm1, work the slipped st pattern as established to m2, sm2, k to 1 st before mB, M1R, k1, smB, k1, M1L, k to m3, sm3, work the slipped st pattern as established to m4, sm4, k to 1 st before mC, M1R, k1, smC, k1, M1L, k to m5, sm5, work the slipped st pattern as established to m6, sm6, k to 1 st before mD, M1R, k1, smD, k1, M1L, k to end (8 st inc + CO).

ROW 14 (WS): CO 1 (1, 2, 2, 4, 4), then p across, but when you reach the slipped st from the previous row, swyif, slipping all m as you work across the row.

STITCH COUNT CHECK-IN
FRONTS (EA): 10 (10, 12, 12, 14, 14)
SLEEVES (EA): 23 (25, 25, 32, 37, 37)
BACK: 49 (55, 61, 61, 71, 77)

ROW 15 (RS): CO 2 (2, 2, 2, 4, 4) st, k to 1 st before mA, M1R, k1, smA, k1, M1L, k to m1, sm1, work the slipped st pattern as established to m2, sm2, k to 1 st before mB, M1R, k1, smB, k1, M1L, k to m3, sm3, work the slipped st pattern as established to m4, sm4, k to 1 st before mC, M1R, k1, smC, k1, M1L, k to m5, sm5, work the slipped st pattern as established to m6, sm6, k to 1 st before mD, M1R, k1, smD, k1, M1L, k to end (8 st inc + CO).

ROW 16 (WS): CO 2 (2, 2, 2, 4, 4) st, then p across remainder of row, slipping m as you go (no slipped st this row).

ROW 17 (RS): CO 4 (4, 4, 4, 4, 6) st, k to 1 st before mA, M1R, k1, smA, k1, M1L, k to m1, sm1, work the slipped st pattern as established to m2, sm2, k to 1 st before mB, M1R, k1, smB, k1, M1L, k to m3, sm3, work the slipped st pattern as established to m4, sm4, k to 1 st before mC, M1R, k1, smC, k1, M1L, k to m5, sm5, work the slipped st pattern as established to m6, sm6, k to 1 st before mD, M1R, k1, smD, k1, M1L, k to end (8 st inc + CO).

ROW 18 (WS): CO 4 (4, 4, 4, 4, 6), then p across, but when you reach the slipped st from the previous row, swyif, slipping all m as you work across the row.

STITCH COUNT CHECK-IN
FRONTS (EA): 18 (18, 20, 20, 24, 26)
SLEEVES (EA): 27 (29, 29, 36, 41, 41)
BACK: 53 (59, 65, 65, 75, 81)

ROW 19 (RS): CO 15 (21, 23, 23, 25, 27) st. K to 1 st before mA, M1R, k1, smA, k1, M1L, k to m1, sm1, work the slipped st pattern as established to m2, sm2, k to 1 st before mB, M1R, k1, smB, k to m3, sm3, work the slipped st pattern as established to m4, sm4, k to mC, smC, k1, M1L, k to m5, sm5, work the slipped st pattern as established to m6, sm6, k to 1 st before mD, M1R, k1, smD, k1, M1L, k to end (8 st inc + CO).

CUT yarn, leaving a tail.

STITCH COUNT CHECK-IN
FRONT: 53 (59, 65, 65, 75, 81)
SLEEVES (EA): 29 (31, 31, 38, 43, 43)
BACK: 53 (59, 65, 65, 75, 81)

NECKLINE JOIN: Rejoin yarn just after mD, leaving a tail to weave in later. This marks the new BOR. Slide the stitches after mD to the left needle so they "meet" with the other stitches on the front section (all stitches between mD and mA are now the "front")— 53 (59, 65, 65, 75, 81) st between mD and mA. K this round (this takes the place of the ws/non-slip st row, so you will not slip st on this round), joining the front stitches when you reach the gap (be careful not to twist stitches) and knit to end of round (no inc).

NOTE: On the next round you will begin the slipped st pattern on the front. Also make note that the increases on the front/back stop until you begin to get closer to the sleeve divide. Increases on the sleeves will continue at regular intervals.

NEXT ROUND: At new BOR (just after mD), k11 (14, 14, 14, 16, 19), pm7, slwyib [k5, slwyib] rep bet brackets 5 (5, 6, 6, 7, 7) times total, pm8, k11 (14, 14, 14, 16, 19), smA, k1, M1L, k to m1, sm1, work the slipped st pattern as established to m2, sm2, k to 1 st before mB, M1R, k1, smB, k to m3, sm3, work the slipped st pattern as established to m4, sm4, k to mC, smC, k1, M1L, k to m5, sm5, work the slipped st pattern as established to m6, sm6, k to 1 st before mD, M1R, k1 (4 st inc)

*You should have 31 (31, 37, 37, 43, 43) st between m7 and m8.

NEXT ROUND (NO INC): K to m7, work in slipped st pattern as established to m8, sm8, k to mA, smA, k to m1, sm1, work in slipped st pattern as established to m2, sm2, k to mB, smB, k to m3, work the slipped st pattern as established to m4, sm4, k to mC, smC, k to m5, sm5, work in slipped st pattern as established to m6, sm6, k to mD.

NEXT ROUND (INC): K to m7, work in slipped st pattern as established to m8, sm8, k to mA, smA, k1, M1L, k to m1, sm1, work in slipped st pattern as established to m2, sm2, k to 1 st before mB, M1R, k1, smB, k to m3, sm3, work in slipped st pattern as established to m4, sm4, k to mC, smC, k1, M1L, k to m5, sm5, work in slipped st pattern as established to m6, sm6, k to 1 st before mD, M1R, k1 (4 st inc).

STITCH COUNT CHECK-IN
FRONT: 53 (59, 65, 65, 75, 81)
SLEEVES (EA): 33 (35, 35, 42, 47, 47)
BACK: 53 (59, 65, 65, 75, 81)

REP the last two rounds, working inc only on the sleeves and maintaining the 4-round slipped st pattern as established in all sections until you reach the following st count on the sleeves: 49 (51, 53, 60, 65, 65).

WORK one round without increases, then move ahead to the next inc round.

NOTE: Inc on the front/back sections begin again on the next round to establish arm and bust shaping.

NEXT ROUND (EXTRA INC): K1, M1L, k2, M1L, k to m7, sm7, work slipped st pattern as established to m8, sm8, k to 3 st before mA, M1R, k2, M1R, k1, smA, k1, M1L, k to m1, sm1, work in slipped st pattern as established to m2, sm2, k to 1 st before mB, M1R, k1, smB, k1, M1L, k2, M1L, k to m3, sm3, work in slipped st pattern as established to m4, sm4, k to 3 st before mC, M1R, k2, M1R, k1, smC, k1, M1L, k to m5, sm5, work in slipped st pattern as established to m6, sm6, k to 1 st before mD, M1R, k1 (12 st inc).

NEXT ROUND (NO INC): K to m7, work in slipped st pattern as established to m8, sm8, k to mA, smA, k to m1, sm1, work in slipped st pattern as established to m2, sm2, k to mB, smB, k to m3, work the slipped st pattern as established to m4, sm4, k to mC, smC, k to m5, sm5, work in slipped st pattern as established to m6, sm6, k to mD.

REP these two rounds 2 (3, 2, 3, 3, 4) times more.

STITCH COUNT CHECK-IN
FRONT: 65 (75, 77, 81, 91, 101)
SLEEVES (EA): 55 (59, 59, 68, 73, 75)
BACK: 65 (75, 77, 81, 91, 101)

NEXT ROUND (DOUBLE EXTRA INC): K1, M1L, k2, M1L, k2, M1L, k to m7, sm7, work slipped st pattern as established to m8, sm8, k to 5 st before mA, M1R, k2, M1R, k2, M1R, k1, smA, k1, M1L, k to m1, sm1, work in slipped st pattern as established to m2, sm2, k to 1 st before mB, M1R, k1, smB, k1, M1L, k2, M1L, k2, M1L, k to m3, sm3, work in slipped st pattern as established to m4, sm4, k to 5 st before mC, M1R, k2, M1R, k2, M1R, k1, smC, k1, M1L, k to m5, sm5, work in slipped st pattern as established to m6, sm6, k to 1 st before mD, M1R, k1 (16 st inc).

NEXT ROUND (NO INC): K to m7, work in slipped st pattern as established to m8, sm8, k to mA, smA, k to m1, sm1, work in slipped st pattern as established to m2, sm2, k to mB, smB, k to m3, work the slipped st pattern as established to m4, sm4, k to mC, smC, k to m5, sm5, work in slipped st pattern as established to m6, sm6, k to mD.

REP these two rounds 2 (2, 3, 4, 4, 4) times more.

STITCH COUNT CHECK-IN

FRONT: 83 (93, 101, 111, 121, 131)
SLEEVES (EA): 61 (65, 67, 78, 83, 85)
BACK: 83 (93, 101, 111, 121, 131)

DIVIDE FOR SLEEVES: K to m7, sm7, work slipped st pattern as established (picking up where you left off in the embossed pattern) to m8, sm8, k to mA, rem mA and place sleeve st on waste yarn (loosely, so you can try it on later). CO 2 (2, 4, 4, 4, 5) st underarm and join to next section, removing mB in the process, work across back section to m3, sm3, work in slipped st pattern as established to m4, sm4, k to mC, rem mC and place sleeve st on waste yarn (loosely, so you can try it on later). CO 2 (2, 4, 4, 4, 5) st underarm and join to next section, keeping mD to denote BOR.

STITCH COUNT CHECK-IN

170 (190, 210, 230, 250, 272) stitches in lower body

LOWER BODY: Knit the lower body in the round, maintaining slipped st pattern on front and back where established until body measures 14.5" (36.8 cm) from underarm. Transition to U.S. size 6/4 mm (24–32" [60–80 cm]) circular needle (or needle one size smaller than that used for body) and work one round in pattern. At

Seascape back detail.

the same time, dec 0 (0, 0, 0, 0, 2) st evenly using k2tog. On the next round begin lower ribbing as follows: [k3, p2] rep bet brackets to end of round. Continue in established [k3, p2] ribbing for 2.5" (6.4 cm). Bind off with medium/loose tension in pattern. Lower edge should not feel restrictive; if it does, bind off more loosely.

TEST YOUR BIND-OFF EDGE: Don't settle for a lower edge (or any edge, for that matter) that isn't as flexible as you would like it to be. If you feel that the lower edge feels restrictive, take the time to re-work it more loosely, giving yourself a little more room on each stitch as you go. You'll love your sweater so much more (and be more likely to wear it) if the lower edge lays comfortably. I've had sweaters that were never worn and couldn't figure out what I didn't like about them, only to realize it was a pesky tight bind-off that ruined an otherwise great sweater.

SLEEVES: With U.S. size 7/4.5 mm (12" [30 cm]) circular needle or DPN (or same size used for body), pick up sleeve st from waste yarn, as well as those cast-on under the arm—63 (67, 71, 82, 87, 90) st. Pm at the center of the underarm to denote BOR. Work the sleeves in stockinette st in the round, maintaining the embossed slipped st panel where established as you work down the length of the sleeve. Work in this manner for 2" (5 cm).

DEC ROUND: K2, k2tog, work in pattern as established to 4 st before m, ssk, k2 (2 st dec).

CONTINUE in pattern, working a dec round approximately every 1.5" (1.5, 1.5, 1, 1, 1) (3.75 cm [3.75, 3.75, 2.5, 2.5, 2.5]) until sleeve measures 19" (48 cm) and you have 40 (40, 45, 45, 50, 60) st (you may need to work a single dec on the last row to reach this count). Transition to U.S. size 5/3.75 mm (12" [30 cm]) circular needle (or DPN) and work one round in stockinette (there are no further slipped stitches). On the next round transition to ribbing as follows: [k3, p2] rep bet brackets to end of round. Continue in established [k3, p2] ribbing until cuff measures 2" (5 cm). Bind off in pattern with medium tension. Note: Cuff should not be restrictive; if it is, bind off more loosely.

NECKLINE: With U.S. size 5/3.75 mm (24" [60 cm]) circular needle (or two sizes smaller than used for body), pick up nearly every st around the neckline (adjust as needed for best results) to achieve a multiple of 5. Work in [k3, p2] ribbing, rep bet brackets every round, until neckline measures 2" (5 cm). Bind off in pattern with medium tension.

WET block flat, turning as needed for even drying.

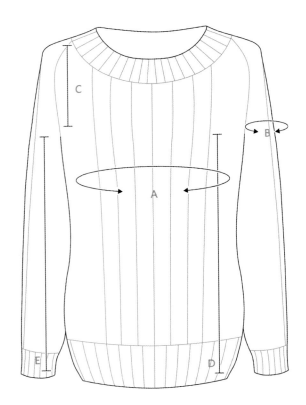

FINISHED MEASUREMENTS

A) BUST:
34" (38, 42, 46, 50, 54) (85 cm [95, 105, 115, 125, 135])

B) SLEEVE AT WIDEST POINT:
12" (13, 14, 16, 17, 18) (30 cm [33, 35, 41, 43, 45])

C) TOP OF SHOULDER TO UNDERARM:
9.5" (9.9, 10.5, 11.5, 11.9, 12.4) (24.03 cm [25.2, 26.77, 29.31, 30.28, 31.46])

D) LENGTH OF BODY FROM UNDERARM:
17" (43.18 cm) prior to blocking

E) LENGTH OF SLEEVE FROM UNDERARM:
21" (53.34 cm) prior to blocking

Bayside Garter Lace Pullover

I rarely incorporate lace into my designs; I'm more of a "structured texture" kind of gal. But I love the way this garter/eyelet combination results in a geometric edge that hardly feels like lace. This unique pattern provides an interesting alternative to traditional ribbing, and produces a tidy finish that lays perfectly flat with wear.

TIMELINE

Knit in a slightly lighter weight than most sweaters in this book, Bayside is a Binge Knit primarily due to sheer number of stitches. Though there's nothing terribly fussy to slow you down, you'll want to estimate the full 14 days for this project.

MATERIALS

Yarn	• Sport | Manos Milo | 65% Merino, 35% linen | 380 yards (347 m) per 100 g | 1024 yards (1138, 1264, 1390, 1557, 1744) (936 m [1041, 1156, 1271, 1424, 1595])
Yarn Notes	• Worked in a blend of Merino and linen, the fabric of this design should be soft but structured, with good stitch definition and drape.
Needles	• U.S. size 5/3.75 mm (24-32" [60-80 cm]) circular needle (body) • U.S. size 5/3.75 mm (12" [30 cm]) circular needle or DPN (sleeves) • U.S. size 3/3.25 mm (12" [30 cm]) circular needle or DPN (sleeve cuff) • U.S. size 3/3.25 mm (16-24" [40-60 cm]) circular needle (neckline) • Note: Use needle size necessary to obtain gauge.
Gauge	• 23 st and 30 rows with larger needle over 4" (10 cm) in stockinette stitch
Notions	• Yarn needle • Stitch markers • Waste yarn

STITCH GLOSSARY

bet	between
BOR	beginning of round/row
CO	cast on
dec	decrease
ea	each
inc	increase
k	knit
k2tog	knit 2 st at once (dec 1)
kfb	knit into front and back of st (inc 1)
m	marker/markers
mX	marker "X" indicates which marker (i.e, mA, mB, mC, etc.)
M1L	make one st that leans left (inc 1)
M1R	make one st that leans right (inc 1)
p	purl
pmX	place marker, "X" indicates which marker (i.e, pmA, pmB, pmC, etc.)
rem m	remove marker
rep	repeat
rs	right side
sm	slip marker/markers
smX	slip marker, "X" indicates which marker (i.e, smA, smB, smC, etc.)

(continued)

STITCH GLOSSARY

ssk	slip, slip, knit together (dec 1)
st	stitch/stitches
ws	wrong side
yo	yarn over (inc 1)
[ ]	brackets always indicate a repeat

SIZES

Bust sizes 30/32" (34/36, 38/40, 42/44, 46/48, 50/52) (76/81 cm [86/91, 97/102, 107/112, 117/122, 127/132])

RECOMMENDED EASE

Positive ease is included for a comfortable fit. See finished measurements for final ease as compared to your actual bust measurement. If you are between sizes, refer to the final measurements to determine which size to choose. In many cases you'll find that the smaller of the two sizes will be best.

CONSTRUCTION

Bayside is worked back and forth from the beginning until the neck shaping is complete, then joined to work in the round from there. Garter stitch details at the raglan seams as well as a garter lace bottom border create interest, while providing structure and texture to the overall design. The sleeves and neckline are worked last.

NOTE: Rows and rounds apply to all sizes unless otherwise indicated. Be sure to read ahead and mark sections that are specific to your size before you begin.

QUICK TIP: If you live in a warmer climate, Bayside is easy to modify for three-quarter sleeves and a shorter body. The beauty of knitting top-down is that you can try it on as you go, and stop just before it's your perfect length (to account for growth with blocking).

BAYSIDE PATTERN

With U.S. size 5/3.75 mm (24–32" [60–80 cm]) circular needle, cast on 60 (76, 92, 102, 118, 126) st using cable cast-on method. Do not join.

ROW 1 – SET UP (RS): K2, pmA, kfb, k8 (12, 16, 20, 28, 28), kfb, pmB, kfb, k34 (42, 50, 52, 52, 60), kfb, pmC, kfb, k8 (12, 16, 20, 28, 28), kfb, pmD, k2 (6 st inc).

ROW 2 (WS): P across, slipping m as you go.

ROW 3 (RS): Kfb, k1, smA, k3, M1L, k to 3 st before mB, M1R, k3, smB, k3, M1L, k to 3 st before mC, M1R, k3, smC, k3, M1L, k to 3 st before mD, M1R, k3, smD, k1, kfb (8 st inc).

ROW 4 (WS): P to m, sm, k3, p to 3 st before m, k3, sm, k3, p to 3 st before m, k3, sm, k3, p to 3 st before m, k3, sm, p to end.

ROW 5 (RS) AND 6 (WS): Rep rows 3 and 4 once more.

ROW 7 (RS): CO 1 st using knitted cast-on worked knitwise*, k the new st, k1, then k to 3 st before m, M1R, k3, smA, k3, M1L, k to 3 st before mB, M1R, k3, smB, k3, M1L, k to 3 st before mC, M1R, k3, smC, k3, M1L, k to 3 st before mD, M1R, k3, smD, k3, M1L, k to end (8 st inc + CO).

ROW 8 (WS): CO 1 st using knitted cast-on worked purlwise*, p to 3 st before m (including new st), k3, sm, k3, p to 3 st before m, k3, sm, k3, p to 3 st before m, k3, sm, k3, p to 3 st before m, k3, sm, k3, p to end.

*GOING FORWARD, all stitches cast-on on the right side will be worked using the knitted cast-on method, and all stitches cast-on on the wrong side will be worked using the knitted cast-on worked purlwise. Always knit the new stitch on the right side and purl the new stitch on the wrong side as you work through the row.

ROW 9 (RS): CO 1 st, k to 3 st before mA, M1R, k3, smA, k3, M1L, k to 3 st before mB, M1R, k3, smB, k3, M1L, k to 3 st before mC, M1R, k3, smC, k3, M1L, k to 3 st before mD, M1R, k3, smD, k3, M1L, k to end (8 st inc + CO).

ROW 10 (WS): CO 1 st, p to 3 st before m, k3, sm, k3, p to 3 st before m, k3, sm, k3, p to 3 st before m, k3, sm, k3, p to end.

Bayside trim lace detail.

ROW 11 (RS): Rep row 9.

ROW 12 (WS): Rep row 10.

ROW 13 (RS): CO 2 st, k to 3 st before mA, M1R, k3, smA, k3, M1L, k to 3 st before mB, M1R, k3, smB, k3, M1L, k to 3 st before mC, M1R, k3, smC, k3, M1L, k to 3 st before mD, M1R, k3, smD, k3, M1L, k to end (8 st inc + CO).

ROW 14 (WS): CO 2 st, p to 3 st before m, k3, sm, k3, p to 3 st before m, k3, sm, k3, p to 3 st before m, k3, sm, k3, p to 3 st before m, k3, sm, k3, p to end.

STITCH COUNT CHECK-IN

FRONTS (EA): 13
SLEEVES (EA): 24 (28, 32, 36, 44, 44)
BACK: 50 (58, 66, 68, 68, 76)

ROW 15 (RS): CO 4 st, k to 3 st before mA, M1R, k3, smA, k3, M1L, k to 3 st before mB, M1R, k3, smB, k3, M1L, k to 3 st before mC, M1R, k3, smC, k3, M1L, k to 3 st before mD, M1R, k3, smD, k3, M1L, k to end (8 st inc + CO).

ROW 16 (WS): CO 4 st, p to 3 st before m, k3, sm, k3, p to 3 st before m, k3, sm, k3, p to 3 st before m, k3, sm, k3, p to 3 st before m, k3, sm, k3, p to end.

ROW 17 (RS): CO 5 (7, 5, 5, 5, 5) st, k to 3 st before mA, M1R, k3, smA, k3, M1L, k to 3 st before mB, M1R, k3, smB, k3, M1L, k to 3 st before mC, M1R, k3, smC, k3, M1L, k to 3 st before mD, M1R, k3, smD, k3, M1L, k to end (8 st inc + CO).

ROW 18 (WS): CO 5 (7, 5, 5, 5, 5) st, p to 3 st before m, k3, sm, k3, p to 3 st before m, k3, sm, k3, p to 3 st before m, k3, sm, k3, p to 3 st before m, k3, sm, k3, p to end.

The following rows have directions specific to certain sizes. Follow the rows for your size in order, moving ahead as directed.

SIZES 30/32, 34/36 ROW 19 (RS): CO 8 (12, -, -, -, -) st, k to 3 st before mA, M1R, k3, smA, k3, M1L, k to 3 st before mB, M1R, k3, smB, k3, M1L, k to 3 st before mC, M1R, k3, smC, k3, M1L, k to 3 st before mD, M1R, k3, smD, k3, M1L, k to end (8 st inc + CO). Cut yarn, leaving a tail. Move ahead to Neckline Join.

SIZES 38/40, 42/44, 46/48, 50/52 ROW 19 (RS): CO - (-, 6, 6, 6, 4) st, k to 3 st before mA, M1R, k3, smA, k3, M1L, k to 3 st before mB, M1R, k3, smB, k3, M1L, k to 3 st before mC, M1R, k3, smC, k3, M1L, k to 3 st before mD, M1R, k3, smD, k3, M1L, k to end (8 st inc + CO).

SIZES 38/40, 42/44, 46/48, 50/52 ROW 20 (WS): CO - (-, 6, 6, 6, 4) st, p to 3 st before m, k3, sm, k3, p to 3 st before m, k3, sm, k3, p to 3 st before m, k3, sm, k3, p to 3 st before m, k3, sm, k3, p to end.

SIZES 38/40, 42/44, 46/48 ROW 21 (RS): CO - (-, 12, 14, 14, -) st, k to 3 st before mA, M1R, k3, smA, k3, M1L, k to 3 st before mB, M1R, k3, smB, k3, M1L, k to 3 st before mC, M1R, k3, smC, k3, M1L, k to 3 st before mD, M1R, k3, smD, k3, M1L, k to end (8 st inc + CO). Cut yarn, leaving a tail. Move ahead to Neckline Join.

SIZE 50/52 ROW 21 (RS): CO - (-, -, -, -, 6) st, k to 3 st before mA, M1R, k3, smA, k3, M1L, k to 3 st before mB, M1R, k3, smB, k3, M1L, k to 3 st before mC, M1R, k3, smC, k3, M1L, k to 3 st before mD, M1R, k3, smD, k3, M1L, k to end (8 st inc + CO).

SIZE 50/52 ROW 22 (WS): CO - (-, -, -, -, 6) st, p to 3 st before m, k3, sm, k3, p to 3 st before m, k3, sm, k3, p to 3 st before m, k3, sm, k3, p to 3 st before m, k3, sm, k3, p to end.

SIZE 50/52 ROW 23 (RS): CO - (-, -, -, -, 14) st, k to 3 st before mA, M1R, k3, smA, k3, M1L, k to 3 st before mB, M1R, k3, smB, k3, M1L, k to 3 st before mC, M1R, k3, smC, k3, M1L, k to 3 st before mD, M1R, k3, smD, k3, M1L, k to end (8 st inc + CO). Cut yarn, leaving a tail. Move ahead to Neckline Join.

NECKLINE JOIN: Rejoin yarn just after mD, leaving a tail to weave in later. This marks the new BOR. Slide the stitches after mD to the left needle so they "meet" with stitches on the other front section (all stitches between mD and mA are now the "front"). P3, k across, joining the front stitches as you reach the gap (be careful not to twist stitches), and continue to k to 3 st before mA, p3, smA, p3, k to 3 st before mB, p3, smB, p3, k to 3 st before mC, p3, smC, p3, k to 3 st before mD, p3.

STITCH COUNT CHECK-IN
FRONT: 56 (64, 74, 76, 76, 86)
SLEEVES (EA): 30 (34, 40, 44, 52, 54)
BACK: 56 (64, 74, 76, 76, 86)

NEXT ROUND (INC): K3, M1L, k to 3 st before mA, M1R, k3, smA, k3, M1L, k to 3 st before mB, M1R, k3, smB, k3, M1L, k to 3 st before mC, m1R, k3, smC, k3, M1L, k to 3 st before mD, m1R, k3 (8 st inc).

NEXT ROUND (NO INC): P3, k to 3 st before mA, p3, smA, p3, k to 3 st before mB, p3, smB, p3, k to 3 st before mC, p3, smC, p3, k to 3 st before mD, p3.

REP these two rounds until you have the following:

STITCH COUNT CHECK-IN
FRONT: 94 (106, 114, 112, 110, 120)
SLEEVES (EA): 68 (76, 80, 80, 86, 88)
BACK: 94 (106, 114, 112, 110, 120)

NEXT ROUND (EXTRA INC): K3, M1L, k2, M1L, k to 5 st before mA, M1R, k2, M1R, k3, smA, k3, M1L, k to 3 st before mB, M1R, k3, smB, k3, M1L, k2, M1L, k to 5 st before mC, M1R, k2, M1R, k3, smC, k3, M1L, k to 3 st before mD, m1R, k3 (12 st inc).

Bayside front view.

NEXT ROUND (NO INC): P3, k to 3 st before mA, p3, smA, p3, k to 3 st before mB, p3, smB, p3, k to 3 st before mC, p3, smC, p3, k to 3 st before mD, p3.

SIZES 30/32, 34/36 Move ahead to Divide for Sleeves.

SIZES 38/40, 42/44, 46/48, 50/52 NEXT ROUND (EXTRA INC): K3, M1L, k2, M1L, k to 5 st before mA, M1R, k2, M1R, k3, smA, k3, M1L, k to 3 st before mB, M1R, k3, smB, k3, M1L, k2, M1L, k to 5 st before mC, M1R, k2, M1R, k3, smC, k3, M1L, k to 3 st before mD, m1R, k3 (12 st inc).

NEXT ROUND (NO INC): P3, k to 3 st before mA, p3, smA, p3, k to 3 st before mB, p3, smB, p3, k to 3 st before mC, p3, smC, p3, k to 3 st before mD, p3.

SIZE 38/40 Move ahead to Divide for Sleeves.

Bayside shoulder and neck detail.

SIZES 42/44, 46/48, 50/52 NEXT ROUND (EXTRA INC): K3, M1L, k2, M1L, k to 5 st before mA, M1R, k2, M1R, k3, smA, k3, M1L, k to 3 st before mB, M1R, k3, smB, k3, M1L, k2, M1L, k to 5 st before mC, M1R, k2, M1R, k3, smC, k3, M1L, k to 3 st before mD, m1R, k3 (12 st inc).

NEXT ROUND (NO INC): P3, k to 3 st before mA, p3, smA, p3, k to 3 st before mB, p3, smB, p3, k to 3 st before mC, p3, smC, p3, k to 3 st before mD, p3.

SIZES 42/44, 46/48, 50/52 NEXT ROUND (DOUBLE EXTRA INC): K3, M1L, k2, M1L, k2, M1L, k to 7 st before mA, M1R, k2, M1R, k2, M1R, k3, smA, k3, M1L, k to 3 st before mB, M1R, k3, smB, k3, M1L, k2, M1L, k2, M1L, k to 7 st before mC, M1R, k2, M1R, k2, M1R, k3, smC, k3, M1L, k to 3 st before mD, m1R, k3 (16 st inc).

NEXT ROUND (NO INC): P3, k to 3 st before mA, p3, smA, p3, k to 3 st before mB, p3, smB, p3, k to 3 st before mC, p3, smC, p3, k to 3 st before mD, p3.

SIZE 42/44 Move ahead to Divide for Sleeves.

SIZES 46/48, 50/52 NEXT ROUND (DOUBLE EXTRA INC): K3, M1L, k2, M1L, k2, M1L, k to 7 st before mA, M1R, k2, M1R, k2, M1R, k3, smA, k3, M1L, k to 3 st before mB, M1R, k3, smB, k3, M1L, k2, M1L, k2, M1L, k to 7 st before mC, M1R, k2, M1R, k2, M1R, k3, smC, k3, M1L, k to 3 st before mD, m1R, k3 (16 st inc).

NEXT ROUND (NO INC): P3, k to 3 st before mA, p3, smA, p3, k to 3 st before mB, p3, smB, p3, k to 3 st before mC, p3, smC, p3, k to 3 st before mD, p3.

SIZES 46/48, 50/52 Repeat the above two rounds, one more time. Then move ahead to Divide for Sleeves.

STITCH COUNT CHECK-IN
FRONT: 98 (110, 122, 130, 140, 150)
SLEEVES (EA): 70 (78, 84, 88, 98, 100)
BACK: 98 (110, 122, 130, 140, 150)

DIVIDE FOR SLEEVES: K across front to mA, rem mA and place sleeve st onto waste yarn (loosely, so you can try it on later). CO 0 (0, 0, 3, 4, 6) st underarm and join to back section, removing mB in the process. K to mC and remove m, place sleeve st onto waste yarn (loosely, so you can try it on later). CO 0 (0, 0, 3, 4, 6) st underarm and join to front. Replace mD at the center of the underarm to denote BOR.

STITCH COUNT CHECK-IN
196 (220, 244, 266, 288, 312) st in lower body

LOWER BODY: Work lower body in the round in stockinette stitch until body measures 12" (30 cm) from sleeve divide. On the next round, work 6 (2, 6, 3, 8, 4) increases using kfb method along the front. Repeat on the back section, increasing another 6 (2, 6, 3, 8, 4) st for a total of 12 (4, 12, 6, 16, 8) stitches increased. You should end with a multiple of 16 for the lower border.

LOWER BORDER ROUND 1: *K7, [ssk, yo] rep bet brackets four times total, k1. Rep from * to end of round.

ROUND 2: *P8, k7, p1; rep from * to end.

ROUNDS 3–8: Repeat rounds 1 and 2.

ROUND 9: *[Yo, k2tog] rep bet brackets four times total, k8. Rep from * to end of round.

ROUND 10: *K8, p8. Rep from * to end.

ROUNDS 11–16: Rep rounds 9 and 10.

REP rounds 1–16 once more. Then, begin the Lower Body series a third time, binding off on round 10 in pattern with medium tension (leaving rounds 11–16 unfinished).

SLEEVES: With U.S. size 5/3.75 mm (12" [30 cm]) circular needle or DPN (or the same size as used for the body), pick up sleeve stitches from waste yarn (including st cast-on under the arm where applicable)—70 (78, 84, 91, 102, 106) st. Pm at center of underarm to mark BOR. Work in the round in stockinette st (knitting every row) for 2" (5 cm).

NEXT ROUND: K2, k2tog, k to 4 st before m, ssk, k2 (2 st dec).

CONTINUE in stockinette st in the round, working a dec round as indicated approximately every 1–1.5 inches (2.5–8 cm) until you have 50 (55, 60, 65, 75, 75) st and sleeve measures approximately 14" (35.5 cm) from underarm. Work an additional dec or so as needed to end with a multiple of 5 for the ribbing. Transition to U.S. size 3/3.25 mm (12" [30 cm]) circular needle or DPN (or needle two sizes smaller than that used for sleeve) and k one last round before beginning ribbing as follows:

NEXT ROUND: Begin cuff ribbing as follows: [k3, p2] rep between brackets to end of round. Continue in established ribbing (repeating [k3, p2] on every round) until cuff measures 5" (12.5 cm). Bind off in pattern with medium tension.

REP for second sleeve.

IS YOUR CUFF TOO TIGHT? Your cuff shouldn't feel tight when you slide your hand through the sleeve of your sweater. If you find that this happens, try binding off a little more loosely by relaxing your grip on your needles and leaving a little more space between each stitch while you bind off. Even if it looks a little sloppy initially, blocking can smooth out the cuff edge and you'll find it easier to slide your sweater off and on without fiddling over an unforgiving cuff.

NECKLINE: With U.S. size 3/3.25 mm (16–24" [40–60 cm]) circular needle, pick up every stitch along the upper shoulders and back, and 7 of every 8 st along the front, ending with a multiple of 5 (adjust as needed for best results). Work in [k3, p2] ribbing in the round on the rs until neckline measures 1.5–2" (3.8–5 cm). Bind off in pattern with medium tension.

WEAVE-IN ends and wet block, pinning flat until dry.

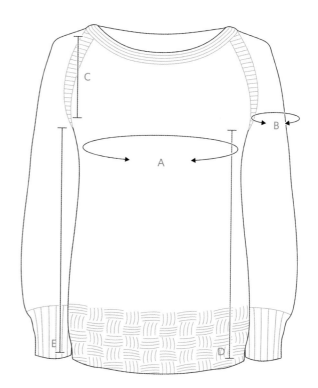

FINISHED MEASUREMENTS

A) BUST:
34.1" (38.3, 42.4, 46.3, 50.1, 54.3) (85.2 cm [95.7, 106.1, 115.7, 125.2, 135.7])

B) SLEEVE AT WIDEST POINT:
12.2" (13.6, 14.6, 15.8, 17.7, 18.4) (30.4 cm [33.9, 36.5, 39.6, 44.3, 46.1])

C) TOP OF SHOULDER TO UNDERARM:
8.8" (9.6, 10.1, 10.6, 11.5, 11.9) (22.35 cm [24.38, 25.74, 26.92, 29.13, 30.14])

D) LENGTH OF BODY FROM UNDERARM:
16" (40.64 cm) prior to sleeve divide

E) LENGTH OF SLEEVE FROM UNDERARM:
19" (48.26 cm) prior to sleeve divide

North Channel Collared Cardigan

There were many incarnations of North Channel before I settled on "the one." Yarn has a mind of its own sometimes, and won't cooperate until you clue-in to what it wants to be. When this version finally came to life on the needles, I was smitten. North Channel features vertical ridges of slipped-stitch ribbing on the front panels, and a wide ribbed collar. Picking up fewer stitches than normal on the front bands works strategically with the slipped-stitch texture to draw the fronts slightly upward, leaving length in back. This flattering, versatile shape is a twist on a standard cardigan.

TIMELINE

North Channel will likely be one of the quicker Binge Knits in this chapter, but the tall collar and slipped-stitch pattern do add a bit of time to the project. Estimate 10 to 12 days if you have ample knitting time available.

Gauge	• 19 st and 25 rows with largest needle over 4" (10 cm) in stockinette st
Notions	• Yarn needle
	• Stitch markers
	• Waste yarn

MATERIALS

Yarn	• DK | Knitted Wit Polwarth Shimmer DK | 85% Polwarth wool, 15% silk | 330 yards (302 m) per 115 g | 1067 yards (1185, 1304, 1434, 1577, 1735) (976 m [1084, 1192, 1311, 1442, 1586])
Yarn Notes	• Worked in hand-dyed, non-superwash Polwarth silk, your sweater should have light drape, medium sheen and relaxed fit. Take care to work your swatch with both colors, and wet block to check color-fastness before you begin.
Needles	• U.S. size 7/4.5 mm (24-32" [60-80 cm]) circular needle (body)
	• U.S. size 7/4.5 mm (12" [30 cm]) circular needle or DPN (sleeves)
	• U.S. size 6/4 mm (24-32" [60-80 cm]) circular needle (lower body ribbing/neck ribbing)
	• U.S. size 5/3.75 mm (24-32" [60-80 cm]) circular needle (front ribbing)
	• U.S. size 5/3.75 mm (12" [30 cm]) circular needle or DPN (sleeve cuff)
	• Note: Use needle size necessary to obtain gauge.

STITCH GLOSSARY

bet	between
BOR	beginning of round/row
CO	cast on
dec	decrease
ea	each
inc	increase
k	knit
k2tog	knit 2 st at once (dec 1)
kfb	knit into front and back of st (inc 1)
m	marker/markers
M1L	make one st that leans left (inc 1)
M1R	make one st that leans right (inc 1)
mX	marker "X" indicates which marker (i.e, mA, mB, mC, etc.)
p	purl

(continued)

STITCH GLOSSARY

pmX	place marker, "X" indicates which marker (i.e, mA, mB, mC, etc.)
rem m	remove marker
rep	repeat
rs	right side
sl	slip
sm	slip marker/markers
smX	slip marker, "X" indicates which marker (i.e, smA, smB, smC, etc.)
ssk	slip, slip, knit together (dec 1)
st	stitch/stitches
ws	wrong side
wyif	with yarn in front
[ ]	brackets always indicate a repeat

SIZES

Bust sizes 30/32" (34/36, 38/40, 42/44, 46/48, 50/52) (76/81 cm [86/91, 97/102, 107/112, 117/122, 127/132])

RECOMMENDED EASE

Positive ease is included for a comfortable fit. See finished measurements for final ease as compared to your actual bust measurement. If you are between sizes, refer to the final measurements to determine which size to choose. In many cases you'll find that the smaller of the two sizes will be best.

CONSTRUCTION

North Channel is worked flat from top to bottom with subtle neck shaping in the early set-up rows. Front bands and sleeves are worked next, with the wide ribbed collar worked last.

NOTE: Rows apply to all sizes unless otherwise indicated. Be sure to read ahead and mark sections that are specific to your size before you begin.

QUICK TIP: If the upward angle of the front panels doesn't suit your style, simply pick up more stitches along the button band and the front sections will lay straight.

NORTH CHANNEL PATTERN

With U.S. size 7/4.5 mm (24–32" [60–80 cm]) circular needle and MC, cast on 32 (42, 64, 76, 80, 90) st using cable cast-on method. Do not join.

ROW 1 – SET UP ROW (RS): K2, pmA, kfb, k0 (2, 8, 12, 14, 16), kfb, pmB, kfb, k22 (28, 38, 42, 42, 48), kfb, pmC, kfb, k0 (2, 8, 12, 14, 16), kfb, pmD, k2 (6 st inc).

ROW 2 (WS): P across, slipping m as you go.

SIZE 30/32 ONLY ROW 3 (RS): K2, smA, K1, M1L, k2, M1R, k1, smB, k2, M1L, k to 2 st before mC, M1R, k2, smC, k1, M1L, k 2, M1R, k1, smD, k2 (6 st inc).

SIZES 34/36, 38/40, 42/44, 46/48, 50/52 ROW 3 (RS): K2, smA, k2, M1L, k to 2 st before mB, M1R, k2, smB, k2, M1L, k to 2 st before mC, M1R, k2, smC, k2, M1L, k to 2 st before mD, M1R, k2, smD, k2 (6 st inc).

ALL SIZES continue.

ROW 4 (WS): P across, slipping m as you go.

ROW 5 (RS): K1, M1R, k1, smA, k2, M1L, k to 2 st before mB, M1R, k2, smB, k2, M1L, k to 2 st before mC, M1R, k2, smC, k2, M1L, k to 2 st before mD, M1R, k2, smD, k1, M1L, k to end (8 st inc).

ROW 6 (WS): P across, slipping m as you go.

ROW 7 (RS): CO 0 (0, 0, 0, 0, 1) st using knitted cast-on worked tightly*, k to 2 st before mA, M1R, k2, smA, k2, M1L, k to 2 st before mB, M1R, k2, smB, k2, M1L, k to 2 st before mC, M1R, k2, smC, k2, M1L, k to 2 st before mD, M1R, k2, smD, k2, M1L, k to end (8 st inc + cast on).

ROW 8 (WS): CO 0 (0, 0, 0, 0, 1) st using knitted cast-on worked purlwise*, p across (including newly cast-on st), slipping m as you go.

ROW 9 (RS): CO 0 (1, 1, 1, 1, 1) st using knitted cast-on worked tightly, k to 2 st before mA, M1R, k2, smA, k2, M1L, k to 2 st before mB, M1R, k2, smB, k2, M1L, k to 2 st before mC, M1R, k2, smC, k2, M1L, k to 2 st before mD, M1R, k2, smD, k2, M1L, k to end (8 st inc + cast on).

ROW 10 (WS): CO 0 (1, 1, 1, 1, 1) st using knitted cast-on worked purlwise, p across (including newly cast-on st), slipping m as you go.

STITCH COUNT CHECK-IN

FRONTS (EA): 5 (6, 6, 6, 6, 7)
SLEEVES (EA): 12 (14, 20, 24, 26, 28)
BACK: 34 (40, 50, 54, 54, 60)

*GOING FORWARD, all stitches cast-on on the right side will be worked using the knitted cast-on method, and all stitches cast-on on the wrong side will be worked using the knitted cast-on worked purlwise. Always knit the new stitch/es on the right side and purl the new stitch/es on the wrong side as you work through the rows.

ROW 11 (RS): CO 0 (1, 2, 2, 2, 2) st, k to 2 st before mA, M1R, k2, smA, k2, M1L, k to 2 st before mB, M1R, k2, smB, k2, M1L, k to 2 st before mC, M1R, k2, smC, k2, M1L, k to 2 st before mD, M1R, k2, smD, k2, M1L, k to end (8 st inc + cast on).

ROW 12 (WS): CO 0 (1, 2, 2, 2, 2) st and p across, slipping m as you go.

ROW 13 (RS): CO 1 (1, 2, 2, 2, 4) st, k to 2 st before mA, M1R, k2, smA, k2, M1L, k to 2 st before mB, M1R, k2, smB, k2, M1L, k to 2 st before mC, M1R, k2, smC, k2, M1L, k to 2 st before mD, M1R, k2, smD, k2, M1L, k to end (8 st inc + cast on).

North Channel neck and front detail.

ROW 14 (WS): CO 1 (1, 2, 2, 2, 4) st and p across, slipping m as you go.

ROW 15 (RS): CO 1 (2, 4, 4, 4, 4) st, k to 2 st before mA, M1R, k2, smA, k2, M1L, k to 2 st before mB, M1R, k2, smB, k2, M1L, k to 2 st before mC, M1R, k2, smC, k2, M1L, k to 2 st before mD, M1R, k2, smD, k2, M1L, k to end (8 st inc + cast on).

ROW 16 (WS): CO 1 (2, 4, 4, 4, 4) st and p across, slipping m as you go.

ROW 17 (RS): CO 4 (4, 4, 6, 6, 6) st, k to 2 st before mA, M1R, k2, smA, k2, M1L, k to 2 st before mB, M1R, k2, smB, k2, M1L, k to 2 st before mC, M1R, k2, smC, k2, M1L, k to 2 st before mD, M1R, k2, smD, k2, M1L, k to end (8 st inc + cast on).

North Channel back and shoulder view.

ROW 18 (WS): CO 4 (4, 4, 6, 6, 6) st and p across, slipping m as you go.

ROW 19 (RS): CO 18 (19, 19, 19, 19, 20) st, k to 2 st before mA, M1R, k2, smA, k2, M1L, k to 2 st before mB, M1R, k2, smB, k2, M1L, k to 2 st before mC, M1R, k2, smC, k2, M1L, k to 2 st before mD, M1R, k2, smD, k2, M1L, k to end (8 st inc + cast on).

ROW 20 (WS): CO 18 (19, 19, 19, 19, 20) st, and p across row, slipping m as you go.

STITCH COUNT CHECK-IN

FRONTS (EA): 34 (38, 42, 44, 44, 48)
SLEEVES (EA): 22 (24, 30, 34, 36, 38)
BACK: 44 (50, 60, 64, 64, 70)

NEXT ROW (INC) RS: K4*, [sl2wyif, k4] rep bet brackets three times total, pmE, then k to 2 st before mA, M1R, k2, smA, k2, M1L, k to 2 st before mB, M1R, k2, smB, k2, M1L, k to 2 st before mC, M1R, k2, smC, k2, M1L, k to 2 st before mD, M1R, k2, smD, k2, M1L, k to 22 st before end, pmF, k4, [sl2wyif, k4] rep bet brackets to end (8 st inc).

NEXT ROW (WS): K1*, sl2wyif, k1, [k3, sl2wyif, k1] rep bet brackets to next m, sm, p to last m (slipping m as you go), then k1, sl2wyif, k1, [k3, sl2wyif, k1] rep bet brackets to end.

TIP:* Pull the first st of each row very tight after you've knit it, before you work across the rest of the row. This will help maintain even tension at the front edge and will make it tidier and easier to pick up your button band later.

REP these two rows until you have the following number of stitches:

STITCH COUNT CHECK-IN

FRONTS (EA): 50 (55, 59, 61, 60, 64)
SLEEVES (EA): 54 (58, 64, 68, 68, 70)
BACK: 76 (84, 94, 98, 96, 102)

NEXT ROW (EXTRA INC) RS: K4, [sl2wyif, k4] rep bet brackets three times, smE, k to 4 st before mA, M1R, k2, M1R, k2, smA, k2, M1L, k to 2 st before mB, M1R, k2, smB, k2, M1L, k2, M1L, k to 4 st before mC, M1R, k2, M1R, k2, smC, k2, M1L, k to 2 st before mD, M1R, k2, smD, k2, M1L, k2, M1L, k to mF, smF, k4, [sl2wyif, k4] rep bet brackets to end (12 st inc).

NEXT ROW (WS): Maintain rib texture as established over the first 22 and last 22 st, and p remainder of row, slipping m as you go.

REP these two rows 0 (0, 0, 0, 1, 1) more times. You should have the following number of stitches:

FRONTS (EA): 52 (57, 61, 63, 64, 68)
SLEEVES (EA): 56 (60, 66, 70, 72, 74)
BACK: 80 (88, 98, 102, 104, 110)

SIZES 30/32, 34/36, 38/40 Move ahead to Divide for Sleeves.

SIZES 42/44, 46/48, 50/52 NEXT ROW (DOUBLE EXTRA INC) RS: K4, [sl2wyif, k4] rep bet brackets three times, smE, k to 6 st before mA, M1R, k2, M1R, k2, M1R, k2, smA, k2, M1L, k to 2 st before mB, M1R, k2, smB, k2, M1L, k2, M1L, k2, M1L, k to 6 st before mC, M1R, k2, M1R, k2, M1R, k2, smC, k2, M1L, k to 2 st before mD, M1R, k2, smD, k2, M1L, k2, M1L, k2, M1L, k to mF, smF, k4, [sl2wyif, k4] rep bet brackets to end (16 st inc).

NEXT ROW (WS): Maintain rib texture as established over the first 22 and last 22 st, and p remainder of row, slipping m as you go.

SIZES 42/44, 46/48, 50/52 Rep the above two rows - (-, -, 0, 1, 1) times, then move ahead to Divide for Sleeves.

STITCH COUNT CHECK-IN

FRONTS (EA): 52 (57, 61, 66, 70, 74)
SLEEVES (EA): 56 (60, 66, 72, 76, 78)
BACK: 80 (88, 98, 108, 116, 122)

NOTE: Maintain the slipped rib texture on both fronts down the remainder of the body until stated otherwise. Remember to continue to pull the first st tight after working it at the beginning of each row (on the rs and the ws).

DIVIDE FOR SLEEVES: Work in pattern to mA, rem mA and place sleeve stitches onto waste yarn (loosely, so you can try it on later). CO 2 (2, 2, 2, 4, 6) st at the underarm and join to back section, removing mB in the process and replacing it at the center of the underarm. K to mC and rem mC, place sleeve stitches onto waste yarn (loosely, so you can try it on later). CO 2 (2, 2, 2, 4, 6) st at the underarm and join to front, removing mD in the process and replacing it at the center of the underarm (in the center of the newly cast-on st), k to end.

STITCH COUNT CHECK-IN

188 (206, 224, 244, 264, 282) st in lower body

LOWER BODY: Work the lower body in stockinette st with slipped rib panels down both fronts (as established) until body measures 12.5" (31.75 cm) from underarm. Transition to needle one size smaller on next ws row and purl this row on the smaller needle. At the same time, inc 2 (2, 2, 0, 4, 4) st somewhat evenly using kfb to end with a multiple of 6 + 4 (it will seem noticeable at first, but will disappear into the texture on the next row).

LOWER TEXTURE (RS): [K4, sl2wyif] rep bet brackets to last six st, k4.

LOWER TEXTURE (WS): K1, sl2wyif, k1 [k3, sl2wyif, k1] rep bet brackets to end.

REP these two rows until lower border measures 2.5" (6.4 cm). Bind off with medium tension in pattern. Bottom edge should not feel tight and restrictive. If it does, bind off more loosely.

SLEEVES: With U.S. size 7/4.5 mm (12" [30 cm]) circular needle or DPN (or the same size as used for the body), pick up sleeve st from waste yarn as well as st cast-on under the arm—58 (62, 68, 74, 80, 84) st. Pm at center of underarm to mark BOR. Continue in the round in stockinette st for 2" (5 cm).

DEC ROUND: K2, k2tog, k to 4 st before m, ssk, k2 (2 st dec).

CONTINUE sleeve in stockinette st in the round, working a dec round as indicated above approximately every 1.5–2" (3.8–5 cm) until sleeve measures approximately 18" (46 cm) from underarm, and you have the following number of stitches: 36 (42, 48, 48, 54, 60). On the last round, transition to U.S. size 5/3.75 mm (12" [30 cm]) circular needle (or two sizes smaller than used for sleeve/body) for cuff and begin ribbing as follows: [k4, p2] rep between brackets to end of round. Continue in established ribbing (repeating [k4, p2] on every round) until cuff measures 3" (7.6 cm). Bind off in pattern with medium tension—cuff should not be restrictive. If it is, bind off more loosely.

REP for second sleeve.

FRONT BANDS (TO BE WORKED BEFORE THE COLLAR): With U.S. size 5/3.75 mm (24-32" [60-80 cm]) and starting at the right front lower edge of the sweater on the rs (starting at the bottom edge, working toward the top), pick up roughly 5 of every 6 st along the front edge, ending up with a multiple of 4 + 2 for the ribbing. Refer to page 162 for button band tips and tricks. Work in [k2, p2] ribbing, ending k2 on the rs, and [p2, k2] ribbing, ending p2 on the ws and rep bet brackets until band measures 1-1.5" (2.5-3.8 cm). Bind off in pattern with medium tension. Rep for the left front, starting at the top of the sweater on the rs and working downward. Note: Try adjusting the look of your cardigan by adjusting the number of stitches you pick up. Fewer stitches will draw the bands upward, while picking up more stitches will extend the fronts so they align with the length of the back.

NECKLINE: With U.S. size 6/4 mm (24-32" [60-80 cm]) circular needle (or one size smaller than used for body), pick up a multiple of 4 + 2 st around the top edge of front bands and neckline. Work the upper portion in [k2, p2] ribbing, ending k2, until collar measures 7" (18 cm), then bind off in pattern with medium tension.

WEAVE-IN ends and wet block, soaking thoroughly, then rinse well. Pin flat and allow to dry completely, turning as needed for even drying.

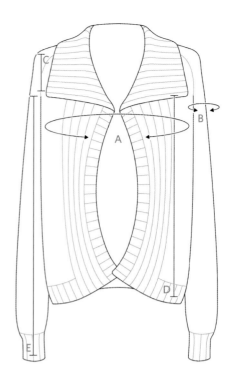

FINISHED MEASUREMENTS

A) BUST:
43.4" (47.2, 51, 55.2, 60.3, 64.9) (108.7 cm [118.1, 127.6, 138.1, 150.8, 162.4])

B) SLEEVE AT WIDEST POINT:
12.2" (13.1, 14.3, 15.6, 16.8, 17.7) (30.5 cm [32.6, 35.8, 38.9, 42.1, 44.2])

C) TOP OF SHOULDER TO UNDERARM:
9.28" (9.76, 10.24, 10.88, 11.68, 12.16) (23.57 cm [24.79, 26.01, 27.64, 29.67, 30.89])

D) LENGTH OF BODY FROM UNDERARM:
15" (38.1 cm)

E) LENGTH OF SLEEVE FROM UNDERARM:
21" (53.34 cm)

Give me minimalism with simple, dramatic details any day of the week. The Scandinavian-inspired texture on Riverbank carves a striking visual into the front of this sweater; it's quite captivating when you look up close. As soon as this one was off the needles I found myself daydreaming about how I'd wear it, and I still can't get enough of the tactile combination of bouncy Targhee wool and plush cables. The versatile cropped length makes for easy layering as well, so you can dress it up or down according to your mood.

TIMELINE

In spite of the shorter length and sleeves, the slightly lighter weight yarn and rich details—like the front cable chart and twisted ribbing—add a little extra time. You may need to refer to the pattern a little more often to make sure your front panel design stays on target. Give yourself 9 to 12 days for this one.

MATERIALS

Yarn	• DK | Brooklyn Tweed Arbor | 100% domestic Targhee wool | 145 yards (133 m) per 50 g | 713 yards (792, 880, 968, 1084, 1214) (652 m [724, 805, 885, 991, 1110])
Yarn Notes	• The recommended yarn is a hearty Targhee wool with bouncy twist and excellent stitch definition. The non-superwash qualities of the yarn will help the sweater maintain its shape. The desired fabric should be soft with medium density and minimal drape.
Needles	• U.S. size 6/4 mm (24-32" [60-80 cm]) circular needle (body) • U.S. size 5/3.75 mm (24-32" [60-80 cm]) circular needle (lower body ribbing) • U.S. size 6/4 mm (12" [30 cm]) circular needle or DPN (sleeves) • U.S. size 4/3.5 mm (24" [60 cm]) circular needle (neck ribbing) • U.S. size 4/3.5 mm (12" [30 cm]) circular needle or DPN (sleeve cuff) • Note: Use needle size necessary to obtain gauge.

Gauge	• 20 st and 28 rows with larger needle over 4" (10 cm) in stockinette stitch
Notions	• Yarn needle • Stitch markers • Waste yarn • Cable needle

STITCH GLOSSARY

bet	between
BOR	beginning of round/row
CO	cast on
dec	decrease
ea	each
inc	increase
k	knit
k2tog	knit 2 st at once (dec 1)
kfb	knit into front and back of st (inc 1)
ktbl	knit through the back loop of the stitch (twisted k st)
m	marker/markers
mX	marker "X" indicates which marker (i.e, mA, mB, mC, etc.)
M1L	make one st that leans left (inc 1)

(continued)

M1R	make one st that leans right (inc 1)
p	purl
pmX	place marker, "X" indicates which marker (i.e, pmA, pmB, pmC, etc.)
rem m	remove marker
rep	repeat
rs	right side
sm	slip marker/markers
smX	slip marker, "X" indicates which marker (i.e, smA, smB, smC, etc.)
ssk	slip, slip, knit together (dec 1)
st	stitch/stitches
ws	wrong side
[ ]	brackets always indicate a repeat

SIZES

Bust sizes 30/32" (34/36, 38/40, 42/44, 46/48, 50/52) (76/81 cm [86/91, 97/102, 107/112, 117/122, 127/132])

RECOMMENDED EASE

Positive ease is included for a comfortable fit. See finished measurements for final ease as compared to your actual bust measurement. If you are between sizes, refer to the final measurements to determine which size to choose. In many cases you'll find that the smaller of the two sizes will be the best choice.

CONSTRUCTION

Riverbank is worked flat until the neckline shaping is complete, then joined and worked in the round from there. The front panel features a repetitive figure-eight cable against a trail of garter stitch. The texture is deceptively easy to work without constant focus on the pattern, but you'd never know it to look at the finished piece. The neckline and sleeves are worked last.

NOTE: Rows and rounds apply to all sizes unless otherwise indicated. Be sure to read ahead and mark sections that are specific to your size before you begin.

QUICK TIP: Stitch definition plays an important role in this design. Yarn substitutions and busy colorways may detract from the overall effect, so use caution when choosing alternatives.

RIVERBANK PATTERN

With U.S. size 6/4 mm (24-32" [60-80 cm]) circular needle (or size to obtain gauge), cast on 30 (46, 72, 80, 88, 98) st using cable cast-on method. Do not join.

ROW 1 – SET UP (RS): K2, pmA, kfb, k0 (4, 12, 14, 18, 20), kfb, pmB, kfb, k20 (28, 38, 42, 42, 48), kfb, pmC, kfb, k0 (4, 12, 14, 18, 20), kfb, pmD, k2 (6 st inc).

ROW 2 (WS): P across, slipping m as you go.

SIZE 30/32 ONLY ROW 3 (RS): K2, smA, p1, M1L, k2, M1R, p1, smB, p1, M1L, k to 1 st before mC, M1R, p1, smC, p1, M1L, k2, M1R, p1, smD, k2 (6 st inc).

SIZES 34/36, 38/40, 42/44, 46/48, 50/52 ROW 3 (RS): K2, smA, p1, M1L, k to 1 st before mB, M1R, p1, smB, p1, M1L, k to 1 st before mC, M1R, p1, smC, p1, M1L, k to 1 st before mD, M1R, p1, smD, k2 (6 st inc).

ALL SIZES continue.

ROW 4 (WS): K the knits (on either side of the raglan m), p the purls, slipping m as you go.

ROW 5 (RS): K to 1 st before mA, M1R, p1, smA, p1, M1L, k to 1 st before mB, M1R, p1, smB, p1, M1L, k to 1 st before mC, M1R, p1, smC, p1, M1L, k to 1 st before mD, M1R, p1, smD, p1, M1L, k to end (8 st inc).

ROW 6 (WS): Rep row 4.

REP these two rows 3 (2, 1, 1, 1, 1) times more.

STITCH COUNT CHECK-IN

FRONTS (EA): 6 (5, 4, 4, 4, 4)
SLEEVES (EA): 14 (16, 22, 24, 28, 30)
BACK: 34 (40, 48, 52, 52, 58)

NEXT ROW (RS): CO 2 st using knitted cast-on worked tightly*, k new st and k to 1 st before mA, M1R, p1, smA, p1, M1L, k to 1 st before mB, M1R, p1, smB, p1, M1L, k to 1 st before mC, M1R, p1, smC, p1, M1L, k to 1 st before mD, M1R, p1, smD, p1, M1L, k to end (8 st inc + CO).

NEXT ROW (WS): CO 2 st using knitted cast-on worked purlwise*, then work across row in pattern (p the purls, k the knits), slipping m as you go.

*GOING FORWARD, all stitches cast-on on the right side will be worked using the knitted cast-on method, and all stitches cast-on on the wrong side will be worked using the knitted cast-on worked purlwise. Always knit the new stitch/es on the right side and purl the new stitch/es on the wrong side as you work through the row.

REP rows 5 and 6 one time more.

STITCH COUNT CHECK-IN

FRONTS (EA): 12 (11, 10, 10, 10, 10)
SLEEVES (EA): 18 (20, 26, 28, 32, 34)
BACK: 38 (44, 52, 56, 56, 62)

NEXT ROW (RS): CO 4 st, k new st and k to 1 st before mA, p1, smA, p1, M1L, k to 1 st before mB, M1R, p1, smB, p1, M1L, k to 1 st before mC, M1R, p1, smC, p1, M1L, k to 1 st before mD, M1R, p1, smD, p1, M1L, k to end (8 st inc + CO).

NEXT ROW (WS): CO 4 st, then work across row in pattern (p the purls, k the knits), slipping m as you go.

REP these two rows 0 (1, 2, 1, 1, 0) times more.

STITCH COUNT CHECK-IN

FRONTS (EA): 17 (21, 25, 20, 20, 15)
SLEEVES (EA): 20 (24, 32, 32, 36, 36)
BACK: 40 (48, 58, 60, 60, 64)

SIZES 30/32, 34/36, 38/40 Move ahead to Neckline Join.

SIZES 42/44, 46/48, 50/52 NEXT ROW (RS): CO - (-, -, 6, 6, 6) st, k new st and k to 1 st before mA, M1R, p1, smA, p1, M1L, k to 1 st before mB, M1R, p1, smB, p1, M1L, k to 1 st before mC, M1R, p1, smC, p1, M1L, k to 1 st before mD, M1R, p1, smD, p1, M1L, k to end (8 st inc + CO).

SIZES 42/44, 46/48, 50/52 NEXT ROW (WS): CO - (-, -, 6, 6, 6) st, then work across row in pattern (p the purls, k the knits), slipping m as you go.

SIZES 42/44, 46/48 Move ahead to Neckline Join.

SIZE 50/52 NEXT ROW (RS): CO - (-, -, -, -, 6) st, k new st and k to 1 st before mA, M1R, p1, smA, p1, M1L, k to 1 st before mB, M1R, p1, smB, p1, M1L, k to 1 st before mC, M1R, p1, smC, p1, M1L, k to 1 st before mD, M1R, p1, smD, p1, M1L, k to end (8 st inc + CO).

SIZE 50/52 NEXT ROW (WS): CO - (-, -, -, -, 6) st, then work across row in pattern (p the purls, k the knits), slipping m as you go.

NECKLINE JOIN: CO 8 (10, 12, 12, 12, 14) st, k new st and k to 1 st before mA, M1R, p1, smA, p1, M1L, k to 1 st before mB, M1R, p1, smB, p1, M1L, k to 1 st before mC, M1R, p1, smC, p1, M1L, k to 1 st before mD, M1R, p1, smD, p1, M1L, k to end (8 st inc + CO). Cut yarn, leaving a tail.

REJOIN yarn just after mD, leaving a tail to weave in later. This marks the new BOR. Slide the stitches after mD to the left needle so they "meet" with the other stitches on the front section (all stitches between mD and mA are now the "front"). K across, joining the front stitches as you reach the gap (be careful not to twist stitches) and knit to end of round.

STITCH COUNT CHECK-IN

FRONT: 44 (54, 64, 68, 68, 74)
SLEEVES (EA): 22 (26, 34, 36, 40, 42)
BACK: 42 (50, 60, 64, 64, 70)

NEXT ROUND (INC): P1, M1L, k to 1 st before mA, M1R, p1, smA, p1, M1L, k to 1 st before mB, M1R, p1, smB, p1, M1L, k to 1 st before mC, M1R, p1, smC, p1, M1L, k to 1 st before mD, M1R, p1 (8 st inc).

NEXT ROUND (NO INC): P1, k to 1 st before mA, p1, smA, p1, k to 1 st before mB, p1, smB, p1, k to 1 st before mC, p1, smC, p1, k to 1 st before mD, p1.

NEXT ROUND (INC): P1, M1L, k7 (12, 17, 19, 19, 22), pmE, work Center Panel starting with round 1 (in subsequent rounds, rep chart rounds in order down the front of the body), pmF, k7 (12, 17, 19, 19, 22), M1R, p1, smA, p1, M1L, k to 1 st before mB, M1R, p1, smB, p1, M1L, k to 1 st before mC, M1R, p1, smC, p1, M1L, k to 1 st before mD, M1R, p1 (8 st inc).

NEXT ROUND (NO INC): P1, k to mE, smE, work Center Panel next round, smF, k to 1 st before mA, p1, smA, p1, k to 1 st before mB, p1, smB, p1, k to 1 st before mC, p1, smC, p1, k to 1 st before mD, p1.

NEXT ROUND (INC): P1, M1L, k to mE, smE, work Center Panel next round, smF, k to 1 st before mA, M1R, p1, smA, p1, M1L, k to 1 st before mB, M1R, p1, smB, p1, M1L, k to 1 st before mC, M1R, p1, smC, p1, M1L, k to 1 st before mD, M1R, p1 (8 st inc).

NEXT ROUND (NO INC): P1, k to mE, smE, work Center Panel next round, smF, k to 1 st before mA, p1, smA, p1, k to 1 st before mB, p1, smB, p1, k to 1 st before mC, p1, smC, p1, k to 1 st before mD, p1.

REP the above two rounds until you reach the following:

STITCH COUNT CHECK-IN

FRONT: 74 (86, 96, 100, 100, 104)
SLEEVES (EA): 52 (58, 66, 68, 72, 72)
BACK: 72 (82, 92, 96, 96, 100)

NEXT ROUND (EXTRA INC): P1, M1L, k2, M1L, k to mE, smE, work Center Panel next round, smF, k to 3 st before mA, M1R, k2, M1R, p1, smA, p1, M1L, k to 1 st before mB, M1R, p1, smB, p1, M1L, k2, M1L, k to 3 st before mC, M1R, k2, M1R, p1, smC, p1, M1L, k to 1 st before mD, M1R, p1 (12 st inc).

NEXT ROUND (NO INC): P1, k to mE, smE, work Center Panel next round, smF, k to 1 st before mA, p1, smA, p1, k to 1 st before mB, p1, smB, p1, k to 1 st before mC, p1, smC, p1, k to 1 st before mD, p1.

REP the above two rounds one time more (12 more st inc).

SIZES 30/32, 34/36, 38/40 Move ahead to Divide for Sleeves.

SIZES 42/44, 46/48, 50/52 NEXT ROUND (DOUBLE EXTRA INC): P1, M1L, k2, M1L, k2, M1L, k to mE, smE, work Center Panel next round, smF, k to 5 st before mA, M1R, k2, M1R, k2, M1R, p1, smA, p1, M1L, k to 1 st before mB, M1R, p1, smB, p1, M1L, k2, M1L, k2, M1L, k to 5 st before mC, M1R, k2, M1R, k2, M1R, p1, smC, p1, M1L, k to 1 st before mD, M1R, p1 (16 st inc).

Riverbank back view.

SIZES 42/44, 46/48, 50/52 NEXT ROUND (NO INC): P1, k to mE, smE, work Center Panel next round, smF, k to 1 st before mA, p1, smA, p1, k to 1 st before mB, p1, smB, p1, k to 1 st before mC, p1, smC, p1, k to 1 st before mD, p1.

SIZE 42/44 Move ahead to Divide for Sleeves.

SIZES 46/48, 50/52 Rep the above two rounds - (-, -, -, 1, 2) times more. Then move ahead to Divide for Sleeves.

STITCH COUNT CHECK-IN

FRONT: 82 (94, 104, 114, 120, 130)
SLEEVES (EA): 56 (62, 70, 74, 80, 82)
BACK: 80 (90, 100, 110, 116, 126)

DIVIDE FOR SLEEVES: K across front to mA (maintaining Center Panel as established), rem mA and place sleeve stitches onto waste yarn (loosely, so you can try it on later). CO 4 (4, 4, 4, 4, 6) st underarm and join to back section, removing mB in the process. K to mC and rem mC, place sleeve stitches onto waste yarn (loosely, so you can try it on later). CO 4 (4, 4, 4, 4, 6) st underarm and join to front, removing mD in the process. Replace mD at the center of the underarm (in the center of the newly cast-on st)—mD now denotes BOR.

Riverbank front view.

STITCH COUNT CHECK-IN

170 (192, 212, 232, 244, 268) st in lower body

LOWER BODY: Knit the lower body in stockinette st in the round (no inc), maintaining the Center Panel down the front as established until body measures 12.5" (32 cm) from underarm. Transition to U.S. size 5/3.75 mm (24–32" [60–80 cm]) circular needle (or needle one size smaller than that used for the body) and k one round. At the same time, dec 2 (0, 0, 0, 0, 0) st somewhat evenly using k2tog to end with a multiple of 4. Begin lower ribbing as follows: [p3, ktbl] rep bet brackets to end of round. Rep this round until ribbing measures 2.5" (6.4 cm). Bind off with medium/loose tension in pattern, but do not twist the k st, simply k them through the front loop when binding off (twisting them can make the bind-off edge too restrictive).

SLEEVES: With U.S. size 6/4 mm (12" [30 cm]) circular needle or DPN (or the same size as used for the body), pick up sleeve stitches from waste yarn (including st cast-on under the arm) — 60 (66, 74, 78, 84, 88) st. Pm at center of underarm to mark BOR. Knit sleeve in the round in stockinette st for 2" (5 cm).

DEC ROUND: K2, k2tog, k to 4 st before m, ssk, k2 (2 st dec).

WORK a dec round as indicated approximately every 2" (5 cm) until sleeve measures approximately 12" (30 cm) from underarm, and you have the following: 48 (48, 48, 56, 64, 68) st. On the last round, transition to U.S. size 4/3.5 mm (12" [30 cm]) circular needle— or two sizes smaller than used for sleeve/body—and work the last round. Begin ribbing on the next round as follows: [p3, ktbl] rep between brackets to end of round. Continue in established ribbing until cuff measures 3" (7.6 cm). Bind off in pattern with medium tension. Cuff should not feel restrictive. If it is, bind off more loosely.

REP for second sleeve.

NECKLINE: With U.S. size 4/3.5 mm (24" [60 cm])—or needle two sizes smaller than that used for the body—pick up stitches around the neckline in the following manner: Pick up every available stitch along the shoulders and back, and approximately 7 of every 8 st along the front, ending with a multiple of 3. Adjust as needed for best results. Work neckline in [p2, ktbl] ribbing (rep bet brackets) in the round until neck ribbing measures 1.5" (3.8 cm). Bind off in pattern with medium tension.

WEAVE-IN ends and wet block, soaking thoroughly, then rinse well. Pin flat and allow to dry completely, turning as needed for even drying.

CENTER PANEL DIRECTIONS

ROUND 1: K5, p6, k8, p6, k5.
ROUND 2: K5, p2, c8b, c8f, p2, k5.
ROUND 3: P7, k4, p8, k4, p7.
ROUND 4: K5, p2, k16, p2, k5.
ROUND 5: P7, k4, p8, k4, p7.
ROUND 6: K5, p2, k16, p2, k5.
ROUND 7: P7, k4, p8, k4, p7.
ROUND 8: K5, p2, k16, p2, k5.
ROUND 9: P7, k4, p8, k4, p7.
ROUND 10: K5, p2, k16, p2, k5.
ROUND 11: P7, k4, p8, k4, p7.
ROUND 12: K5, p2, k16, p2, k5.
ROUND 13: P7, k4, p8, k4, p7.
ROUND 14: K5, p2, k16, p2, k5.
ROUND 15: K5, p2, c8fp, c8bp, p2, k5.
ROUND 16: K5, p6, k8, p6, k5.
ROUND 17: K5, p6, c8f, p6, k5.

CENTER PANEL CHART

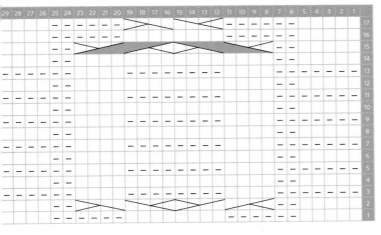

FINISHED MEASUREMENTS

A) BUST:
34" (38.4, 42.4, 46.4, 48.8, 53.6) (85 cm [96, 106, 116, 124, 134])

B) SLEEVE AT WIDEST POINT:
12" (13.2, 14.8, 15.6, 16.8, 17.6) (30 cm [33, 37, 39, 42, 44])

C) TOP OF SHOULDER TO UNDERARM:
8.6" (9.1, 9.7, 10.1, 10.7, 11.1) (21.77 cm [23.22, 24.67, 25.76, 27.21, 28.30])

D) LENGTH OF BODY FROM UNDERARM:
15" (38.1 cm)

E) LENGTH OF SLEEVE FROM UNDERARM:
15" (38.1 cm)

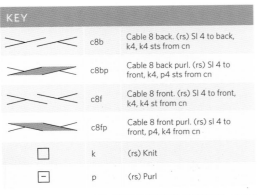

KEY		
⧓	c8b	Cable 8 back. (rs) Sl 4 to back, k4, k4 sts from cn
⧓	c8bp	Cable 8 back purl. (rs) Sl 4 to front, k4, p4 sts from cn
⧓	c8f	Cable 8 front. (rs) Sl 4 to front, k4, k4 st from cn
⧓	c8fp	Cable 8 front purl. (rs) sl 4 to front, p4, k4 from cn
☐	k	(rs) Knit
−	p	(rs) Purl

Basic Techniques

TOOLS FOR SWEATER SUCCESS

CASTING ON

Cable Cast-On

I nearly always use the cable cast-on as the starting point for a top-down sweater. It creates a stable, sturdy edge for the neckline, and is easy to pick up later. Unlike other cast-on methods that start you off working the wrong side first, the cable cast-on method will allow you to begin working on the right side as soon as you finish casting on.

To work this method, begin by casting on 2 stitches using the knitted cast-on method, right. Next, insert your right needle between the two stitches on the left needle (Step 1), wrap the working yarn around the right needle and draw it through the center of the two stitches, draw it out a bit (Step 2) and slide this new stitch over the left needle (Step 3). Repeat this process until you have cast on the appropriate number of stitches.

Knitted Cast-On (Knitwise)

I like to use the knitted cast-on because this method is a bit less bulky and makes for a smoother pick up along the front neckline. To work this method, simply knit into the first stitch—but don't slide the stitch off the needle—and draw the working yarn out slightly. Slide the new stitch back onto the left needle and pull it snug. Repeat this process, always knitting into the newest stitch to create the next stitch. When you've finished casting on the appropriate number of new stitches, knit across them or work them in the pattern as indicated, and continue across the row.

Step 1

Step 2

Step 3

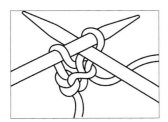

Step 1

Step 2

Step 3

Knitted Cast-On (Purlwise)

When working the knitted cast-on from the wrong side, purl into the first stitch on your left needle and draw the working yarn out slightly. Slide the new stitch back onto the left needle and pull it snug. Repeat this process, always purling into the newest stitch to create the next stitch. When you've finished casting on the appropriate number of new stitches, purl across them or work them in the pattern as indicated, and continue across the row.

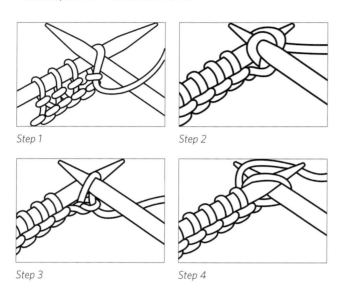

Step 1

Step 2

Step 3

Step 4

BINDING OFF

I have a confession: I'm a boring knitter when it comes to binding off. I've knit hundreds of sweaters in my lifetime, and I almost always use a regular bind-off worked in pattern. There are times a stretchier bind-off or a decorative bind-off are called-for, but I generally get the best results with the old tried-and-true method. With practice you can control your tension—adjusting as needed—to get the results you want. You may find that another bind-off suits you better; feel free to use what works for you.

INCREASING

The make-one, slanted increase is one of my favorites. It's a subtle increase that reinforces the upper body around the arm shaping. A needle with a sharp tip can make these increases easier to work, and you'll find that with practice you'll be able to remember which direction the increase should angle. When first setting up a new project, I like to make note of whether these increases angle toward the raglan/arm "seam" or away from it. By identifying this ahead of time, you'll more easily be able to remember which increase you should work. Ask yourself: Should this increase point toward the marker or away from it?

M1R (Make one, right slanting increase)

Pick up the bar before the next stitch with your left needle (Step 1) or use your right needle to lift it and place it on the left needle, if that's easier. As you knit through this new stitch, pay special attention to the direction you place your needle—it should go through the stitch knitwise with the legs of the new stitch twisting toward the right as you reach through and work the stitch. If done correctly it will twist at the bottom and angle toward the right (Step 2).

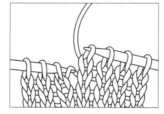
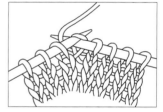

Step 1

Step 2

M1L (Make one, left slanting increase)

Lift the bar before the next stitch and slide it onto the left needle (Step 1). Knit this stitch through the back loop to create an increased stitch that twists at the bottom and angles left (Step 2).

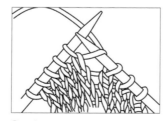
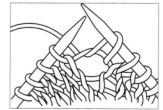

Step 1

Step 2

M1u (Make one under)

This is my own variation of a make-one increase. It results in an increase that looks similar to a yarn over (yo) but creates a smaller, tidier hole. To work this increase, simply knit under the bar between the stitch on your right needle and the stitch on your left needle. Unlike the M1R or M1L increase, this increase is worked by knitting straight through the center of that space under that bar (shown lifted by the left needle below). This creates a new stitch that leaves a very small gap beneath it. The M1u increase provides flexibility to the fabric around it without stressing the surrounding stitches.

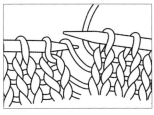 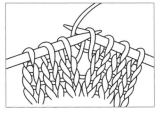

Step 1   *Step 2*

DECREASING

SSK (Slip, slip, knit)

Slip the next two stitches knitwise off the left needle, one at a time (Step 1). Slide them back to the left needle, keeping the new presentation of the stitches. Knit the stitches together as shown in Step 2.

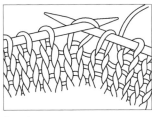 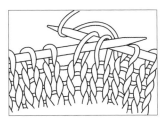

Step 1   *Step 2*

FINISH STRONG: PROFESSIONAL TRICKS FOR A TIDY FINISH

Knitters always seem surprised when I tell them how much I love working the final details on a sweater. Finishing is an opportunity to end on a high note, and it's worth taking the time to hone your technique. It's not difficult to get professional results; it just takes the right approach and a little practice. The more you do it, the easier it gets.

Neckline Finishing

After years of answering questions from worried knitters, the most important advice I can give you is this: necklines aren't naturally perfect. Seeing little variations in your neckline is normal and is part of creating a handknit sweater. The same goes for underarm gap—it happens. Just weave it closed with a strand of yarn. Too often we focus on the perceived "flaws" in our work, not realizing that variations are normal, and we all have them. Our goal is beauty, not perfection.

Here are a few tips for creating a lovely neckline:

Casting on new stitches at the neckline can make the edge a bit wonky. The trick is to work them as tightly as possible by keeping your stitches near the needle tips while casting on the new stitches. As you create each new stitch, pull it taut against the needle.

When picking up stitches around the neckline, think of it like paving a highway over a slightly bumpy path. Rather than picking up under whole stitches—which creates more bulk than necessary and tends to prevent the neckline from laying as flat as it could—I like to pick up just half of each stitch as I work my way around. You can pick up the top half or bottom half of the stitch, as you prefer—sometimes one or the other looks best with the design. This method helps tighten-up those neckline stitches and gives you the freedom to adjust as needed.

Picking up Stitches Around the Neckline

Sometimes the next stitch presented isn't the best one to pick up. Remember, you're paving a highway over a bumpy path, so don't let divots deter you. Sometimes skipping over a gap to pick up the next stitch will help close unsightly gaps.

 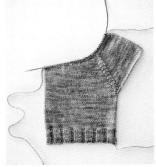

Picking up neckline.   *Neckline pick-up complete.*

Don't fret. If you pick up once and find that you didn't get the results you wanted, it's easy to pull it out and start again. Before you do, make note of the trouble spots and where you might be able to pick up the stitch next to it or one leg of the stitch below it to even things out.

Block it. We're our own worst critics when it comes to noticing flaws in our work, and I recommend that if you have just a few tiny spots that bother you, wait and see if blocking makes a difference. Many yarns will bloom when blocked, which can improve your results dramatically.

Front (Button) Bands

It is amazing what a proper front button band can do for a sweater, regardless of whether you include buttons or not. Here are my favorite tips and tricks for beautiful bands.

First, many patterns won't tell you exactly how many stitches to pick up along the front bands of a sweater, and if a pattern does tell you, I recommend you take the suggestion with a grain of salt. How many stitches you should pick up is entirely dependent on your row gauge; if your row gauge varies from the row gauge in the pattern or if you've added even slightly more or less length to your sweater, an exact number of stitches can lead you astray quickly. This count will vary from knitter to knitter, sweater to sweater. I always recommend a general stitch range (5 of every 6, for example) based on the row gauge in the pattern, but this is only a suggestion and should be adjusted as needed for best results.

NOTE: Unless a pattern specifically tells you to slip the first stitch of each row, don't be tempted to do it. This will leave you with too few stitches to work this technique properly. Also note, I almost always pick up on the right side, unless otherwise stated in the pattern.

When you pick up along the front bands of your garment, you'll be working perpendicular to the body of the sweater. This means you are trying to align stitches (in ribbing) with existing rows (on the body). You may already know that knit stitches aren't square; they're wider than they are tall, so trying to match perpendicular stitches with horizontal rows requires a little strategy. It starts with knowing your row gauge, which may vary from the stated row gauge in the pattern. Measure your own row gauge first and then use this handy reference to determine how many stitches you'll want to pick up. Keep in mind that some patterns—such as the North Channel Collared Cardigan (page 144)—may employ a unique strategy for the front bands, and in that case, follow the directions as they're given in the pattern.

HERE'S MY CHEAT SHEET: HOW MANY STITCHES SHOULD I PICK UP?

If you have 3 rows per inch (2.5 cm) in the body, pick up 3 of every 4 stitches along the front band.

If you have 4 rows per inch (2.5 cm) in the body, pick up 4 of every 5 stitches along the front band.

If you have 5 rows per inch (2.5 cm) in the body, pick up 5 of every 6 stitches along the front band.

If you have 6 rows per inch (2.5 cm) in the body, pick up 6 of every 7 stitches along the front band.

If you have 7 rows per inch (2.5 cm) in the body, pick up 7 of every 8 stitches along the front band.

Always begin with your row gauge and use it to follow this general guideline. But remember, this is knitting; nothing is truly set in stone, and you must learn to bend the rules to make them work for you. You may find that your stitches are looser on the edges and you need to pick up fewer stitches to compensate, or that you need a few more. This is only a suggestion and you should always adjust appropriately for your needs.

Keep in mind: There's a difference between "pick up" and "pick up and knit." My technique is to pick up first by grabbing just one leg of each edge stitch, rather than going below each whole stitch to pick up in the space beneath. It's a unique method, but it gives tidy results. Get all the stitches on your needle first, then you are free to begin working your ribbing on the right side, and can easily drop a stitch (or rather, a leg of the stitch) if you realize you've picked up one too many. Or on the contrary, you can pick up an extra if you realize you're short a stitch or two.

A tip about picking up the correct multiple: If the pattern indicates to pick up a specific multiple (such as a multiple of 4 + 2) as seen in the North Channel Collared Cardigan (page 144), here's an easy way to do it. First, try my technique for picking up without knitting and get your stitches on your needle per your row gauge (see previous instructions above). Next, take your total stitch count on your needle and subtract 2 stitches, then divide the remainder by 4. If it works out evenly, you have a multiple of 4 + 2. If not, you can easily drop or add a stitch as you work through the first ribbing row in order to end up with the correct number.

Here's an example:

Let's say you picked up a total of 85 stitches on your front band and your goal is a multiple of 4 + 2 for the ribbing to work out properly. Here's how to check your math:

85 stitches - 2 = 83 stitches

83 stitches ÷ 4 = 20.75 stitches

This multiple doesn't quite work out for what we need. Take the final number and round it up or down to the nearest whole number (in this case it would be 21). Now we'll work backwards.

21 stitches x 4 = 84 stitches

84 stitches + 2 stitches = 86 stitches

Step 1

Step 2

Back View

This tells me I need 1 extra stitch in order to fit the multiple of 4 + 2. You can check your math the same way:

86 stitches - 2 = 84 stitches

84 stitches ÷ 4 = 21 stitches

BLOCKING

Whatever you do, don't skip this important last step. Blocking helps to remove excess dye, chaff and debris—yarn-making and dyeing isn't always a tidy process. Blocking also allows the fiber to relax and bloom. It can enhance the stitch pattern, soften the transitions between the body and the ribbing and compensate for inconsistencies in the stitches. Final sizing in the pattern instructions are based on blocked results, so you will not get the true fit, drape or finished look of the pattern until the blocking is complete.

For best results: Use a very mild, gentle wool wash that is especially designed for hand knits. Soak your garment in cool water without agitation and use just a small amount of wool wash per the package directions. Let the sweater soak for at least 20 minutes; you want the fibers to be fully saturated.

Gently express the water and press the garment into a towel, rolling it up gently and pressing out as much extra water as possible.

Lay the garment out flat on blocking mats; I like to use the interlocking puzzle mats from my local home improvement store. Pin the sweater flat, smoothing out the details and pinning the sweater into shape. Use pins to follow the curves around the arms, as well as any details (such as cables or lace) that may benefit from a little shaping.

Let the sweater dry in a warm spot—away from direct sunlight unless you're confident about the yarn and know it's color-safe. Turn as needed for even drying.

Resources

BROOKLYN TWEED

135 NE 12th Avenue
Portland, Oregon 97232
www.brooklyntweed.com

KNITTED WIT

19959 E Burnside
Portland, Oregon 97233
https://www.etsy.com/shop/KnittedWit

LOLODIDIT

8545 W Warm Springs Rd
A-4 239
Las Vegas, NV 89113
www.lolodidit.com

MAGPIE FIBERS

5711 Industry Lane
Unit 28
Frederick, Maryland 21704
www.magpiefibers.com

MALABRIGO

Montevideo, Uruguay
www.malabrigoyarn.com

MANOS

Uruguay
www.manosyarns.com
U.S. distributor: fairmountfibers.com

SHERWOOD YARN

Southwell, England
www.sherwoodyarn.com

SHIBUI

1500 NW 18th Avenue
Portland, OR 97209
www.shibuiknits.com

SKACEL KNITTING

8041 S. 180th Street
Kent, Washington 98032
www.skacelknitting.com

THE FIBRE CO.

Cumbria, U.K.
www.thefibreco.com

THREE IRISH GIRLS

Superior, Wisconsin
www.threeirishgirlsyarn.com

WOOLFOLK

Portland, Oregon
www.woolfolkyarn.com

Acknowledgments

This book would not have been possible without an incredible team of people behind the scenes. Many thanks to the companies who provided yarn support: Skacel Collection, Woolfolk, Brooklyn Tweed, Malabrigo, Knitted Wit, Lolodidit, The Fibre Co., Three Irish Girls, Sherwood Yarn and Magpie Fibers. Thank you to my team of sample knitters, most especially my friends-turned-volunteers Lisa Kirk, Erika Close and Sarah Keller, whose kind hearts and quick needles helped me cross the finish line on time. Thank you to my photographer, Belen Mercer, for maintaining a sense of humor during endless photo sessions. A big thank you (and a hug) to my son, Jonah Greene, for providing the schematics and illustrations. Thank you to my team of willing test knitters and to my tech editor, Cathy Susko, for helping me create the best patterns possible. Thank you to Page Street Publishing for inviting me to join their family of authors and for tirelessly supporting me along the way. A huge thank you to my husband Scott for his unwavering support, which—frankly—leaves me speechless. And last but not least, a lifetime of thanks to my Grandma Margery for giving me the gift of knitting.

About the Author

Marie Greene is an independent knitwear designer and teacher whose innovative approach to seamless sweaters has gained notice around the world. Her designs have been featured in collections for The Fibre Co., Skacel Collection and Making Stories, as well as *Laine* magazine. You can find her technique classes at yarn shops and fiber festivals worldwide, and see more of her work online at www.oliveknits.com. Marie lives in the Pacific Northwest with her husband and three sons. *Seamless Knit Sweaters in 2 Weeks* is her first book.

Index